Open Plan

CULTURAL HISTORIES OF DESIGN

Series editors:
Grace Lees-Maffei of the University of Hertfordshire, UK
Kjetil Fallan of the University of Oslo, Norway

The Cultural Histories of Design series presents rigorous and original research on the role and significance of design in society and culture, past and present. From a vantage point in the heart of the humanities, the series explores design as the most significant manifestation of modern and contemporary culture.

In the series:
Modern Asian Design
D. J. Huppatz
Norman Bel Geddes: American Design Visionary
Nicolas P. Maffei
Soviet Critical Design: Senezh Studio and the Communist Surround
Tom Cubbin
The New Typography in Scandinavia: Modernist Design and Print Culture
Trond Klevgaard
Open Plan: A Design History of the American Office
Jennifer Kaufmann-Buhler

Forthcoming titles:
Jugendstil Women and the Making of Modern Design
Sabine Wieber

Open Plan

A Design History of the American Office

Jennifer Kaufmann-Buhler

BLOOMSBURY VISUAL ARTS
LONDON · NEW YORK · OXFORD · NEW DELHI · SYDNEY

BLOOMSBURY VISUAL ARTS
Bloomsbury Publishing Plc
50 Bedford Square, London, WC1B 3DP, UK
1385 Broadway, New York, NY 10018, USA

BLOOMSBURY, BLOOMSBURY VISUAL ARTS and the Diana logo are trademarks of
Bloomsbury Publishing Plc

First published in Great Britain 2021

© Jennifer Kaufmann-Buhler, 2021

Jennifer Kaufmann-Buhler has asserted her right under the Copyright, Designs and Patents Act, 1988, to be identified as Author of this work.

For legal purposes the Acknowledgments on p. viii constitute an extension of this copyright page.

Cover design: Louise Dugdale
Cover image: Westinghouse, *Westinghouse ASD Group*
(Grand Rapids, MI: Westinghouse, 1972).
Trade catalog from the William Pahlmann Papers at the Hagley Museum and Library: Series 25, Box 23

All rights reserved. No part of this publication may be reproduced or transmitted in any form or by any means, electronic or mechanical, including photocopying, recording, or any information storage or retrieval system, without prior permission in writing from the publishers.

The author and publisher gratefully acknowledge the permission granted to reproduce the copyright material in this book.

Every effort has been made to trace copyright holders of images and to obtain their permission for the use of copyright material. The publisher apologizes for any errors or omissions in copyright acknowledgment and would be grateful if notified of any corrections that should be incorporated in future reprints or editions of this book.

Bloomsbury Publishing Plc does not have any control over, or responsibility for, any third-party websites referred to or in this book. All internet addresses given in this book were correct at the time of going to press. The author and publisher regret any inconvenience caused if addresses have changed or sites have ceased to exist, but can accept no responsibility for any such changes.

A catalogue record for this book is available from the British Library.

Library of Congress Cataloging-in-Publication Data
Names: Kaufmann-Buhler, Jennifer, author.
Title: Open plan : a design history of the American office / Jennifer Kaufmann-Buhler.
Description: New York : Bloomsbury Publishing, 2021. | Series: Cultural histories of design | Includes bibliographical references and index.
Identifiers: LCCN 2020024164 (print) | LCCN 2020024165 (ebook) |
ISBN 9781350044739 (paperback) | ISBN 9781350044722 (hardback) |
ISBN 9781350044715 (ePDF) | ISBN 9781350044746 (ePub)
Subjects: LCSH: Office layout–History. | Offices–United States–Design and construction–History. | Work environment–United States–History.
Classification: LCC HF5547.2 .K38 2021 (print) | LCC HF5547.2 (ebook) |
DDC 725/.23–dc23
LC record available at https://lccn.loc.gov/2020024164
LC ebook record available at https://lccn.loc.gov/2020024165

ISBN: HB: 978-1-3500-4472-2
PB: 978-1-3500-4473-9
ePDF: 978-1-3500-4471-5
eBook: 978-1-3500-4474-6

Series: Cultural Histories of Design

Typeset by Newgen KnowledgeWorks Pvt. Ltd., Chennai, India

To find out more about our authors and books visit www.bloomsbury.com and sign up for our newsletters.

Contents

List of Figures vi
Acknowledgments viii

Introduction 1

1 Designing Hierarchy 15

2 Managing Change 39

3 Negotiating Privacy and Communication 63

4 Personalizing the Workstation 89

5 Supporting Technology 117

6 Facilitating Movement 141

Conclusion 165

Notes 173
Index 197

Figures

1 Original office landscape interior in the newly built administration offices (Freehafer Hall) at Purdue University, 1971. 2
2 Office interior featuring new workstation mock-up at Freehafer Hall at Purdue University, 2016. 3
3 Drawing showing various common office design concepts used in the 1978 Steelcase/Louis Harris and Associates survey. 5
4 Sales office for Deering, Milliken and Co. designed by the Knoll Planning Unit, 1958. 18
5 DuPont Freon Division layout, designed by the Quickborner Team, 1967. 27
6 Action Office 2 installation at Citizens and Southern National Bank in Atlanta, Georgia, 1968. 28
7 Eppinger's TRM workstations in the McDonald's Office, 1971. 31
8 Meditation room in the McDonald's "Think Tank," 1971. 32
9 Technical drawing of Herman Miller's Action Office 2, 1972. 46
10 Image of a hand screwing the top of a panel in Steelcase's Movable Wall system, 1976. 47
11 Detailed drawing of a Steelcase Movable Wall, 1970s. 48
12 Image of the Haworth Places system, 1989. 51
13 Quickborner Team's communication chart for Purdue University, 1968. 67
14 Quickborner Team's interior layout of Purdue's Freehafer Hall. 68
15 Photograph of the interior of Freehafer Hall, 1971. 71
16 Herman Miller's Acoustic Conditioner, 1976. 76
17 Illustration of the movement of sound in Action Office, 1975. 78
18 An Action Office workstation in the offices of JFN Associates, 1968. 92
19 Steelcase 9000+ furniture installation showing a model office populated with workers. 95
20 Action Office storage in a mailroom, 1979. 97
21 Steelcase Mobiles storage wall workstations. 99
22 A wheelchair user working in Haworth's Unigroup system, 1982. 108
23 Krueger raceway, 1988. 125
24 Worker using a computer in Freehafer Hall, 1991. 126

25 Kimball's CETRA furniture with VDT corners, 1988. 127
26 Herman Miller computer turntable, 1982. 128
27 Herman Miller's Action Secretary advertisement, 1974. 130
28 Ergonomic workstation from Haworth's UniTek line. 135
29 TBWA/Chiat/Day Los Angeles offices, 1999. 155

Acknowledgments

This research began as part of my doctoral dissertation at the University of Wisconsin-Madison. I want to thank my dissertation committee William Jones, Pascale Carayon, Roberto Rengel, Anna Andrzejewski, and Jung-hye Shin each of whom had a mark on the shape and direction of this research and on my own thinking throughout the early development of this project. I especially want to thank my dissertation advisor and mentor Virginia T. Boyd whose unwavering guidance and support carried me through the research and writing process of the dissertation.

I have been fortunate to receive significant financial support for my research including a university fellowship and two research grants from the University of Wisconsin during my time as a graduate student, an Exploratory Grant and a Henry Belin du Pont Research grant from the Hagley Museum and Library, and support from Purdue University including a Purdue Research Foundation summer research grant, a College of Liberal Arts Aspire grant, and a Library Scholars grant. I wish to thank Columbus College of Art and Design in Columbus, Ohio, which generously supported my research while I was a faculty member there. I would also like to thank the numerous librarians, archivists, and other staff at the Hagley Museum and Library, Purdue University Special Collections, Yale University Special Collections, the Wisconsin Historical Society, the Computer History Museum Archive, the Art Institute of Chicago, the Chicago Public History Museum and Library, the Western Reserve Library, and the Benson Ford Research Center.

Thank you also to the various corporate entities and their staff that have been so instrumental to this project particularly Amy Auscherman and Alexa Hagen at the Herman Miller Corporate Archives and Kathy Reagan and Justine Bailey at the Steelcase Corporate Archives for their help in providing information, materials, and images to support my research. I would also like to thank Herman Miller, Steelcase, Haworth, Knoll, Krueger International, Kimball, Westinghouse, ASD|Sky, TBWA/Chiat/Day, and Combine Consulting for their generous permission to reproduce images used in this book. Thank you also to Purdue's Office of Physical Facilities for allowing me research access to the plans and other materials associated with Freehafer Hall.

Thank you to Michelle Niemann who read multiple drafts of this book at various stages and helped me unravel my brain and unsnarl my writing countless times. I would like to thank my Purdue colleagues particularly Maren Linett, Rebekah Klein-Pejšová, Erin Moodie, Cara Kinnally, Toni Rogat, and Stephanie Zywicki for reading and commenting on various chapter drafts and related conference papers. I am grateful to my colleagues and friends in the field of design history particularly: Carma Gorman, David Raizman, Victoria R. Pass, Bess Williamson, Elizabeth Guffey, and Maggie Taft for their support, encouragement, and critical eyes at various stages of this process and various iterations of this research (proposals, articles, conference papers, etc.). Thank you also to Marsely Kehoe for crafting a beautifully organized and thorough index for this volume. Thank you to Rebecca Barden, Olivia Davies, and Claire Collins of Bloomsbury for their help in developing and managing this project and Grace Lees-Maffei and Kjetil Fallan for their comments and advice, and for including my book in the Cultural Histories of Design series.

Finally, I want to thank my parents Mary Birnbaum and Robert Birnbaum and my brother, Scott Birnbaum, for their constant love, support, and encouragement. Most of all, I want to thank my husband, Toby Kaufmann-Buhler, for serving as my pacesetter and cheerleader, and for holding my hand through the ups and downs of this long journey.

Introduction

In the fall of 2016, as I was just starting in my new role as an assistant professor at Purdue University, a new colleague told me about a large and rather old open plan office on campus called Freehafer Hall. Meeting with a Purdue staff member with some knowledge of the building's history, it was on that very first visit to Freehafer Hall that learned that it had been one of the first purpose-built office landscapes in the United States. In 1967, as Purdue was planning a new administration building, it sought an office solution that would spatially integrate various administrative units that were scattered across campus and provide a comfortable and attractive working environment that would also support a high level of flexibility for future change. After attending a seminar on the new office landscape concept in Chicago, two administrators from Purdue presented the idea of adopting it for the new building to the board of trustees. On the administrators' enthusiastic recommendation, the board voted unanimously to contract with the Quickborner Team to handle the layout and interior design concept of the new building (Figure 1).[1]

Office landscaping or *burolandschaft* was an open office planning concept developed in the late 1950s by German brothers Eberhard Schnelle and Wolfgang Schnelle (the founders of the Quickborner Team), which utilized an analysis of communication patterns as the basis for office planning, ensuring that workers were placed nearest to those they communicated with most frequently. In their designs, the Quickborner Team eliminated all interior partitions (fully enclosed offices) and arranged all workers in a loose amorphous configuration with simple tables and desks, free-standing curving screens, and plants to provide modest privacy. The office landscaping concept spread across Western Europe through the early 1960s, and in 1967, the Quickborner Team expanded into the US market, opening their first US offices and taking their very first American clients including DuPont, Eastman Kodak, and John Hancock, just as Purdue was starting to plan their new administration building. When it was first introduced in the United States, office landscaping was quite controversial. Some in the

Figure 1 Photograph of the interior of the original office landscape in the newly built administration offices at Purdue University from 1971. The image shows a typical office landscape interior with its curving screens, simple furniture, and liberal use of plants to define the space.
Source: Purdue University Special Collections UA 153 Box 1 Folder 2.

architectural, design, business, and popular press heralded the new design as a radical reimagining of office space and office work, while others were deeply critical and even strongly resistant to the new office design concept.[2] Meanwhile, just as office landscaping was getting significant attention in the American architecture and design community, the American furniture manufacturer Herman Miller released their new open plan furniture line, Action Office, which would upend the American office furniture industry through the 1970s. Together, office landscaping and this new class of systems furniture became the conceptual and technical underpinning for the American open plan office, which would transform the design of American offices for decades to come.

In light of this history, I found it truly astonishing that Purdue University had been such an early adopter of the office landscape in the United States. Of course, the Freehafer Hall that I visited in 2016 looked nothing like the initial design. Some of the original furniture was still around, but the office landscape design, with its curving screens in red, green, and yellow stripes, and its lush plants, was long gone, and in its place was a sea of cubicles with aging blue, cream, and beige partitions with wood trim enclosing hundreds of individual workstations. The furniture was not the only thing that was different—in the intervening years, the workers, the organization, and the structure of office work itself had all changed significantly. Where once the office had been filled with clattering typewriters and ringing telephones, it now contained computers, printers, and copiers. Walking around, I noticed long runs of tangled wires running haphazardly along the floor, and I even saw a snarl of cables draped awkwardly across the front of an old lateral filing cabinet. While this was still a working office, there was a visible mismatch between the work underway and the design and use of the office interior.

When I started visiting in the fall of 2016, Freehafer was already slated to be torn down in the upcoming year and all the workers inside were expected to relocate to one of two newly built open plan offices on campus. On one of my research trips, a worker at Freehafer showed me a mock-up workstation for one of the new offices (Figure 2). Next to the old and rather drab cubicle partitions in Freehafer, this newer iteration of an open plan workstation looked bright and crisp with its clean gray partitions and bright-white trim and a light wood veneer work surface. The 64-inch (162 cm) cubicle walls of the older workstations in Freehafer seemed to tower over this new workstation with its panels that were

Figure 2 Photograph of an office interior featuring the new workstation mock-up surrounded by the older cubicle style workstations with their higher partitions in Freehafer Hall at Purdue University in 2016.
Source: Photograph taken by author.

at least a foot lower in height. Inside this model workstation, someone had added a few pretend personal items as props to make the new workstation look a little more hospitable including a framed photograph of a dog, a pink plastic high-heeled shoe, a snowman coffee mug, and, providing a bit of meta-humor, a flyer taped to a shelf describing the "12 commandments of cubicle etiquette" along with a laminated cartoon featuring a cubicle joke. Standing in Freehafer Hall on that day, looking at this modern open plan workstation inside of the older 1980s-era cubicle office which in turn was inside of a former 1970s office landscape, I felt as though three generations of the open plan office were converging around me.

One of the challenges of this project about the history of the open plan office in the United States is that the open plan is like a many-headed hydra. Although it stems from some shared ideas about office work and office design, it also had a number of different iterations and manifestations that were visually, conceptually, and technically distinct from each other. In fact, even the term open plan office is a catchall that has sometimes been used to refer to an architectural design (an unpartitioned office space), sometimes signifies an office-planning process (such as office landscaping), and other times is used to indicate a special class of office furniture (systems furniture). In practice, these diverse expressions of the open plan office design concept were used in combination to produce a variety of office spaces that were all considered "open plan." For example, in 1978, Steelcase and Louis Harris and Associates conducted a survey on office design and offered respondents three distinct iterations identified explicitly as open plan designs including an office landscape arrangement with low-curving screens and plants, a storage wall design which used storage cabinets to separate rows of workers, and a design featuring individually partitioned workstations using systems furniture (Figure 3). Notably, one of the alternative types of office interiors included in the drawing features an open space with rows of desks and is pointedly referred to as a "pool" design, a reference to its common use in centralized clerical divisions such as typing pools and steno pools. This distinction between the open plan and the pool arrangement reflects a common belief among architects and designers at the time that the new open plan was something truly different from more conventional office designs. By showing several distinct versions of an open plan, and by differentiating the open plan from conventional office designs of the period, the survey points to the various ways in which the term "open plan" was used both technically and textually. Even as the open plan was becoming increasingly common in American offices, its definition remained quite fluid and ill-defined.[3]

The term "open plan office" flattens and unifies, while in actual practice the open plan office was never a single or universal idea fixed at a point in time. As the Freehafer example illustrates, the various iterations and generations of the open plan often overlap with one another historically and even spatially. As

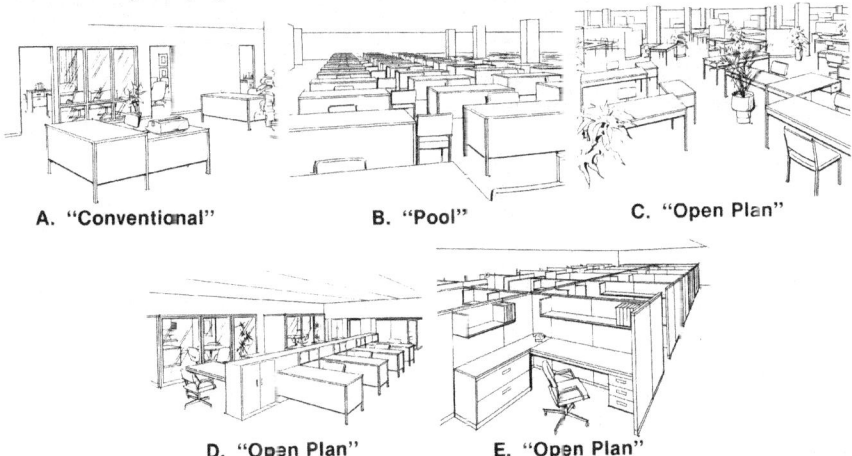

Figure 3 Drawing showing various common office design concepts used in the 1978 Steelcase/Louis Harris and Associates survey. These reflect the competing definitions of open-plan designs at the time.
Source: Louis Harris and Associates, *Office Environments. Do They Work*, 28. Steelcase Corporate Archives.

architects and designers built new offices using the latest iteration of the open plan and the newest lines of systems furniture, older offices with older furniture continue to be used. The adoption of the latest version of the open plan in some offices did not negate or end the life of the older versions still in use by many other organizations and their workers. Throughout this book, I use the "open plan office" as a deliberately generic term that refers to a constellation of diverse office design concepts, practices, and processes that have overlapped and coexisted over many decades. I also frequently use the colloquial term "cubicles," to distinguish the open plan office designs of the 1980s and 1990s from earlier open plan layouts. That term did not originate with the open plan office, and in fact has long been used to describe all types of small spatial enclosures from bathroom stalls to library carrels.[4] In postwar popular culture and media, references to cubicles as fully enclosed spaces were common, and notably, when the open plan first became popular in the United States in the late 1960s it was often described by its advocates as a rejection of the small enclosed office cubicle.[5] By the late 1970s, the term cubicle began to be used in relation to open plan office workspaces, and that usage along with the shortened "cube" became common in American media through the 1980s and 1990s.[6] Though its meaning has changed over time, the term "cubicle" has long had a negative connotation in office design, and using that term here acknowledges that historically negative association.

The history of office design is deeply intertwined with the history of management and managerial ideas. As architectural critic and writer James Russell argues, office design is a tool of management and a spatial embodiment of managerial ideals. Russell traces the evolving design of offices from the "moral uplift" of Frank Lloyd Wright's 1904 Larkin Building to the buzzing "coffee bar" culture of Silicon Valley in the late 1990s to show how management theories have been reborn and reproduced in office architecture time and time again.[7] The concept of the open plan workspace originated in the late nineteenth and early twentieth centuries when large open work spaces were commonly used in offices and factories. These early open plan offices were typically designed to facilitate a high degree of efficiency of the work process along with a high capacity for surveillance over the work and working process of both white- and blue-collar workers.[8] Among the most iconic examples from the early twentieth century is Frank Lloyd Wright's 1939 Johnson Wax building with its dramatic open work room in Racine, Wisconsin. In his office design for Johnson Wax, Wright created a spacious and well-lit workspace that could house a large group of clerical workers and was designed to promote efficiency as well as create a supportive working environment that would foster a sense of belonging and cooperation.[9] Even in these early iterations, the open plan was often celebrated as a progressive solution that promised to provide a comfortable and attractive work space for workers.[10] In the postwar period, new approaches to organizational management in the United States continued to inform the ideals of the open plan office design and its uses, as new technical developments particularly the use of air conditioning, fluorescent lighting, and suspended ceilings allowed architects and designers to create wider and deeper interior spaces that could be arranged more freely to accommodate the work process.[11]

These technical and conceptual developments in mid-twentieth-century American corporate architecture formed the essential underpinning for the development of the new open plan concepts of the 1960s, which took advantage of the resulting large unpartitioned spaces to create a new kind of interior arrangement that reimagined the relationship between the organization and its office. When the architecture and design press first began promoting the new open plan office concept in the United States, it was hailed by some as a major intervention into the entrenched bureaucracy and hierarchy of the postwar corporate office.[12] Its proponents viewed office landscaping and the new class of systems furniture as transformative concepts that together embodied larger changes in the structure and culture of work at the time including the growth of new office technology, the emergence of knowledge work, and the increased pace of organizational change. According to its advocates, this new kind of office would not only support and reflect the changes underway in office work at the time, but also help to initiate larger organizational, social, and cultural change.

Although the open plan office was not really a new kind of architectural space, its advocates nonetheless viewed this new approach to office design as something truly different and distinct from the design ideas that came before. Furthermore, many architects and designers of the 1960s viewed the new open plan as a spatial manifestation of a larger transformation of work and the workplace that was directly linked to a larger transformation of society. Their starry-eyed optimism for the possibilities and potentials of the future may seem naive to our modern eyes, but the architects and designers describing this future were echoing ideas that were widely circulating in management, business, and intellectual circles at the time. As Howard Brick has argued, writers and scholars of the era such as Kenneth Galbraith, Talcott Parsons, Daniel Bell, Peter Drucker, and David Riesman among others saw the possibility of transforming the material and economic abundance of the postwar period into a more collective and egalitarian vision of American society.[13] As part of this vision of the future, these writers and thinkers described an imminent transformation of work away from a Fordist industrial system, toward "knowledge work" characterized by the management and production of information and ideas rather than the production of goods.[14] In this emerging culture of work, workers would supposedly have greater autonomy and independence in their working process, and as a result, top–down management structures, organizational hierarchy, and corporate bureaucracies would disappear and organizations would become flatter, more dynamic, and more dependent on worker interaction and communication. Architects, designers, furniture manufacturers, and organizations enthusiastically embraced these ideas about the possibility of radical social, cultural, political, and economic change, and viewed the open plan as a manifestation of these ideas. By the early 1970s there were already dozens of new open plan furniture systems on the market, and American organizations began adopting the new open plan design concepts in significant numbers.

This new open plan emerged out of the idealism and economic prosperity of the late postwar period, but it came of age in the more austere 1970s when these idealistic visions for the future began to fade. As historian Judith Stein has argued in her book, *Pivotal Decade*, the 1970s were an era of enormous social, political, and economic change that had a lasting influence on American society and politics. It was a period of nation-wide belt-tightening including multiple energy crises, rampant inflation, a drop in productivity, and growing unemployment.[15] Public and private organizations navigating this landscape of increased economic uncertainty were in search of cost-saving strategies to reduce their overhead expenses and increase their flexibility. At the time, many companies were implementing office automation, centralizing their clerical divisions, reducing their energy usage, laying off workers, and reorganizing to reduce costs and increase productivity and efficiency, and the new open plan was directly tied to these larger changes in the structure and culture of work.

The open plan promised organizations a means of quickly transforming the space of the office to adapt to these new structures, technologies and processes of work, but it was also a means of achieving some of these same cost-cutting goals in that it generally decreased overhead costs by increasing office density (fitting more workers into less space), made office space changes faster to implement and significantly cheaper, and even reduced overall energy costs. Organizations often implemented the open plan by promising workers a more egalitarian office in which they would have greater autonomy, a more attractive and dynamic workspace, and easier communication with colleagues. In practice, the ever shrinking and moving workstations reflected this era of economic and organizational upheaval in which jobs were continuously in flux and could even disappear (along with one's entire workspace) overnight.

The design and marketing of the new systems furniture reflected this persistent tension between the original ideals of the open plan as an expression of progressive organizational change, and its implementation as part of a larger effort to cut costs and increase productivity. Through the 1970s and 1980s, office furniture manufacturers often tried to simultaneously project an image of the open plan as a progressive office design solution while also speaking to the technical and economic benefits of the new furniture and this new way of designing the office. The partitions of systems furniture embodied open-ness and egalitarianism and they were an efficient use of space that made space changes easier, faster, and cheaper. The marketing copy portrayed these benefits as simultaneous and coexistent, but this fixation on cutting costs and making the space more efficient often meant implementing the open plan in ways that ran directly counter to the idealistic vision of its earliest champions.

Architectural histories about the open plan office have often examined changes in corporate architecture and its relationship to new technical developments in architecture alongside larger social and organizational changes in the workplace. In their book *Tower and Office*, Iñaki Ábalos and Juan Herreros provide a rich analysis of the technical and conceptual evolution of office architecture, including an in-depth discussion regarding the development of the open plan in the postwar period.[16] Other research in architectural history has examined the direct influence of cybernetics and new management theory on the development and use of the open plan, for example in the work on office landscaping by Andreas Rumpfhuber and Olga Pantelidou's research on Kevin Roche.[17] This type of scholarship has laid an important foundation for conceptualizing the technical and theoretical significance of the open plan office as a spatial intervention into the midcentury organization and its structure.

The architectural space of the open plan office of the postwar era was a vital precondition to the creation of the open plan office concept, and further, as I argue, the design of the architectural space had significant implications for the implementation and use of the open plan. Yet, this book is not an architectural history, but rather it is a design history. While architectural history and practice is often grand in its scale, orientation, and theoretical lens, interior design history and practice tends to be more intimate in its scale, and generally more focused on the social and cultural aspects of interior space.[18] My focus is primarily on the design and arrangement of the interior spaces and furniture of the office and its use by organizations and workers over time. This project builds significantly on a vernacular architecture approach, which encourages the study of more ordinary architectural spaces and structures. In this study, I feature a mix of different architectural examples including writing and works by well-known designers and architects such as John Pile and Kevin Roche, alongside more ordinary architectural spaces such as those built and used by Wisconsin State Government.[19] By incorporating a variety of architectural spaces by a mix of different organizations (private and public, large and small), this work seeks to draw broader connections about the use of the open plan and its meaning for organizations and workers.

Vernacular architectural approaches also emphasize the value of thinking about change over time as a natural and inevitable aspect of use.[20] Rather than fetishizing the initial design as is common in more traditional architectural history, vernacular architecture offers a way of thinking about change over time. This emphasis on change over time is particularly useful and relevant in the study of the open plan office because its advocates believed that rapid organizational, social, and technological change was imminent, and the open plan design promised organizations and workers an office that would be able to keep up with that change for perpetuity. In this way, the first iteration of an open plan office was never supposed to be the final and best solution, but rather a starting point for future change and development. Instead of treating each new open office installation as a perfect time capsule embodying its particular moment in time, this book explores the long-term implications of the design that emerged through its usage, including the ways in which the choices made in the planning stages informed the ways in which organizations and workers adapted the space and furniture to their changing needs. As David Edgerton has argued, a "use-based history" disrupts conventional timelines that too often prioritize progress and innovation in favor of a more diverse and more complex narrative in which older technologies persist in their usage long after a new technology has come and gone.[21] Building on this idea of a use-based history, this book looks beyond the ideals of the open plan as it was imagined by architects and designers to consider the messy reality that emerges through its usage including the mislaid plans, conflicting goals, misguided intentions, and the misfitting parts and pieces of open plan furniture. The real life of the open plan office is in its use over time: the array of mismatched office chairs, dingy systems furniture components, tangled power cords and communication cables under the desk, workstation drawers filled with papers and office supplies, partitions with personal items pinned to their surfaces, and an ever-growing collection of aging computers and other technologies.

As writer Nikil Saval has argued, the utopian ideals of architects and designer have long shaped the history of office design from the nineteenth century to the present, but rarely have those ideals achieved their intended goals from workers' perspectives. Saval's book, *Cubed*, which weaves together social history, design history, and popular culture, vividly captures the gap between the fantasies of office design and its practical and symbolic failures.[22] Like Saval, I too am examining the gap between the ideals of the open plan office and its usage, but my research contributes a greater emphasis on the material and technical aspects of the open plan and systems furniture that manifest through its design, production, specification, and use. My research draws on information and data from dozens of different open plan or "systems" furniture lines ranging from the major names in the industry such as Herman Miller, Steelcase and Knoll to the lesser known systems by companies like Eppinger, Krueger, Kimball, and Hauserman. As part of my original data collection, I even looked at furniture systems manufactured in prisons, such as the furniture products of Badger State Industries often used in Wisconsin State Government offices. Looking across a variety of office furniture systems and components revealed larger patterns of representation and design that serve as the underpinning for my analysis regarding the ideals of the open plan and its use. This book draws on trade catalogs, price lists, installation guides and archival information from manufacturers, architects, designers, and organizations to examine the real logistical, technical, and material challenges embedded in the concept of the open plan and the design of systems furniture. This new type office furniture was not a fixed collection of stable and perfectly interlocking components, but rather a growing miscellany of parts and pieces that did not always coordinate or easily connect with each other, and this material aspect of the open plan had implications for its usage over time, particularly as organizations, their facilities managers and their workers sought to adapt the open plan to new needs. This book treats these technical and material aspects of systems furniture as critical evidence of the gap between the ideals of the most ardent proponents of the open plan and the real usage of the open plan in American offices.

Of course, the open plan is not just a technical system of architecture and interlocking furniture components—it is also a workspace inhabited by organizations and their workers. Advocates of the open plan imagined the organization and its open plan offices as two halves or two manifestations of the same conceptual body, and every social, cultural, political and technological change in the organization should ideally materialize in its spatial body (its office), and any change in the office would in turn reverberate within the organization producing cultural and social change among workers. I treat the open plan as a concept situated within a larger context of work including the broader cultural, social, and economic environment, the experience and identities of diverse workers, changing technologies, the evolving structure and content of office work, and a shifting organizational context. To get at these ideas and their complex interactions, my research draws on the concept of the work system. Developed by industrial systems engineers Michael J. Smith and Pascale Carayon, the "work system" is a tool for analyzing job design. Smith and Carayon argue that each job is shaped and informed by the organization, the environment (including the physical design of the workplace), the tasks of the particular worker, their technology, and the individual characteristics and identity of the person doing the job. According to Smith and Carayon, these elements are interactive and interdependent producing stress and strain for workers in some areas, while also creating support or benefit in others.[23] As the work system model demonstrates, the work, the workplace, and the worker are intertwined, and this model served as an important framework in my own thinking, research, and analysis.

The organization of this book is not a traditional chronology, but rather features a thematic structure to explore the ideals and problems of the open plan. Each chapter focuses on one component or aspect of the open plan as a means for unpacking the concept of the open plan as well as trace the many problems that emerged over time as the open plan became the dominant office design in the United States in the latter part of the twentieth century. The organization does not precisely follow a historical narrative, but there is a chronological structure to the book starting from the conventional offices of the 1950s and 1960s in the very first chapter and stretching to the alternative offices of the 1990s and early 2000s discussed in the very last chapter. In the conclusion, I consider the legacy of this history as it relates to contemporary open plan offices.

The first chapter, "Designing Hierarchy," foregrounds the problem of hierarchy in office design in the postwar period and the parallel transition in office planning from the conventionally designed office to the new open plan offices of the 1960s. By introducing the open plan within the broader social, cultural, and political context of the period, particularly the deeply entrenched and persistent culture of discrimination and exclusion based on gender, race, and ability, this chapter examines the gap between egalitarian ideals of the open plan, and the reality of its use as a tool for maintaining difference in power and status. Though its advocates viewed the new open plan as a transformative design, I argue it was never the radical rejection of hierarchy it was marketed to be; hierarchy and status remained a central part of the design concept, and were deeply embedded not only in the design but in the design process itself.

In the second chapter, "Managing Change," I examine the ways in which architects, designers, and furniture manufacturers characterized the open plan and the new systems furniture lines as tools for supporting and implementing rapid social, cultural, economic, organizational, and technological change. As I argue, even as architects, designers, and manufacturers described the infinite flexibility of the open plan, the material and technical limitations of systems furniture and office architecture created new and unexpected barriers to change for the organizations who adopted it. The promise of infinite flexibility for change also placed pressure on furniture manufacturers as they sought to continuously adapt their furniture to suit the changing spatial and technological requirements of organizations. Although architects and designers had often imagined the open plan in service of progressive organizational change that would improve the workplace and workers' experience, workers experienced organizational change and the parallel space changes of the 1970s and 1980s as largely negative, particularly when they involved organizational restructuring, centralization, the adoption of new technologies, or significant cuts and layoffs.

In the third chapter, "Negotiating Privacy and Communication," I examine the persistent tension between the goal of improving workplace interactions in the open plan by removing physical barriers and workers' need and desire for enclosure and privacy. To support these often-contradictory requirements between these two essential elements of office design, proponents of the open plan sought to reframe the meaning and uses of privacy by arguing that privacy was not a physical state, but rather a psychological one that required the careful management of workers' perceptions of privacy. Despite their claims of optimally providing the best of both worlds (communication and privacy), workers found the open plan office a noisy and distracting space, and by the early 1980s new research from the field of environment and behavior suggested that, contrary to the original ideals of the open plan, workers experienced greater ease of communication with a higher degree of enclosure. This widely publicized but deeply flawed research led to architects, designers, and organizations using more and taller partitions around individual workstations, ultimately producing the frequently maligned cubicle designs of the 1980s and 1990s.

In Chapter 4, "Personalizing the Workstation," I look at the workstation as a vital tool of the open plan office concept. Designer Robert Propst introduced the workstation as part of his Action Office furniture system to support knowledge workers' need for displaying and managing information. As it became a standard part of the systems furniture toolkit, the workstation became critical to the office planning process allowing architects, designers, and space planners to classify and manage the needs of each class of worker by creating a standard template of components. Although the idealized workstation was intended to be highly adaptable to the individual needs of different workers allowing them to swap out components as needed to better support their work, such adaptation was often discouraged by organizations because of the problems it created for facilities managers and their staff who were tasked with maintaining the ever growing inventory of furniture parts. Yet, even in offices where workers were restricted from making changes, I argue that workers in those offices still inhabited and personalized the interior space of the workstation through their ordinary usage.

In Chapter 5, "Supporting Technology," I examine the interaction of the open plan with the rapidly changing office technologies of the 1970s and 1980s, particularly the spread of personal computers in American offices. The open plan was often championed as an ideal tool for supporting the adoption and use of new technologies in the office, but there were significant technical limitations embedded in the open plan office design. As organizations sought to manage the emerging gap between the planned power and cable access in their space and their growing computer usage, systems furniture increasingly became the means of facilitating that interaction. At the same time, new concerns about the interaction of workers' bodies with computers created new pressure to develop and purchase more adjustable and adaptable furniture to better support intensive computer usage. The problems around the introduction of new computing technology in the open plan office reveals the ways in which the assumptions about the present and future needs of the organization and related technologies led to certain architectural and design choices in the open plan that in turn had long-term implications for the introduction and use of future technologies in the office.

Finally, in Chapter 6, "Facilitating Movement," I examine the ways in which movement and circulation were conceptualized and supported in the early open plan, and how those ideals of movement were reanimated and redefined as part of the "alternative office" movement in the 1990s and early 2000s. Though rarely considered an open plan design concept, in part because architects and designers viewed it as an antidote to the cubicle offices of the 1990s, the alternative office was overlaid on the template of the open plan, using the same kinds of spaces and even the same types of furniture. What truly defined the alternative office was its fixation on the role of movement as a tool for the working process, a strategic goal of the organization, and a means of encouraging greater collaboration, particularly among professional workers. Some offices began shifting away from the primacy of the individual workspace (in some cases even eliminating the assigned workspace altogether) and instead used a "club" approach in which workers were encouraged to work in different locations in the office throughout the workday. These new offices, often featuring elaborate amenities including lounges, cafes, gyms, and game rooms, encouraged workers to see the office as a very comfortable and contained urban playground, but were also designed with the express goal of keeping workers at work. As I argue, even as the alternative office celebrated effortless movement for its workers, it often ignored the enormous number of support workers in contract, temporary, service, and administrative positions, whose work enabled the freedom and flexibility of the more mobile professional and full-time staff.

In the conclusion, I consider the legacy of the open plan and its persistence in American offices through so many iterations and evolutions. Like its most vocal champions of the open plan in the late 1960s and early 1970s, advocates of the twenty-first century open plan offices often describe how this "new" open plan naturally supports the elimination of hierarchy, enables organizational and technological change, and encourages a high degree of communication and collaboration among workers. The ideals of the open plan have persisted despite their repeated failures over many decades of use. I argue that this idealized open plan was never just a fantasy about office design, but rather a fantasy about the future of office work and the idealized knowledge worker whose body, identity, and opportunity were conceptualized as universal while excluding workers' whose bodies, identities, or job classifications were outside of that ideal.

Chapter 1
Designing Hierarchy

In the 1980 film *9 to 5*, Lily Tomlin, Dolly Parton, and Jane Fonda played three white-collar workers who kidnap their "sexist, egotistical, lying, hypocritical bigot" boss, played by Dabney Coleman. In his absence from the office, they transform the bureaucratic and deeply sexist corporate culture into a more supportive organization with a host of new feminist policies and benefits including flexible hours, job share, equal pay for equal work, and in-office daycare. Over the course of the movie, office design serves as a direct expression of this transformation. At the start of the film, the office is a dull and monochromatic bullpen with rows and rows of tidy desks arranged in a grid, a spatial reflection of the top–down organizational culture of the corporation. By the end of the film the three women had transformed that same office into a new open plan, featuring a looser arrangement of desks in small groupings separated by low brightly colored orange and yellow partitions. Notably, the image of the new open plan in the film also emphasizes the diversity and inclusiveness of the space—the view of the newly designed office prominently features women, workers of color, and even a worker in a wheelchair pulling up to their open plan workstation reinforcing the idea that this workplace is an entirely different one not only spatially, but also culturally. This symbolic intertwining of an inclusive organizational culture and the open plan office design in the film reflects the image of the open plan as a naturally progressive office design solution and an expression of a more egalitarian organizational culture.

This chapter traces these changing ideas about hierarchy and office design from the conventionally designed offices of the mid-twentieth century with its rigid expression of hierarchy and status to the new and supposedly more inclusive open plan. Architects and designers of the period often treated status in office design as a neutral expression of organizational position and status, but I argue that office hierarchies of this era were intertwined with the long history of discrimination in the workplace, particularly in terms of gender, race, and ability. Advocates in the late 1960s viewed the new open plan as a complete reimagining of organizational culture, management theory, and the office itself, particularly in its rejection of hierarchy and status as organizing structures of the office. Echoing the emerging ideas in management theory of the 1960s, architects and designers promoting the open plan envisioned a future in which workers would have greater ownership over their work and work process, which in turn would benefit the organization by increasing productivity, efficiency, and creativity. Rather than imagining the organization as a system of rationalized boxes reporting up the chain of command (as represented in an organizational chart of the era), new management theory described the modern organization as a flatter system in which all the parts of the organization were important contributors to the larger goal. For proponents of the open plan, the new office concept was the spatial manifestation of this larger transformation in the structure of work that promised a more egalitarian culture.

Even as the open plan projected an image of greater inclusivity, hierarchy was always an integral part of the planning process for the open plan. Though its advocates often described the benefits of worker participation in office planning, the open plan was typically implemented in ways that codified and reinforced the positions, priorities, and preferences of those in power and often left out altogether the experiences and needs of lower level support staff and service workers, who rarely had the opportunity to participate in the design process in a substantive way. Recognizing the long tail of discrimination and exclusion embedded in hiring and promotion practices in American organizations throughout the twentieth century, this system effectively prioritized the voices of predominantly White men in professional roles while ignoring the voices, perspectives, and needs of marginalized workers in lower level positions including women, workers with disabilities, and workers of color. Despite its progressive and countercultural image, the open plan in fact *reinforced* organizational structures and systems of inequality through its design and usage.

Postwar Corporate Hierarchy

The postwar period saw an enormous growth in the design and construction of new corporate offices in the United States.[1] Rather than rehabilitate, remodel, or update their older buildings, American companies of that era invested enormous resources in constructing entirely new office buildings to suit their rapidly expanding organizations. Whether located inside of a towering skyscraper in the central business district of a major city or in a sprawling corporate office in the suburbs, these new offices reflected the organizational priorities and needs of the time. As Louise Mozingo argues, through their design, these new corporate headquarters of the postwar era needed to: serve as an architectural symbol of the organization, impressing investors and banks and conveying their "corporate trustworthiness"; attract and keep top executives, ensuring that those corporate executives felt a connection to the organization as a whole; and reassure the public that their fears about the excessive power of large corporations were unfounded. According to Mozingo, the corporate architecture of the postwar became the public image of the organization, and a "tangible corporate persona."[2] Further, as Alexandra Lange argues, corporate office design of the postwar was not simply "a matter of dressing the old building in a new glass-and-steel wrapper," it was an "overhaul" of the organizational structure by way of architecture.[3]

Architects and designers planned the interior space of new corporate offices around the organizational structure in explicit ways. First, they designed these new offices based on the formal departmental divisions, breaking up the organization into its constituent parts as conceptualized by the organizational chart and arranging the various corporate divisions around their functional and hierarchical relationships with other units. Within each department, the division of space reflected the inner workings of that department as well as the functional and hierarchical relationships among workers. Office planners typically provided workers in elevated positions a private office while they placed workers in lower-level positions, particularly those in technical and clerical roles, in an open "bullpen." Mapping the interior, architects and designers created detailed standards that allocated space, furniture, and accessories based primarily on the organizational status of each worker. The interior standards established for a particular project rationalized the allocation of space and amenities across the organization to reflect differential status from the topmost executives to the lowest-level clerical workers.[4] In her study of a single organization, sociologist Rosabeth Moss Kanter found a "clear system of stratification" in the conventional office materialized through furniture design, stretching from the metal framed desk with a wood top, to solid wood, and finally to a marble top for those at the top of the organization.[5] Desks were not the only attribute of distinction; journalist Vance Packard described the importance of office size and location as well as all of the other accessories and elements of décor that were tied to status including: lounge furniture, ashtrays, filing trays, carafes, carpets, drapes, and even art. Within this elaborate system of office hierarchy, each change in organizational status merited new office décor such that nearly every promotion required a parallel change in office space.[6]

In their corporate office designs, postwar American architects and designers such as Eero Saarinen, Charles and Ray Eames, and Florence Knoll championed a total design approach, applying a modern design aesthetic in a consistent and predictable way as a spatial and material expression of organizational efficiency and modernity. For example, in her work leading the Knoll Planning Unit, designer Florence Knoll created meticulous plans for her office designs. Figure 4 shows an office interior featured in a Knoll catalog, showcasing the orderly arrangement of Knoll desks with their clean geometric forms providing an

Figure 4 Sales office for Deering, Milliken and Co. in New York City, designed by the Knoll Planning Unit, featuring Florence Knoll desks and Eero Saarinen desk chairs, 1958. The image illustrates the meticulous office planning that came to define the modern corporate interior.
Source: Image Courtesy Knoll Archive.

elegant contrast with Eero Saarinen's organic office chairs. According to Bobbye Tigerman, Knoll's approach to design, which used the iconic pieces from the Knoll company's furniture line, became a "visual code" of the modern office.[7] This style of corporate modernism became the common visual and material lexicon of organizational hierarchy and management through the midcentury in the United States.

Architects' and designers' emphasis on creating a rationalized and carefully planned corporate interior explicitly designed around organizational hierarchy was a material expression of an idealized and fetishized corporate bureaucracy.

In *White Collar*, C. Wright Mills describes the office as a "symbol factory" where every action and decision of the organization was rendered material through pieces of paper circulating through the office from one clerk to another, from one floor to the next.[3] From the early-twentieth century through the postwar period, this circulation of paperwork was also a central focus in office design. Manuals on office layout and management emphasized the importance of arranging clerical staff around the idea of paperflow, ensuring that each worker's placement fit with the circulation of paperwork (forms, memos, processes) snaking through the office from worker to worker and division to division.[9]

This design process awarded workers in the upper level positions with the elaborate perquisites of organizational status and treated low-level workers as operational gears in a bureaucratic machine. The workspace was an explicit manifestation of hierarchy, status and position. As Lange argues, this meant that "one's job was visible with a glance at the purpose built desktop; its importance to the firm visible with a glance at its proximity to the powerful."[10] The postwar corporate office was thus conceptualized as a materialization of the working process, a tool in the circulation of work and information, and an outward expression of organizational hierarchy.

Cultures of Conformity and Discrimination

Workers were present in this system of circulating paper, but architects, designers, and managers often treated them as movable and interchangeable components within the larger space of the office and the organizational bureaucracy. This way of thinking about the organization as a system constructed predominantly of paperwork was not new or unique to the postwar era; for example in his research on the expansion of clerical work in mid-nineteenth century America, Michael Zakim analyzes the numerous ways in which the production and circulation of bureaucratic paperwork came to define modern capitalism, modern office work, and the design of the office itself.[11] Throughout the modern era, office design has been conceptualized by architects, designers, and managers as an idealized manifestation of the corporate hierarchy and more specifically as a system composed of workflows, job titles, and organizational relationships embodied by the corporate organizational chart. But the process of designing new corporate buildings in the mid-twentieth century with newly defined space standards created a fresh interpretation of the rationalized and standardized organizational hierarchy. Postwar architects imagined the corporate hierarchy, the organization, and its workers as abstract entities, and treated the new corporate office as the conceptual and material matrix that would draw these disparate components together and create a rational, cohesive, and orderly structure for their containment. Interior layouts neutralized the human workers into movable and interchangeable widgets in the organizational system, and this approach to design reinforced an image of the workplace as one that was inhabited by a universal and illusory worker whose body, identity, and individuality had been scrubbed away.

As Aimi Hamraie has argued in their book *Building Access*, architects and designers have a long history of designing around a universalized figure whose "neutral body" is meant to stand in for an average and idealized user or inhabitant. Hamraie refers to this universal figure at the center of architecture and design practice as the "normate" user whose average body is not only used as an imaginary template for the design process, but also as a kind of prescription of the idealized user who was typically conceptualized as a White, male, and nondisabled user. In the postwar period, women were increasingly included in human factors charts and architectural planning, yet like their male counterpart, her idealized and average form was also imagined as White and nondisabled, again reinforcing this normate idea.[12] Hamraie's analysis of the normate user is useful in thinking about the postwar corporate office because it offers a way of examining the assumptions of identity embedded in this idealized and imaginary worker at its center. Reading an office as a neutral arrangement of walls, partitions, furniture, and accessories without considering the real human bodies and their identities misses the ways in which these spaces reinforced and reproduced the entrenched systems of discrimination of the time.

In the postwar period, the imaginary worker at the center of the corporate office was the so-called organization man. Coined by William Whyte, the term referred to a typical White male worker in the upper levels of the organization, who had become fully enmeshed in the life and culture of the organization and who conformed with the social and cultural norms of the organization. Whyte describes the organization and its workers as one shaped by a culture of conformity that was cultivated by the organization not only in their day-to-day operation, but also through their hiring and promotion practices, which prioritized workers who would "fit in" and systematically weeded out workers who were in any way different from the status quo.[13] In the 1950s and early 1960s, the American public was fixated on the problems of conformity not only in the modernist corporate office, where the sea of men in identical grey flannel suits became a literary and visual trope of the period, but also in the suburban landscape where the houses and families were similarly represented as expressions of the broader culture of visual and social conformity.[14]

The organization man was as much defined by the privileges of his race, gender, ability, and social class as he was by his organizational position. In this sense, the postwar corporate hierarchy, which served as the underpinning of conventional office design, was not merely a materialization of abstract jobs and positions, but an inhabited landscape of privilege and opportunity for some, and exclusion and discrimination for others. As sociologist Joan Acker has argued, organizations are "inequality regimes," shaped by systems of racism, sexism, and classism.[15] Reading the postwar corporate office and its structures of hierarchy through the lens of discrimination highlights the ways in which these spaces were exclusionary by design. The oppression and discrimination of this period cut across numerous social identities, and manifest in many ways, but the burdens of discrimination were not carried equally by all affected by it.

One of the major divisions in American corporate offices of the postwar was along gender lines. White women had a significant presence in the office yet their positions were generally constrained within their own internal hierarchy in which their highest position was often the role of executive secretary, or a managing or supervisory role in a clerical or support unit (generally comprised entirely of women).[16] This was not new to the postwar period, indeed such sexism in office work dates back to the introduction of women in low level clerical roles in the late nineteenth and early twentieth century.[17] Women's work in corporate offices of the midcentury was usually divided between the highly visible front-office work (e.g., serving as a secretary), or back-office work in which workers were typically tied to certain machines and tasks. Women's opportunities for advancement and promotion in this period were often shaped by their education, race, and social class such that highly educated middle class White women received the more plum and visually prominent roles like executive secretary while working-class women and women of color were often relegated to the back-office jobs.[18] Women in clerical and secretarial roles were also frequently evaluated and promoted to higher paid and more visible positions based on their physical appearance (including dress, comportment, grooming, and perceived beauty). This meant that young attractive women were sometimes promoted over women who had more experience, and these systems tended to favor women whose appearance conformed to conventional standards of beauty at the time, which was deeply exclusionary particularly in terms of race, social class, age, body size, and ability.[19]

In addition to gender, American workplaces of this era were starkly divided along racial and ethnic lines. Racial and ethnic identities are themselves complex and intersectional, and different racial and ethnic groups in the United States experienced distinct types of racial oppression. During the final decades of Jim Crow in the United States, American cities, neighborhoods, schools, and workplaces remained structured by a landscape of legally authorized racial segregation that explicitly targeted Black Americans. As Patricia Hill Collins argues, although Black men and women achieved significant gains in civil rights through their activism (protests, sit-ins, marches, demonstrations, boycotts, and legal actions), even their legal successes, from *Brown v. the Board of Education* in 1954 to the passage of the Civil Rights Act in 1964, could not undo the historic systems of discrimination, racism, and exclusion that were deeply embedded in American society.[20]

Alongside Black Americans, Hispanic or Latina/o, American Indian, and Asian American workers also fought to gain greater educational and employment opportunities in the postwar United States with varying degrees of success.[21] In their 1966 annual report on employment patterns in private industry, the Committee on Equal Employment found that compared to their White counterparts, Black, American Indian, and Hispanic or Latino men generally held the lowest paying jobs, and were severely under-represented in the highest paying job categories, particularly white-collar positions (professional, technical, and managerial jobs). Asian American men reportedly had somewhat higher participation in professional and technical positions than other workers of color, though they were also under-represented in managerial roles. Women of color in the United States had higher representation in clerical and service roles than their male counterparts, though they had fewer opportunities for professional, technical, or managerial roles than men of color. One notable exception being Asian American women who had somewhat higher rates of professional and technical employment than other groups, even when compared to White women at the time.[22] Clerical divisions were therefore significantly more racially diverse than other white-collar job categories, but the overwhelming majority of office workers in this era were White. This racial landscape only became more pronounced as many large companies began to move their offices out of the urban centers where people of color were often concentrated and into suburban areas that lacked public transit thereby further deepening the entrenched racial segregation of white-collar work at the time.[23]

Workers with disabilities also encountered significant barriers to jobs and opportunities in this era including outright discrimination as well as a lack of accessibility. Disability activists and organizations fought for greater inclusion and opportunity in the postwar, but opportunities for disabled workers remained limited.[24] As Bess Williamson describes in her book *Accessible America*, veterans injured in the war had some government support geared toward rehabilitation and the goal of a productive career following their military service, but civilians with disabilities had far fewer resources or support in navigating housing, jobs, and transportation. As Williamson argues, for both veterans and civilians, access was often further restricted based on race, social class, and gender.[25] At the same time, the lack of architectural standards to support access in the mid-twentieth century meant that people with disabilities were not only excluded from certain types of jobs (and the educational opportunities to get those jobs), but in some instances they could not even enter the building.

Beyond gender, race, and ability, workers also experienced discrimination on other aspects of identity such as social class, nationality, education, religion, and sexuality, among others. These various classes of identity intersect and interact with each other such that workers who identified with marginalized identities in multiple categories experienced deeper degrees of discrimination.[26] Returning to our "organization man" that has so defined discussions of postwar offices and postwar corporate culture, we have to recognize the numerous workers whose bodies and identities were expressly excluded from those jobs and their assigned spaces. Further, the presumption of this "organization man" and his normate body was also physically inscribed into the design of the office from the ableist architectural spaces to the sexist office chairs and ambient air temperatures, creating spaces that were optimal for some classes of users, and ill-suited or exclusionary for others.[27] The rigid corporate hierarchies of the postwar, so carefully reproduced in office design and office space, are inseparable from the culture of exclusion, including entrenched racism, sexism, and ableism that served as the understructure of organizational culture.

Corporate Countercultures

In the 1960s, an emerging youth culture challenged these entrenched cultures of conformity, discrimination, and technocratic bureaucracy that had defined postwar culture. The activism associated with the various civil rights movements, the women's movement, the peace movement, and the new counterculture left a significant imprint on American business. The civil rights, disability rights, and women's movements paved the way for increased representation for more diverse workers in a greater array of white-collar jobs, increasing access and opportunities for some women, workers of color, and workers with disabilities, but White able-bodied cisgender men continued to dominate professional, technical, and leadership roles across most industries and in most American organizations.[28] At the same time, corporate advertising of the late 1960s and 1970s increasingly adopted the aesthetics of the counterculture through psychedelic imagery and youthful slogans. They also echoed some of the social activism of the era for example selling their products with the language of women's liberation and Black power even as they failed to meaningfully engage in structural change to increase the diversity of their organizations.[29]

As corporations were transforming their external image to reflect the new counterculture and attract a youthful and more diverse consumer market, many were also refashioning their internal corporate culture throwing off the scourge of top–down bureaucracy in favor of a new and more progressive approach to management and organizational structure. Some corporations began to see their own corporate culture as a hindrance to economic growth. In other words, after years of carefully nurturing and developing an army of "yes men" in grey flannel suits, some organizations began seeking ways to upend those social norms and infuse new energy, fresh ideas, and even construct an entirely new corporate image and corporate culture. At the time, new theories of management, organizational culture, and human motivation were actively challenging many of the assumptions of conventional postwar corporate culture.[30]

Among the most influential of these new management theories was the work of Douglas McGregor. In 1957, McGregor published an article titled "The Human Side of Enterprise," which he expanded into a book published in 1960 of the same title that described two competing theories of management: Theory X and Theory Y. The "Theory X" approach was characterized by several key assumptions about the average worker, who: wants to avoid work; dislikes responsibility; is indifferent to the needs of the organization as a whole; and must be controlled by management through close supervision and micromanagement of all work-related tasks and behaviors. In contrast, so-called "Theory Y" managers believed that the role of management was not to "control" workers, but to foster a more supportive workplace environment in which workers had greater ownership for the work process, greater responsibility in the organization, and more opportunity for development and growth.[31] Through the 1960s, "Theory X" was often framed as a "conventional" management approach characteristic of an old-fashioned corporate bureaucracy, and "Theory Y" was typically heralded as a more progressive approach appropriate for a new age of organizational culture and a new generation of workers.

As the concept of "Theory Y" was gaining ground among forward-thinking managers and administrators, management consultant and theorist Peter Drucker's concept of the "knowledge worker" was also enormously influential. First coined by Drucker in 1959, the term "knowledge worker" was frequently used in the 1960s to describe a new generation of professional workers who were more independent than previous generations of office workers. In contrast to the corporate drone of yore, the "knowledge worker" was characterized by Drucker as a highly educated expert whose work required thinking, collaboration, originality, and creativity rather than paper pushing. Most importantly, Drucker argued that the "knowledge worker" was outside of conventional organizational hierarchies. This new class of worker operated independently, made decisions, and ultimately had more in common with executives than with managers or technical workers, and consequently required managers to adopt a new approach that fostered each worker's need for autonomy and individuality.[32]

These ideas were increasingly popular in business circles through the 1960s and early 1970s. In his bestselling book *Up the Organization*, businessman Robert Townsend described his personal philosophy of management and business as president and chairman of rental car company Avis. In many ways, Townsend embodies the countercultural business approach through his management style, and he specifically cites Douglas McGregor's *Human Side of Enterprise* and Peter Drucker's *Managing for Results* as two of the most important books on management he had ever read. In other words, for Townsend, McGregor and

Drucker were his twin pillars of influence in terms of his overall management and leadership style.[33]

Organizations viewed the adoption of these new theories of management as strategically important because research at the time suggested that young workers in the late 1960s and early 1970s had very different motivational goals than their parents. A national survey conducted from 1968 to 1971 found that a growing number of young people sought work that would be personally fulfilling or "meaningful." The study reported that these young workers were resistant to conventional hierarchies, instead prioritizing jobs that would give them greater autonomy to make decisions and independence in the workplace. As a 1973 US government report *Work in America* described, young workers were not revolting against work, but rather revolting against a culture of "authoritarianism."[34] This idea, that young workers were a new and different class requiring a new organizational culture, led some businesses to rethink their organization to better appeal to them. For organizations, reducing hierarchy through the adoption of new management theory was a strategic change that would ultimately help them attract and keep younger workers.

Together, "Theory Y" and "knowledge work" represented a shift in thinking about the nature, purpose, and structure of organizational hierarchy in the 1960s. Rather than conceptualizing the corporate structure as an army in which all of the workers were marching in bureaucratic lockstep, advocates of this new kind of corporate structure characterized it as more fluid, dynamic, and "organic" in its form. Drawing on the ideas of Ludwig von Bertalanffy's general systems theory and Norbert Wiener's concept of cybernetics, organizational theory increasingly described organizations as complex and interdependent systems.[35] As Reinhold Martin has described, this emerging idea of the organic system in the 1960s challenged the centralized and top–down organizational ideal with a new decentralized and distributed model of the organization, which operated "without hierarchy or center."[36] All of these new ideas challenged conventional notions of corporate hierarchy and required a significant philosophical shift in organizational culture. For advocates of this new way of thinking about management and organizational structure, upending hierarchical practices was not a simple or straightforward process that would transform the organization overnight, but rather an ongoing and evolving set of interactions among workers at all levels, and these new ideas were vital to the development of the new open plan office.

Designing the Egalitarian Office

In the late 1950s, just as Douglas McGregor was first writing about his concept of Theory Y, and Peter Drucker was just introducing the concept of the knowledge worker, German organizational consultants (and brothers) Eberhard Schnelle and Wolfgang Schnelle began experimenting with a new way of designing the office that they called *burolandschaft* or "office landscape." According to Andreas Rumpfhuber, theories of cybernetics inspired the Schnelle brothers leading them to conceptualize the office as a dynamic system of information and people in constant circulation. One of their first experiments in office planning was at a publishing house in Germany in the late 1950s, where the Schnelle brothers used the wide expanse of a warehouse space to reprogram the organization around internal patterns of communication. Rather than breaking up the space with enclosed offices, the Schnelle brothers arranged workers in the open warehouse in loose groupings of simple desks, mixed with a modest number of low movable partitions and plants.[37]

Soon after these early experiments, the Schnelle brothers moved their offices to the Quickborn district of Hamburg, renamed their company the Quickborner Team, and began consulting on office projects across West Germany and eventually throughout Europe. Early reporting from the mid-1960s on the office landscape concept in the United States often treated the idea as an office planning oddity from Europe, but in the late 1960s office landscaping started to get some attention, most prominently from Carroll Cihlar, editor of the journal *Office Design*, who published the first extended article on the concept in March of 1967 and organized a symposium on the new concept held in September 1967.[38] At that same time, Quickborner was just opening their first American office in Millburn, New Jersey headed by Hans Lorenzen and Dieter Jaeger, and installing their first American office landscape in the offices of the Freon division of DuPont, where a single floor in a conventional building was redesigned using the new office concept (Figure 5).[39] It is unclear why Quickborner chose this moment to open a US office, but based on their promotion of the concept in the American press at the time, Quickborner perhaps saw a window of opportunity for the landscaping idea as these new ideas about management theory were gaining ground in American architectural and business circles.[40] Following the highly publicized DuPont installation, the American branch of the Quickborner Team was soon working with a number of organizations around the United Stated including John Hancock Insurance, Eastman Kodak, Port Authority of New York, and Purdue University.[41]

As the Schenlle brothers were initially developing their office landscaping concept in the late 1950s, American designer Robert Propst was also becoming interested in the problems of office work and office design. A design consultant, Propst joined Herman Miller as the head of their Research division in 1960, and promptly started work on the problem of office furniture and office design. The result of his early experimentation, research, and thinking about the needs of workers and the problems of modern work was a new kind of furniture called Action Office.[42] The first iteration of Action Office, released in 1965, was a

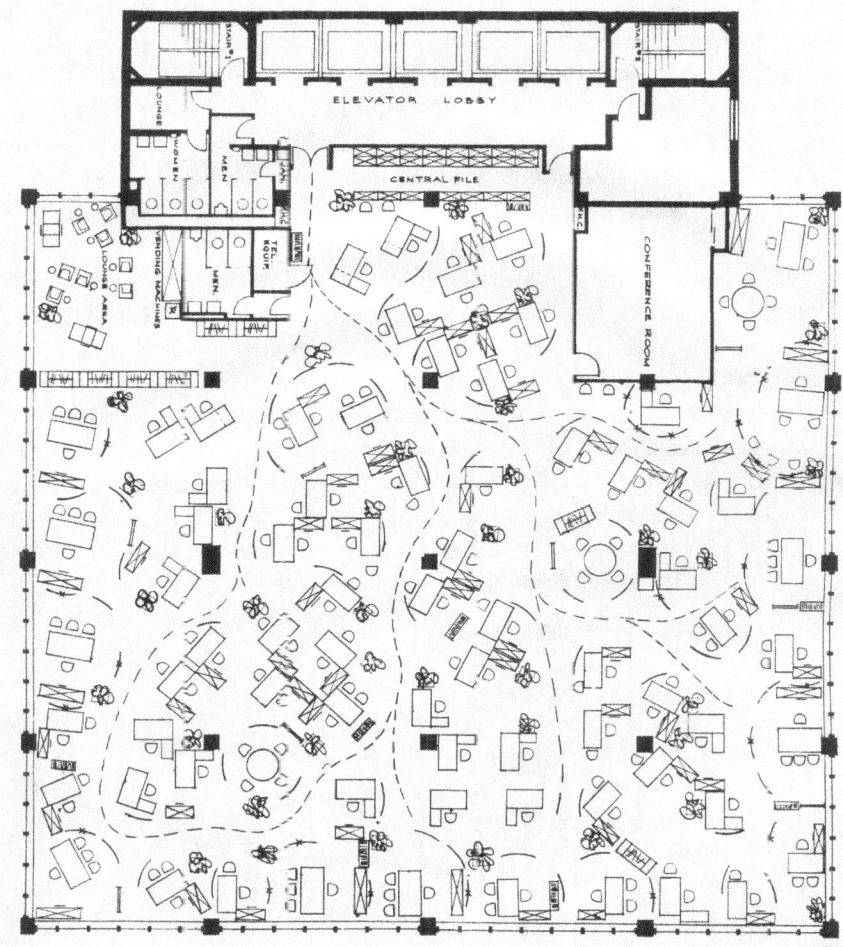

Figure 5 DuPont Freon Division layout, designed by the Quickborner Team in 1967. The design is characteristic of the office landscape layout with its loose arrangement of desks and curving screens creating modest privacy.
Source: Office Landscaping: An Open Plan Concept of Office Design, 71. Image used with permission of Combine Consulting.

series of elegant wood and metal office furniture pieces that were designed to support the unique needs of executives in the office, particularly their need for manipulating information, supporting natural clutter (as a manifestation of the thinking process), and their need for physical movement within their workspace. Action Office 1 was not a market success, but Robert Propst and his research team soon began work on an expanded version of Action Office that would take some of the same ideals embedded in the original series into a modular furniture system suitable for everyone in the office. At the time, Propst was aware of the work of the Quickborner Team and their office landscaping concept, which was just starting to gain significant attention in the United States. In May of 1967 he attended a conference on office landscaping in Stockholm and spoke at the symposium later that same year on office landscaping organized by the American journal *Office Design*. For Propst, the office landscape concept represented an exciting new direction in office design that reinforced much of his own thinking about the future of work.[43]

In 1968, Herman Miller released Action Office 2, a novel furniture system featuring a series of low freestanding partitions that could support work surfaces and storage components. As a system, Action Office offered a suite of interchangeable and interlocking components that could be assembled in many configurations and combinations to meet the individual working needs of any worker in the office. Figure 6 shows an early installation of the new Action Office furniture system in the Citizens and Southern National Bank in Atlanta from 1968. Like office landscaping, Action Office imagined the workplace as an open interior defined through the careful placement of modular furniture components rather than defined by walls. In tandem with the release of the new modular furniture system, Robert Propst published a kind of manifesto called *Action*

Figure 6 Image of Action Office 2 installation at Citizens and Southern National Bank in Atlanta, Georgia, 1968. In the image, the modular partitions and storage of Action Office serve to define the individual workstations, while still maintaining an open interior.
Source: Courtesy of Herman Miller Archives.

Office: A Facility Based on Change, which described the furniture concept and its underlying philosophy.

The coincidental timing of the release of Action Office 2 just as office landscaping was taking off in the American architecture and design press meant that the articles introducing the office landscaping concept to an American audience often referenced the new Herman Miller furniture as a related and even complementary idea.[44] Despite their technical differences, Action Office and office landscaping shared some common ideas including a belief in the need to support the new developmental management approaches embodied by the work of Douglas McGregor and Peter Drucker, and a desire to reduce the role of hierarchy in office design.[45]

The American architecture and design press described these new open plan office concepts as naturally egalitarian. For example, a 1969 article in *Office Design* described the newly landscaped offices of a jewelry company in Rhode Island as "democratic" because of its minimal distinction among workers in the office. According to the article, the furniture used for the executive offices was the same as that for the "humblest office boy's work station." The most elaborate private office was not for the president, but for the personnel department who required it for interview purposes. Describing their broader intention, the Research and Design Institute, an architecture and design office responsible for the project, described how the new plan was meant to "provide superior working conditions" and an expression of a "progressive" business culture. According to a published statement from one of the designers, the new building "is organized on a democratic basis, expressed in office landscape, which supports individual initiative, team effort and a feeling of human dignity for the occupants."[46] Throughout both the article and designer statement, office landscaping is treated as a natural expression of this new culture of work that upended conventional ideas about organizational hierarchy and status in office planning. By rejecting private offices and sharply reducing the gradations of hierarchy in office design as well as their symbolic indicators, advocates of these new open plan concepts promised to reimagine the office as a more egalitarian space in which the markers of hierarchy were all but eliminated.

This rejection of hierarchy embedded in early open plan designs manifest primarily through the elimination of private offices. Of course, advocates of the open plan recognized that some workers were reluctant to give up their private offices. For example, *Progressive Architecture* described how the more established workers in upper positions may not mind leaving their "prestigious den" for an open plan design but the "lesser fry" of the office who were just able to get a private office in the conventional system were likely to feel "deprived of the door and the rug that have been their symbols of success and the tangible goals of their striving."[47] In other words, according to the article, those whose status was clear unambiguous, and well established would be able to accept this change in space, but those just on the margins of earning a private office were most likely to balk at the loss. This typical framing reinforced the belief among advocates of the open plan that the private office was not a functional requirement or necessity for these upper level workers, but rather an empty status symbol and even a barrier to effective communication and interaction.

The aesthetics of these early open plan concepts also rendered the organizational structure and its hierarchy almost illegible by its design. In contrast with conventional office planning which followed the form of the organizational chart, new open plan offices had a visually chaotic appearance in which the myriad divisions and areas appear to merge and flow into each other. This deliberately disordered quality of the open plan office reduced the spatial prominence of organizational hierarchy. Although hierarchy was still present and visible, the differences of status in these early open plan designs were subtler than in conventional office design, typically conveyed through individual floor space, the adjacent number of partitions and plants, and the specified furniture. As environmental psychologist Franklin Becker argued, the increased use of the new class of systems furniture such as Action Office provided a common design vocabulary across the space in open plan offices that often overpowered the differences such that the various workspaces looked more similar than different.[48] Simply by eliding the familiar signifiers of status, the open plan challenged the conventional uses of hierarchy in office design, and by extension its emphasis on organizational culture. According to architect Frank Duffy, in these early types of open plan or office landscaping designs "egalitarianism was worn conspicuously as a badge of progress" symbolizing an office's democratic culture and their flat organizational hierarchy.[49]

As the open plan became popular, advocates of the concept viewed its egalitarian associations as naturally youthful and even inherently countercultural by design. When McDonald's chose an open plan office for its corporate headquarters completed in 1971 in Oak Brook, Illinois, descriptions of their office in the press characterized their choice of an open plan as a reflection of their progressive corporate culture. In news stories, reporters even described the McDonald's office as youthful, with rock music playing in the cafeteria and workers dressed in fashionable "mod" clothing.[50] For McDonald's the youthful organizational culture was an important strategy for attracting and keeping young talented workers. In the words of one of the executives at McDonald's, " 'if you are going to hire young people … you've got to motivate them and these days little cubicles and superficial status symbols like northeast corner offices just don't motivate people'."[51] The new offices featured interiors designed by Associated Space Design (ASD), an Atlanta interiors firm led by William Pulgram. They adopted a new furniture system originally created for the McDonald's offices called TRM or Task Response Module, which was designed by Pulgram and manufactured by Eppinger.[52] The TRM system (Figure 7), with its natural

Figure 7 Eppinger's TRM workstations in the McDonald's Office, 1971. ASD arranged the elegant wood furniture to create individual professional workstations with integrated partitions and storage components.
Source: ASD|SKY.

wood grain and case furniture aesthetics, was expressly designed to appeal to executives by providing a more sophisticated appearance relative to the other classes of systems furniture available at the time.[53] As an article in *Interiors* described, the "wall free corporate democracy" of McDonald's offers a space where "every member of the work force enjoys high-echelon amenities, views, and space." As many of the stories emphasized, even founder Ray Kroc worked in one of the TRM open plan workspaces. Yet, the supposedly "status-free space" also maintained clear distinctions of status in terms of the allocation of floor space, the selection of furniture, and the height and degree of enclosure afforded by the furniture; secretaries and clerical staff, for example, worked at regular Steelcase 5200 line desks.[54]

Perhaps nothing embodied this countercultural aspect of the McDonald's open plan corporate office more prominently than the "think tank" space—a futuristic padded spaceship-like structure on the eighth floor of the building. Prefiguring the playful and immersive office designs associated with Silicon Valley of the 1990s and early 2000s, the McDonald's think tank was designed to provide workers privacy for thinking and escape during the work day. The space had a labyrinth leading to a work room with beanbag chairs and a kind of hatch opening into a round "meditation room" featuring a circular 700-gallon waterbed, fully enclosed with curving walls, and containing a stereo system

Figure 8 Image of a man sitting cross legged on a waterbed in the round meditation room inside the McDonald's "Think Tank," 1971. The think tank offered workers a retreat from the office that would support creative thinking.
Source: ASD|SKY.

and a projection system for images. Available to anyone in the company by appointment, the think tank gave workers a place to unwind, reflect, and escape from office distractions (Figure 8). The space was used both by individuals and small groups (up to six workers) for meeting and brainstorming, and it was even reportedly used for some personnel interviews. Just imagine the strange and perhaps unnerving experience of a job candidate showing up for an interview at the McDonald's headquarters and finding themselves escorted into the think tank room where they might be expected to crawl through a hatch and plop down on a waterbed. While such a scenario might have been a bit odd for a male candidate applying for a job, the same situation for a female job candidate would have likely felt much more unsettling because of the sexual implications of being interviewed on a waterbed; imagine the awkwardness of sitting on an undulating waterbed in a skirt and tights. There is even some suggestion in the reporting that McDonald's "think tank" space was used for sexual dalliances between co-workers.[55] In this sense, the "think tank" waterbed in McDonald's open plan office implicitly referenced the sexual revolution of the 1960s and provided a prominent symbol of McDonald's youthful corporate culture, which in turn reinforced the countercultural aspects of their open plan office. The framing of the open plan office as not only egalitarian but also inherently youthful and countercultural meant that the open plan itself was often seen as a spatial expression of this new type of organizational culture.

The Politics of Planning

In August 1972, the Bureau of Planning and Budget in the State of Wisconsin requested a remodel of their office space in the Hill Farms building in Madison, Wisconsin. The original Hill Farms office space, completed in 1964, had utilized full-height movable partitions for private offices, but the Bureau of Planning and Budget asked for those old partitions to be removed entirely to implement a new "office landscape" with no private offices at all. In the memo, the assistant director of the office cited the numerous benefits of the office landscaping approach, particularly its relationship to the "management philosophy" of the planning office and the "developmental nature" of planning program's work. The memo indicated that the staff was so enthusiastic about this proposed change that if not approved it would be a significant blow to their morale.[56]

At around the same time (in February of 1973) another division in the State of Wisconsin, the Board of Vocational, Technical & Adult Education in the very same building had a "delicate internal management problem." Their recently remodeled offices were reportedly quite lovely with "judicious uses of color and plant material to create a pleasing environment," but according to an internal memo there were "dimensional worms in Eden." One of the bureau directors had a private office that was 6 linear feet (182 cm) larger than the others because of the unfortunate placement of a radiator which was too expensive to move, and the other directors were very upset about this perceived inequity in office sizes. The original memo from the agency head to the Department of Administration (DOA) asked for permission to spend the additional funds to move the radiator and wall allowing the director offices to be the same size. In their response, the head of the DOA responded, "We are not unaware of the degree to which space layout matters tend to take on a seriousness of concern disproportionate to their relative importance in the overall responsibility of governmental management." He continued stating, "we will proceed with the changes you have requested, but in all honesty with a general feeling of reluctance in so doing. Sorrow might even be a better word—for, in this instance, those of us who are attempting to fight the war of negativism about bureaucracy have lost a small battle in that process."[57]

As one group of workers in the State of Wisconsin was enthusiastically eliminating their private offices in favor of a new open plan design, another group was struggling with infighting over the equitable representation of hierarchy in terms of office size. Together, these two stories reflect the emerging debate of this period about the meanings and uses of hierarchy in office design as the open plan became mainstream in the United States. Like many organizations around the country, in the early 1970s the State of Wisconsin had already begun to recognize the burden of bureaucracy and cost associated with the obsessive fixation on status in office design associated with conventional planning, and the new open plan was increasingly attractive to organizations like Wisconsin State Government in part because it upended those conventions. By the late 1970s, the State of Wisconsin would eventually adopt the open plan concept as a standard for all state government office buildings.[58] Yet, even as it became a state standard in Wisconsin, a number of individual workers and even entire divisions remained reluctant to accept the open plan and the parallel loss in space and status that it represented.[59] The leadership of the DOA in the State and some units and their workers readily adopted the open plan concept in the late 1970s and early 1980s, but there was also significant internal resistance at all levels and across numerous units, and the resistance was constantly being negotiated through internal debates about the relative allocation of space for divisions and their workers and the specification of furniture.[60]

These kinds of organizational tensions over office design were not unique to the State of Wisconsin. As noted above, early discussions about the open plan often referenced the potential angst and dissatisfaction of workers who would typically receive a private office. Even as the open plan became mainstream through the 1970s, concerns remained about worker resistance to the new design particularly with regards to the representation of hierarchy and status. According to their 1978 study, Steelcase and Louis Harris and Associates found that 88 percent of business executives surveyed acknowledged that they viewed the loss of status associated with the open plan as a drawback of the design concept.[61] In the business journal *Administrative Management*, an article titled "Getting the Holdouts to Accept the Open Plan" describes how some workers experienced significant apprehension about the new design concept, and that some organizations continue to encounter "resistance and even hostility" from workers, particularly low level and mid-level executives "who may regard their private offices as 'status symbols'."[62]

In part to address these kinds of concerns, office furniture manufacturers marketed systems furniture lines in ways that showcased its ability to express status and position through the specification of components and finishes that offered a visual language of hierarchy even in the open plan. For example, systems furniture price lists of the 1970s and 1980s provided increasingly elaborate gradations of finishes, textiles, and other materials creating an index of status embedded in the furniture specification process. From the laminate finishes to wood grain, from basic nylon to natural fibers or even leather, and from plastic accents to gleaming metal, the language of materials was not just one of aesthetics but also of relative cost and perceived value. Nearly every furniture system could be specified with different materials along with different components throughout the space to ensure a clear and explicit representation of hierarchy. In addition to using the furniture as an expression of status, some projects also maintained a clear spatial separation between upper level executives and general office workers. At the new Montgomery Ward building completed in 1973, designed by architect Minoru Yamasaki with open plan interiors by Rodgers and Associates, top executives had an exclusive space on the twenty-sixth floor of the building. Although the twenty-sixth floor was also an open plan in its design, it featured an elegant wood furniture system that was also different in style and form from the standard Steelcase 9000 furniture used in the rest of the building.[63]

Despite concern about the plight of the professional or executive worker in the open plan and their perceived loss of status, there was comparatively little concern about general office workers, particularly low-level clerical and support staff. In fact, most writings characterized the open plan as a net benefit for low-level workers because it was more egalitarian, more humane, and more supportive of work than the conventional office design.[64] For the lower-level workers in clerical and support roles (who again were predominantly women), the biggest status issue in office design was not the aesthetics and intricacies of status, but rather the degree of inclusion in the planning and design process.

Early advocates of the open plan often championed the idea of participation as an important attribute of the new concept. In office landscaping, the Quickborner Team surveyed all workers in an office-wide communication assessment that tracked the real interactions among workers and liked to include workers at all levels on the planning team. Similarly, Herman Miller provided its clients a detailed survey template to assess the individual working and spatial needs for all workers as part of the planning process. In his 1978 handbook, *Open Office Planning*, designer and writer John Pile cautioned architects and designers that in the design process for an open plan office both of these models could produce an overwhelming amount of data that in the end might not be very usable. Pile further states that such detailed surveys of low-level clerical and support staff are not useful because those workers are essentially "interchangeable units whose personal requirements do not differ in any important way from person to person." Because this class of employees often had a high turnover rate, he argues, "efforts to identify personal needs and work patterns are often pointless." For these reasons, Pile instructed designers and architects that there was little value in collecting such detailed information from all staff. Yet, Pile also acknowledges that involving workers could help encourage user acceptance.[65] How do we square this seeming contradiction?

When prominent advocates and practitioners of open planning like John Pile describe the benefits of user participation, they often meant upper level professional workers such as managers and executives, not low-level support staff. Architects and designers in the 1970s and 1980s increasingly included upper-level workers in office planning, in some cases even giving those workers significant choice regarding their individual preferences. The Union Carbide office in Danbury, Connecticut designed by architect Kevin Roche in the late 1970s and completed in 1982 has often been characterized as an example of high user participation.[66] As part of the planning process for that project, Roche and his team conducted hundreds of interviews in the early planning stages with various (overwhelmingly male) executives and managers and most of those workers were given the opportunity to choose their own furniture from some thirty different options for their private offices. The mostly female clerical staff in the same building were only given minimal opportunities to participate in the planning and design. They were invited to visit a mock-up of the proposed furniture and fill out a simple survey evaluating the selected furniture (a fairly standard practice at the time), but the basic layout and open plan workstation design had already been more or less decided by the architect and corporate leadership.[67] Unlike their professional colleagues whose opinions and needs were carefully assessed and who were even allowed to choose their own office furniture, the clerical staff were given no real choices and few opportunities to participate. The entrenched social inequities of the workforce which were mapped into the allocation and design of space were also reflected in the design process itself through participation (or lack thereof).

The available evidence of the 1970s and 1980s suggests that in most office design projects, general office workers were not included in the design process much at all. Even when workers were involved it was in a very limited capacity, sometimes providing data in an initial survey, and sometimes providing comments on specific aspects of a workstation mockup, as in the Union Carbide example. The 1978 Steelcase survey found that the majority of general office workers had minimal participation in the design process, and even a majority of architects and designers surveyed acknowledged that they felt the users (general office workers) were not included sufficiently in the process.[68] Yet, post occupancy studies on participation at the time had shown a strong correlation between real participation in the design process and satisfaction with the completed building. In 1972, the General Services Association sponsored an experiment in the Federal Aviation Administration (FAA) offices in Seattle where the employees designed their own workstations. While the overall design was reportedly "very heterogeneous," a phrase that suggests a lack of visual cohesion from a design perspective, one year later, after the building was occupied, the workers in that building were generally more satisfied with their space than were the workers in a conventionally planned FAA office in Los Angeles.[69] Perhaps not surprisingly, design manuals of the period encouraged architects and designers to create opportunities for workers to participate in the planning process in some way, but the inclusion of workers in the process was often framed as an effort to encourage their acceptance of the new office rather than as an opportunity to receive meaningful feedback on their needs and preferences.[70] In other words, inviting worker participation was not even necessarily about gaining important insights from the worker to improve or otherwise change the design concept, but rather strategically deployed as a means of ensuring that the workers felt heard even if their ideas or comments were not reflected in the final design at all. Even when general office workers were included, they were rarely told or able to see how their input in the design process was used or addressed in the final design, which often only made workers more frustrated that their feedback, though solicited, was not taken seriously.[71]

This suggests the ways in which hierarchy, power, and status were not just reflected in the physical arrangement of the office, the combination of components, or the choice of materials used in a particular workspace, but it was also produced through the design process itself. Every office design was a negotiation between the organization, its space planners (architects, designers, facilities managers, etc.), its various divisions or units, and its workers across the organization. Those who had a voice in the process had an opportunity to shape the outcome to their benefit, or at least air grievances as part of planning, but for every worker included in the design process, there were often hundreds and even thousands of workers that were not included at all. Because corporate hierarchy remained shaped by discrimination and exclusion, participation in the design was also tied to identity such that White cisgendered and able-bodied men in leadership roles continued to have more voice in the process than women, workers of color, disabled and other marginalized or disenfranchised workers.

Exclusion by Design

When architects and designers first promoted the open plan in the United States, they saw this new office design idea as a transformation of the office and a reflection of a larger shift in thinking about the structure and culture of organizations. Some architects, designers, and organizations saw the conventional office with its "total design" aesthetic and carefully delineated corporate hierarchies as out of step with the new culture of office work in which the trappings of status were no longer useful or even relevant. For its advocates, the open plan was an expression of these new theories of management and organizational culture. Echoing the countercultural idealism of the late 1960s, advocates of the open plan in the United States saw this radical approach to office design as an almost utopian office concept that would promote a more egalitarian organizational culture through its design.

Champions of the open plan often characterized this egalitarian ideal as a transformation of the organization, but the idealized vision of the future of work was one that privileged and prioritized the needs, concerns, and priorities of upper level workers. Despite their gratuitous nods toward supporting the file clerk in the open plan, architects' and designers' idealized open plan was never a place in which all workers and all positions were treated or even imagined as equal. This gap between the language of egalitarianism and its practical application manifest in the design of the open plan, which often continued to silo top level executives from other classes of workers, and also in the planning process in which low-level workers including clerical and service workers were rarely given the opportunity to meaningfully participate in the design process. The hierarchical aspects of the open plan office persisted both materially and conceptually through the design process, which reinforced and reproduced organizational privilege. As organizational theorists Karen Dale and Gibson Burrell write, architects were mediators between the building and their corporate clients, and the resulting organizational architecture thereby reproduces and reinforces a "web of power relations" within the organization. According to Dale and Burrell, this reification of power, status, and hierarchy in architecture is an artifact of these deeply rooted power relations that are endemic to the architectural process itself.[72]

Office design has historically inscribed hierarchy and power into space, but through their use, offices are inscribed with human bodies whose identities also shape the meaning and use of that space. The space of the office, though technically planned as a system of interlocking workspaces designed for abstract positions, was always eventually inhabited by workers whose bodies and identities were as much a part of the space and the organization as their jobs. The legacy of discriminatory hiring and promotion practices in American organizations produced a landscape of inequality and exclusion based on markers of identity including gender, race, and ability. Despite its egalitarian idealism, the open plan was never a neutral description of an abstract organizational entity, but rather a materialization of the systems and structures of power that were themselves shaped by a long history of discrimination.

Chapter 2
Managing Change

For advocates of the open plan, the rejection of organizational hierarchy and the embrace of new management theory was an essential underpinning of the concept, but in selling the open plan to clients, the most frequently referenced benefit was the open plan's flexibility to support change. Architects and designers argued that the office should be as nimble, flexible, and adaptable to change as the organization itself, and offices should ideally reflect and support organizational change. In office landscaping, the Quickborner Team deliberately favored light simple furniture and movable pieces (in some cases on wheels) that would allow the entire space and its contents to easily and quickly adjust to changing organizational needs. Similarly, Robert Propst and his team designed Action Office as a highly modular system of components that would allow organizations to make quick changes to their entire layout to support ongoing change. Proponents of the open plan imagined a future in which office change was constant and immediate; the office and the organization were locked together in perpetual synchronicity—the one immediately changing in response to the other. In their fixation on the importance of change, advocates of the open plan conceptualized the office as an ever-evolving and changing space that was nimble and responsive to every organizational, technological, and social change.

To think about change is inevitably to consider time as a dimension and factor in the use of space. Of course, office design itself exists in time—every office space reflects the assumptions and needs of its particular moment, and those assumptions are reproduced materially and spatially. Office design is also a process that takes time, often requiring many years of planning and discussion before the builders place the first stone in the foundation. The open plan imagined the office not as a sealed time capsule that would exist unchanging for decades, but rather as a dynamic system that would continue to change and evolve in the days, weeks, months, and years following the initial installation. Advocates of the open plan viewed change as a practical necessity in office design, and as an organizational value that reflected the progressive management ideals of its time.

Yet, the meaning and purpose of organizational change evolved significantly from the late 1960s when advocates first began heavily promoting the open plan in the United States to the 1970s when the open plan and systems furniture became mainstream in American offices. Though born in an era of economic prosperity that treated change as an expression of growth and innovation, by the 1970s, the changes underway were markedly different. A significant economic downturn, rising inflation, a loss of productivity, and multiple energy crises helped create a deeply unstable economic climate. Change in the 1960s was framed as optimistic and forward-thinking, but change in the 1970s was often implemented by organizations in a reactionary and defensive manner, frequently with the express goal of increasing productivity, decreasing energy usage, reducing space usage, and cutting operational expenses. The design, evolution, and use of the open plan reflect both the idealism of its early development as well as the pragmatic concerns of organizations that adopted the open plan in large numbers through the 1970s and 1980s.

While the open plan remained an expression of change, the meaning and purpose of organizational change in the 1970s was altogether different from the idealistic vision of change so often described in the 1960s. As I argue, this gap between the original vision and the reality of implementation was materialized in the design of systems furniture which was conceptualized and promoted as a tool for easy change, but was by design a complex system of components that only became more cumbersome as it grew and changed to address emerging technical needs. For organizations, managing office changes required a facilities management team to maintain the ever-growing inventory of systems furniture and to plan, manage, and implement ongoing organizational, technological, and spatial change. For workers, this constant change manifest in significant technological, social, economic, and organizational upheaval that produced an increasingly unstable environment in which workers jobs or units might cut, create, or change entire units overnight. The perpetually shifting partitions of the open plan were a spatial manifestation of the growing economic and social instability.

Designed for Change

The idea that change was an important attribute of office design was not really a new idea in the 1960s. From the early twentieth century through the postwar period a significant number of American corporate offices, factories, schools, and hospitals were designed with full-height movable partitions. Among the major manufacturers of full-height movable partitions was the E. F. Hauserman Company founded in 1913 in Cleveland, Ohio. The Hauserman Company marketed their partitions as a valuable amenity that would afford organizations the flexibility to adapt their interior space to inevitable changes over time. Integrating interior raceways for running electrical wiring and telephone lines inside the panel, and providing hardware for doors, windows, and other architectural details, the partitions functioned like regular interior walls with the added benefit of movability allowing organizations to more easily adapt the space to their ever-changing needs. In their marketing materials from the 1930s, Hauserman described how their steel walls could be rearranged again and again making them "permanent assets" that would actually "outlive the building."[1]

By the postwar period, Hauserman boasted a sophisticated range of partition types suitable for every kind of space from the executive suite to the dispensary and featuring a range of materials, colors, and options to provide architects and organizations a robust and flexible system suitable for specification throughout a building. Hauserman described their movable walls as prefabricated and modular by design, featuring standard posts and components that allowed easy and efficient assembly and disassembly. One brochure from the 1950s even depicts the walls being changed in just thirty minutes as a secretary and executive continue their work, apparently undisturbed by the team of Hauserman workmen dismantling and reassembling the wall system in their midst.[2] In fact, even as they celebrated the ease with which their partitions could move, Hauserman also emphasized the value, importance, and even necessity of using Hauserman's own installers not only for the original installation but for any subsequent move. In buying Hauserman partitions, the organization was not just buying the partition hardware, they were also purchasing Hauserman's installation services for its lifetime of usage.[3] They celebrated their nation-wide system of representatives and installers, and the Hauserman logo prominently featured a workman holding up a panel in the shape of the letter "H", reinforcing the service orientation of the company.

Architectural historians and theorists have often characterized the prominent use of movable walls in postwar architecture as part of a modular understanding of architectural space. In his book *The Organizational Complex*, architectural historian Reinhold Martin describes how postwar corporate architecture embraced standardized modules as key components of architectural design. Martin argues that the concept of the "module" served to structure office space in standardized or prefabricated components within the architectural envelope allowing for some flexibility but constrained by the rigidity of modular standardization. While ostensibly designed to enable change, that change was circumscribed as a system of fixed components that could only be arranged in a limited set of configurations.[4] According to Martin, this emphasis on modular systems was tied to the use of grids as the architectural ideal, embodied visually by the curtain wall with its glittering grid of glass.[5] Creating structures of "organized flexibility" allowed architects to use standardized building components as an architectural language made up of pre-fabricated assemblies, modules, and parts.[6]

New York City's Union Carbide building designed by Skidmore Owings & Merrill (SOM), completed in 1960, was significant because of its embrace of this type of architectural modularity. The floor plan of the 52-story building, designed to house some 5,000 Union Carbide workers, featured a continuous run of carpeting and a ceiling comprised of a grid supporting lighting, air conditioning, and a Hauserman movable partition system.[7] SOM's design allowed Union Carbide to rearrange the walls freely along the grid expanding and moving offices as needed within the modular system.[8] Yet, Union Carbide found that despite the emphasis on flexibility that was built into the original design, making changes to the space was quite cumbersome and even expensive. According to Kevin Roche's project statement for the planning of their new suburban headquarters, Union Carbide was spending an estimated 1.5 million dollars a year in the mid-1970s (the equivalent of nearly 7 million dollars today) just on moves and reorganizations to accommodate regular status changes in their SOM-designed building in New York City.[9] While the total number of moves represented by that figure are not specified, the Chemical and Plastics division reported that in 1976 alone 740 out of 888 workers in their area experienced a move or change to their space with around 20–30 percent of those changes requiring some form of new construction. Leadership from that division indicated that it cost around 150 dollars per workspace when no construction was required and an additional 10 dollars per square foot (30 cm) with construction costs.[10] Those numbers combined with the total figure regarding moves in a year suggests that Union Carbide was moving thousands of workspaces a year in their New York City headquarters. Part of the expense associated with even small space changes was that nearly every change, for example, enlarging even a small 10 feet by 10 feet (304 cm by 304 cm) office to accommodate a promotion created a domino effect on the run of offices adjacent to that office in order to maintain space standards. Although the concept of modularity in postwar architecture provided some flexibility to organizations, it was also bounded and inhibited by the internal space standards that imposed limits on how the space could be changed. Thus, one of the central limitations of the Union Carbide building was not just the technical mechanics of the interior partitions, which were of course cumbersome and expensive to move, but also the set of rules or conditions under which those walls were required or allowed to move.

The modular interiors of postwar corporate architecture, however, were an important precursor and even a prerequisite of the open plan itself which depended on a conceptual shift in thinking about the relationship of the building to its interior arrangement. In their 1976 book, *Planning Office Space*, Francis Duffy, Colin Cave, and Frank Worthington differentiate the "shell" of the building (essentially the architectural envelope) from its interior scenery (furnishings). They argue that in the modern office, these two building elements, though interconnected, had very different life spans and purposes, with the shell serving as a more permanent exterior of the building, and the scenery reflecting the shifting and evolving short term needs of the building's occupants.[11] In the open plan office concept, the shell of the building ideally offered an undifferentiated expanse of office space that could be freely arranged based on the needs of the organization and its workers.[12]

As the Quickborner Team's office landscaping and Herman Miller's Action Office were just gaining notice in the American architectural press in the late 1960s, E. F. Hauserman Company realized that their full-height movable partitions, though still in demand, were out of step with the emerging interest in these new office design concepts. The metal partitions that Hauserman had made for decades were movable, but they did not provide the kind of granular adjustability and instant flexibility associated with the office landscape and the emerging classes of systems furniture like Action Office. Recognizing the rapidly changing market, Hauserman began reimagining its product line to better address this new approach to office design and this new expectation of instant and constant change. In 1969, they produced a new brochure titled, "A New Concept to Manage Change in Business Interiors," which described how their low-height Divider Wall system in tandem with their full-height Ready Wall system could be used to create new landscape or open plan arrangements providing

> the flexibility to change to the office layout you need to improve work flow and communications, to use space more efficiently, to experiment with new management techniques or departmental organization. And the change is not irreversible. If you find the previous layout was better you can go back to it ... easily and without incurring heavy labor costs.[13]

There was no specialized labor or additional costs required to make a change. Hauserman also developed a small line of accessories designed to turn their vertical partitions into active surfaces for projecting images, making notes with a water-soluble marker, supporting a chalkboard or corkboard, or even adding shelves. According to the Hauserman brochure, "Your thinking, your plans are not tied to the structure. You can change. You can manage change."[14] Using Hauserman's new partition concept, companies were invited to try on a new arrangement, tinker with the organization, and explore new approaches to management in an inexpensive and quick manner without being locked into those changes. Hauserman thus characterized the office as a kind of sandbox of experimentation, and their partition system was a toolkit of flexible walls that would allow for effortless and ongoing organizational and spatial change.

Hauserman's fixation on the value of supporting organizational change was not just a marketing ploy. At the time, the Hauserman Company was in the process of implementing organizational change to help their own company adapt to this rapidly shifting marketplace that no longer wanted full-height partitions and conventional office design. In their internal memos and meeting notes, Hauserman's leadership referred to Douglas McGregor's Theory Y concept and talked about the Drucker concept of "management by objectives" in which workers set their own individual goals, which were tied to larger organizational priorities. In one meeting from 1968, a management team at Hauserman described how they wanted to: (1) "be a growth company"; (2) "grow through managing change and finding the opportunities this presents"; (3) "manage change with people who are constantly growing in her capabilities"; and (4) provide "a climate of challenge for people to grow in."[15] In transforming their product and promoting it as a tool for organizational change, Hauserman was reflecting their own organizational transformation that was underway at the time. As they describe in a 1970 annual report, "Some say there is nothing permanent except change. We at Hauserman agree wholeheartedly. The changing form of your business—your changing needs for space—represent our business opportunities."[16] For Hauserman, organizational change was not just a pie-in-the-sky idea or a marketing gimmick, but something they were actively seeking for their own organization as they sought to take their company in a new direction, away from manufacturing building components (movable walls) and into the new systems furniture industry.

By 1971, Hauserman was already working on prototypes for their new office furniture concept when they invited a relatively new workplace design research group called Buffalo Organizations for Social and Technological Innovation (BOSTI) to consult on their new project. Following their initial consultation, Hauserman asked BOSTI to produce an analysis specifically looking at the problems of change in work environments, creating a set of requirements for a productive office, examining the economic issues for "high performance, adaptable office interiors," and identifying specific ways in which the new Hauserman product could respond to changing needs.[17] The resulting report titled *The Management of Change for Productive Interiors* explored in detail the emerging problems of change in contemporary workplaces and the ways in which office space and office furniture could facilitate and support change in an active and ongoing manner. BOSTI concluded their report with eight practical design requirements that emerged from their findings. Drawing on these concrete recommendations from BOSTI, Hauserman's design team created their new Office Interior System (OIS) furniture to facilitate and support ongoing organizational and spatial change.[18]

From the outset, Hauserman conceptualized their systems furniture as an adaptable material intermediary between their human and organizational inhabitants and the architectural spaces they inhabited. The promise of instant and constant flexibility for change was embedded in the design, and was central to the ways in which the new furniture was marketed and sold. Hauserman was just one example, but their investment in this idea of change as an organizational value and their emphasis on change in the development of the OIS system illustrates how these ideals of organizational change and the possibility of change, as conceptualized in this new class of office furniture, were interconnected. Of course, Hauserman was not unique in this regard. Many other furniture companies in the late 1960s and early 1970s were similarly trying to upend their own product lines to compete in this emerging market of systems furniture, and like Hauserman, companies like Westinghouse and Steelcase highlighted the easy flexibility and adjustability of their furniture, which was designed to support and facilitate ongoing space change.

Systems Furniture and the Materiality of Change

Early manufacturers characterized this new class of open plan furniture as a modular system of components that would provide organizations infinite flexibility to make changes to their space and to reflect organizational changes. In practical terms, this new class of office furniture was a collection of individual components including writing surfaces, storage, panels, and shelves that organizations, architects, designers, and users could assemble and combine in a variety of different configurations. The modularity of systems furniture and its emphasis on supporting change was dependent on visual continuity among the various parts and pieces of the system.[19] The desks, storage, and panels all had to coordinate visually (as well as technically) to ensure that the image of the office remained attractive and professional regardless of the configuration in use. In fact, this concept of visual continuity in office planning was itself an expression of modularity in that it reflected the coherent application of materials, finishes, and components that could easily mask the many iterations of change. Aesthetic coherence ensured that the various parts of the system would always fit together and would be visually attractive and complete no matter how they were assembled (Figure 9).

In marketing materials, systems furniture often included assembly images with a hand using a standard tool to assemble a panel; for example, Figure 10 shows a hand tightening a screw on a Steelcase Movable Walls panel. This kind of image reinforced the ideal of easy assembly. Yet in practice, the technical aspects of the system were actually quite complicated; Figure 11 shows a detailed technical drawing of a Steelcase Movable Wall panel and all of its parts and pieces. In general, panels by most systems furniture manufacturers required "connectors," a type of post that linked the panels to one another. Top caps and end caps gave the partitions a finished appearance (disguising the connections and the unfinished ends of the panels), and "glides" added to the feet supported

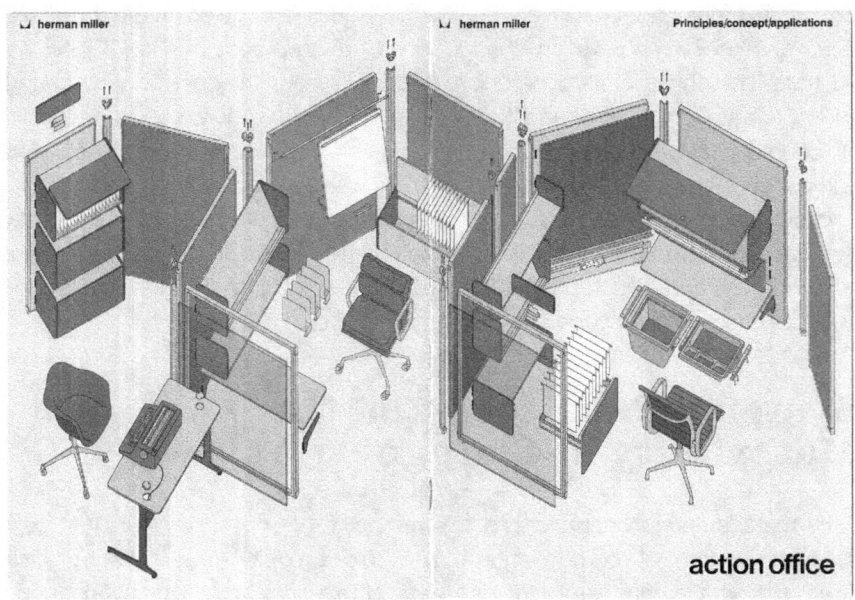

Figure 9 A technical drawing of Herman Miller's Action Office 2 from 1972 illustrating the modular design of the components. As can be seen in this image, all of the components of Action Office were stylistically similar and attached by simple connectors and basic hardware to facilitate easy assembly and change.
Source: Courtesy of Herman Miller Archives.

the panel, allowing it to move and adjust to accommodate uneven floors. Writing surfaces attached to partitions by brackets, cantilevers, or stretchers, and the drawers and other storage elements mounted underneath the writing surfaces or connected to the panels directly. At an even more granular level, each of these parts were attached to each other using very small standard hardware such as screws, nuts, and bolts, each of a particular size and weight necessary for each component. A survey of thirty-seven different lines of furniture from 1974 illustrates the sheer variety of connectors across the various lines describing complex systems of brackets, bolts, screws, clips, hooks, key holes, and even specialized (manufacturer specific) hardware.[20] If this list of hardware used to assemble systems furniture is dizzying to read, just imagine the challenge of actually assembling this furniture with all of these parts and all of their fussy hardware.

Because each system was designed to allow multiple configurations, some components might have several different ways in which they could be connected, with each iteration requiring its own set of specialized hardware. In every systems furniture line, the different component pieces offered a number of possible configurations, and as a result, ordering systems furniture

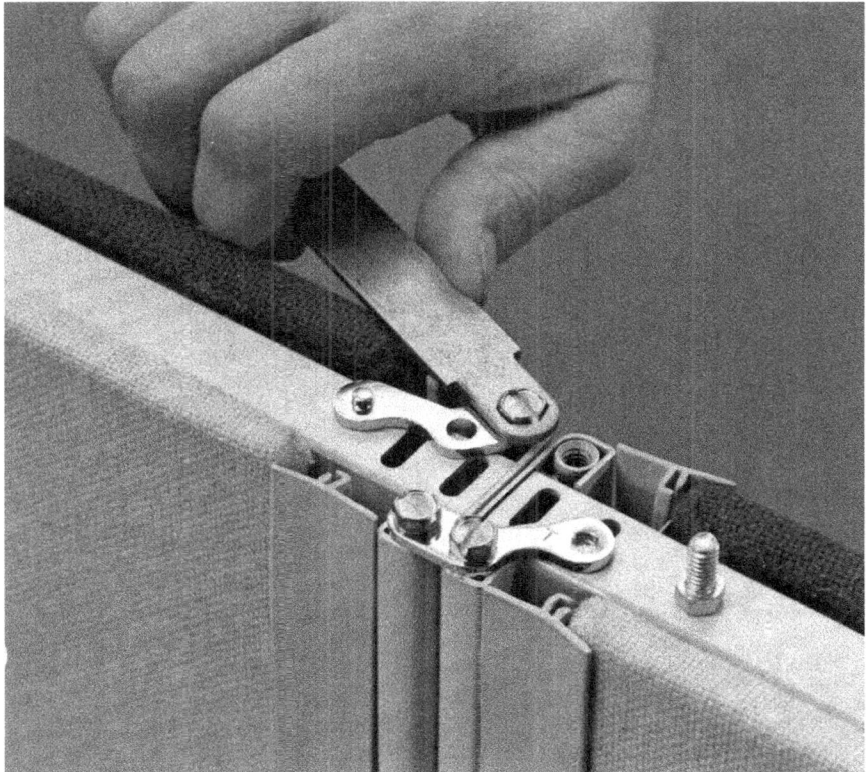

Figure 10 Image of a hand screwing the top of a panel in Steelcase's Movable Wall system from 1976. This kind of photograph with a close up of a hand attaching a panel was a common type of image in systems furniture brochures in the 1970s.
Source: Steelcase Corporate Archives.

was sometimes incredibly complicated requiring careful planning to ensure that the correct hardware was on hand to support the planned installation. Knoll's Stephens line had different hardware "kits" depending on the particular connecting workstations and arrangements of panels and work surfaces, and those kits had to be specified as part of the original furniture order.[21] If one type of kit was used in the original installation, and a later space change required a different hardware combination, that new kit would need to be ordered for the planned change to be implemented. Systems furniture was often portrayed in the furniture catalogs as an adaptable, flexible, and infinitely changeable system, but the materiality of that change was constrained by particular configurations and options. In other words, manufacturers designed the components to connect in predetermined ways; the furniture thus prescribed certain types of installations and inhibited (or even precluded) others.

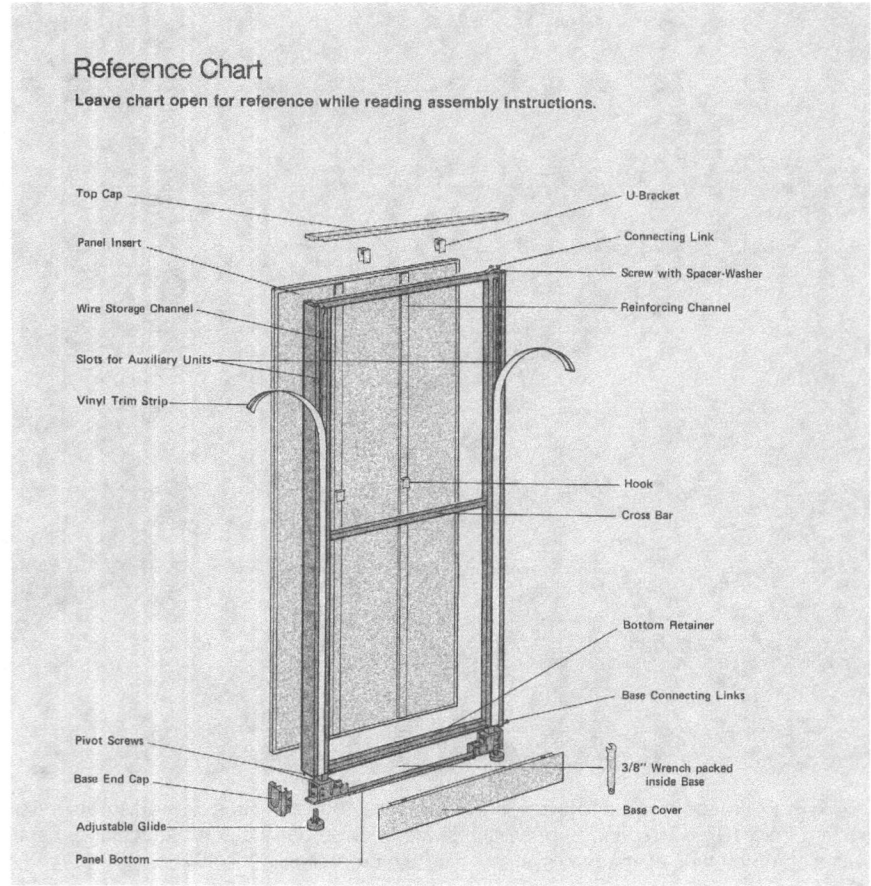

Figure 11 Detailed technical drawing of a panel assembly for the Steelcase Movable Wall system from the 1970s. This illustrates the basic components and hardware of a standard Movable Wall partition; note that Steelcase packed a special wrench for assembly into the base of the partition for shipping.

Source: Steelcase, *Assembly Manual Steelcase Movable Wall System* (n.d.). Trade catalog from the William Pahlmann Papers Series 25 Box 29 at the Hagley Museum and Library and used with permission of Steelcase Corporate Archives.

Systems furniture components, though designed to integrate with other pieces in the same system, were not generally well suited to mix with other unrelated systems. The parts of Knoll's Stephens System could not be easily intermingled or connected with Herman Miller's Action Office, Hauserman's OIS, or Steelcase's 9000 line. Not only did the various systems have their own finishes and fabrics, making them visually and materially distinct from each other, they were also technically distinct; a work surface from one system could not be easily connected to a panel from a different manufacturer.[22] By choosing a systems furniture line, organizations were making a long-term investment with a particular manufacturer, and even after their initial purchase of furniture for a new installation, organizations would often have to purchase additional components and parts to augment their inventory over time. As a result, long-term support and ongoing production and expansion of the system (with new parts to accommodate new needs) were critical criteria for organizations in choosing a systems line.[23] The open plan office was often described by manufacturers as a system designed for change and flexibility, but organizations adopting these open plan systems were immediately locked into a certain furniture line with specific components and predetermined configurations.

Just as the systems lines could become a limitation over time for customers who had adopted a certain type of furniture, the system also imposed constraints on the manufacturer. As systems furniture manufacturers expanded their furniture lines to offer new types of installations and new amenities, they needed to integrate those new parts with the system and ensure that organizations could use the new components with their older generations of furniture. In other words, manufacturers were also locked into their systems as they needed to continue to support their previous clients (who still needed to purchase furniture components for their offices) while also staying competitive in the market as they acquired new clients and addressed new needs and emerging problems. For example, in the early 1970s, integrated lighting systems were a custom concept in office furniture, but by the mid-1970s many of the major furniture lines had added their own integrated lighting systems. These newly designed furniture lighting components often featured a combination of ambient "up lighting" (with lighting elements that created reflected light on the ceiling) and downward task lighting at the workstation itself that could be added post-installation if necessary.[24] When Steelcase created a new lighting component for their systems furniture in 1977, they ensured that it would work with either of their systems lines to allow their legacy clients to retrofit the new lighting system to their older furniture.[25]

Perhaps nothing was more challenging in the logistics of the open plan and systems furniture design than the provision of power. Early systems furniture relied on architecture for adequate access to power and phone lines, but over time this dependence on the architecture for essential utilities became a barrier to change. As architectural journalist Donald Canty described, this issue of providing access to power and telephone cables served to effectively "anchor work spaces" ultimately inhibiting much of the purported flexibility in systems furniture.[26] Part of the reason this became so problematic is that even through the 1970s, most American office buildings were still being designed and constructed with relatively modest power and communication access intended for general office work (typewriters, telephones, and other such common devices). As I will discuss in more detail in Chapter 5, the proliferation of "power-hungry" equipment, particularly computers, required architects, designers, and organizations to give more consideration to the problem of electrical distribution in the office.[27] To address this growing problem of power and communication access in the office, systems furniture began to evolve over the course of the 1970s from light-weight partitions into an architectural power grid providing universal office access to electricity, communication cables, as well as lighting.

The earliest iterations used auxiliary raceways, channels mounted on the front or bottom of a partition accommodating runs of cables for power and communication. For example, both the Steelcase Mobiles and Steelcase 9000 lines in the 1970s had a means of integrating cable runs within the furniture in order to make power more accessible, but also to keep the visual clutter of power and telephone cords out of sight.[28] This type of furniture was not actually "powered," it was merely a conveyance of power, in some instances even relying on a daisy chain of extension cords to connect to a floor, wall, or ceiling power outlet. It was not uncommon for multiple workstations to rely on power access from a single outlet or tombstone in the 1970s; designer John Pile describes "stringing wiring" through raceways and plugging in clusters of workstations into a shared outlet.[29] This method of handling wiring, using runs of extension cords, was not only poor in terms of power issues (creating overloaded circuits) it was also a fire hazard that was even illegal according to some local electrical codes.[30] Any change in office design often required an electrician to manage parallel changes to the power thus limiting the purported flexibility of the furniture significantly.[31]

In 1976, furniture company Haworth released their ERA-1 system, which created the first powered (electrically pre-wired) partition system. In an advertisement for the new powered system, Haworth invited architects and designers to "plan your spaces for the people, not the building." Featuring internal wiring, compartmentalized raceways, and flexible connectors that "snapped" into place completing a circuit, the ERA-1 represented a fundamental shift in thinking about the provision of power in the office.[32] Soon the other major furniture manufacturers were scrambling to create their own integrated powered components to compete with Haworth's revolutionary system.

Haworth's ERA-1 transformed systems furniture into a critical part of the power infrastructure of the office, and by the early 1980s all of the major furniture manufacturers boasted their own integrated power elements designed to support both communication and power needs. Yet, specifying and installing these powered elements only made the systems furniture planning more complicated. A 1988 planning guide for the CETRA system by furniture manufacturer Kimball offers exhaustive detail of the important considerations and caveats in planning powered furniture from identifying the source of power (ceiling, floor, or wall) to determining the placement of the raceway in each panel. To even connect the electrical supply from one panel to the next, designers had to specify the jumper cables that would be used, and those could vary based on both the angle of the connector or (straight, 90°, 120°, 135°) as well as the size of the panels.[33] The integration of powered elements in the design of systems furniture thus made the furniture itself much more complex in its design, much more challenging to specify in a given project, more complicated to install, and increasingly difficult to change.

In fact, by the 1980s, as systems furniture lines were becoming more architectural in their functionality and form, some new furniture lines embraced this idea of the furniture as interior architecture. In the release of their new furniture line Ethospace in 1984, Herman Miller used the language of architecture to describe the new furniture: the partitions were "walls," the glazed panels were "windows," and the interior arrangement was called a "skyline."[34] Similarly, Haworth augmented their Places line with a new line of "Architectural Elements" including fanlights, French doors, gabled panels, and various muntin options (window panes) creating a distinctly architectural aesthetic for the workspace (Figure 12).[35] Buildings in turn became even more skeletal providing only an empty shell of an office with basic power and heating ventilation and air conditioning (HVAC), while increasingly relying on systems furniture to create the entire interior

Figure 12 Image of a Haworth Places workstation which shows the integration of architectural elements into systems furniture. Note the panel featuring window panes with rectangular muntins and a pediment-style top.
Source: Image from Haworth *Places*, 1989. Trace catalog from the Hagley Museum and Library and used with permission of Haworth.

arrangement, and provide lighting, power, and communication cabling for all workstations.

Facilities Management and the Logistics of Organizational Change

The consistent marketing of this new open plan furniture as a flexible "system" designed to support and facilitate change suggests that organizations adopting the open plan valued that attribute. Obviously, the architecture and design press and office furniture manufacturers regularly discussed this idea of flexibility in the new open plan and systems furniture, but the business and mainstream press described the benefits of the open plan and systems furniture in very similar ways. An article from the business journal *Administrative Management* from 1973 describes how the new "modular" workstations were only of value if organizations installed them in a manner that allowed some flexibility in their arrangement enabling change and allowing for growth. Describing the practical uses of this new type of systems furniture, the article described how organizations could arrange the furniture in a variety of configurations, and emphasized that the components were interchangeable, allowing organizations to easily swap out elements of the workstation and quickly add on additional workstations as needed.[36]

The promise of instant and constant space change to support organizational change was appealing at the time in part because public and private organizations alike were navigating an enormous amount of change in real time. The new theories of management at the time promised to create more engaged and productive workers but required a parallel cultural change. New organizational structures promised to make the organization flatter and more dynamic, but that often required a parallel reorganization of the company and its divisions. New office technologies, particularly computers and automation, promised increased efficiency and productivity but required entirely new ways of organizing and structuring work. Meanwhile, the economic climate in the United States was also rapidly changing from the seemingly endless growth and expansion that characterized the 1960s to the belt tightening recessions of the 1970s and 1980s that required still further organizational change to stay competitive.

Private organizations were typically tight-lipped about the nature of organizational change underway, but public organizations were often quite transparent, documenting, referencing, and discussing organizational change in countless memos, letters, and reports. In the State of Wisconsin there were numerous organizational changes through the 1970s and 1980s; the Department of Administration alone had five major reorganizations between 1968 and 1979. From 1978 to 1989 there were more than twenty different formal reorganizations across various agencies throughout Wisconsin State Government, many in connection to proposed space changes.³⁷ In addition to formal reorganizations and programmatic changes, other types of change were also underway at the State including efforts to decentralize certain activities (personnel and payroll), and efforts to centralize others (word processing and data processing).³⁸ Many of these kinds of organizational changes truly did require a space change, from just moving around a few workers to creating or dismantling entire organizational divisions. In this context, it is not surprising that the open plan's promise of easy and inexpensive space change resonated with business executives and management at the time.³⁹ For organizations, the office itself was a tool for change, facilitating the shifting around of people and divisions, supporting the creation of new teams or departments, and reflecting the cuts and expansions of staff. Public and private organizations alike were strongly attracted to this purported ability of the open plan to make change quickly, cheaply, and with minimum disruption in part because they believed that the design of the office should reflect the design of the organization.

Early reports about the open plan often cited the huge percentage of moves and changes or space "churn" for the companies in the months and years following its adoption. In their 1977 story about the Weyerhaeuser open plan offices, *AIA Journal* indicated that roughly a third of Weyerhaeuser's 900 workers were moved each year, and some workers even said that they had been moved three to six times since their move into the new building in 1971.⁴⁰ A report from *Progressive Architecture* from 1977 found that American advertising agency Young and Rubicam made changes to their open plan offices every sixty to ninety days, and IBM estimated that some 25 percent of their work stations were relocated each year in their corporate headquarters.⁴¹ Similarly, an *AIA Journal* story from 1980 reported that Citibank in New York City moved 20 percent of their workers each year, and in some divisions the move rate was as high as 50–75 percent.⁴²

Organizations also used the open plan as a tool for implementing space reductions. For example, in the early 1980s the Department of Administration at the State of Wisconsin had to reduce their office space by an additional 12,466 feet (approximately 3,800 meters) just a few years after moving into their newly designed open plan office.⁴³ The description of seemingly unending space changes in the State of Wisconsin from the late 1970s through the early 1980s reads like an elaborate game of Tetris in which the various units, departments, and agencies were "shoehorn[ed]" into spaces with the express goal of squeezing as many people as possible into the available space.⁴⁴ This kind of squeeze on office space was not unique to the State of Wisconsin; in the words of one space planner in 1979, "all employers want to know is how many people they can jam in there."⁴⁵

These ongoing changes were rarely handled by the architect or designer who created the original layout.⁴⁶ Instead, private and public organizations increasingly relied on an internal facilities management unit to handle these regular space changes. While the idea of having a dedicated space manager or administrator was not really new, the field of facilities management (and their associated responsibilities) grew significantly in the 1970s and 1980s, at least in part because of the widespread adoption of the open plan and systems furniture that required a new approach to managing and coordinating office space.[47] As noted above, systems furniture was marketed by manufacturers as "easy" to change and move, but in reality it was a complex and messy collection of components and hardware that had to be managed and maintained. Even a single workstation might have fifty or more components associated with it, and a large corporate office might have hundreds or even thousands of individual workstations that needed to be managed and maintained.

In 1978, a facilities manager at Hallmark told Herman Miller that managing the growing collection of parts and pieces of the furniture system was one of the biggest challenges in using the Action Office system. They further describe how designing a new space with all new equipment was relatively easy to plan and implement, but the changes over time were much more complicated due to the continuous shuffling and repurposing of the system components. This dynamic aspect of the system made the inventory process not only more challenging but also even more essential. Frequently the components necessary for a planned change were not on hand, creating delays as they scrambled to locate or order the necessary pieces.[48] Every space change therefore required a careful accounting of the furniture on hand in order to make a new layout, and creating an in-house inventory system to track those pieces became essential. The furniture inventory was a functional necessity in the planning process, and facilities managers were often tasked with creating their own inventory system from scratch, which required the creation of an internal tagging system for the parts that would track the identifying information of each component (including its manufacturer, its systems furniture line, its part number, and even color) as well as its physical location whether in storage or on the floor in a specific workstation. Once they had created a working inventory, facilities managers had to constantly update their records to keep track of the growing collection of disparate furniture parts and pieces as they moved around the office.[49] Each furniture component in the office had a double life—simultaneously existing in physical form in a workstation or in storage, and as a piece of data in an inventory. The inventory of systems furniture was a critical backbone for planning and implementing space changes.

Space changes were also challenging for facilities management in part because requests for change often arrived with little notice or forewarning. Units requesting a space change frequently expected a very quick turnaround, and typically required a change to a space that was already occupied by a group of workers, making the planning more complex.[50] In other words, the planning not only involved rearranging the space and the furniture to support the necessary change, it regularly included shifting a whole group of workers already in place to accommodate whatever change was necessary. The architectural space could also impose limits and constraints as older buildings and spaces had to be adapted over time to address new needs, requirements, and expectations.[51] Oddly shaped spaces, inconveniently placed columns or service elements, limited power or lighting access, and other architectural issues could inhibit the planned arrangement in unexpected ways and created regular logistical and technical challenges for facilities managers.

Organizations often had multiple lines and generations of furniture in use and were sometimes using those furniture components in ways that belied the notion of a complete integrated system. This was not an unusual issue—at the time, organizations often adopted systems furniture in a gradual way, starting with a small test case and slowly updating new divisions and areas with the new type of furniture. As a result, new systems furniture would frequently sit side-by-side with older furniture types and even different makes and models of furniture.[52] In an era of tight budgets, facilities managers often tried to reuse older furniture as much as possible, and so the patchwork quality of systems furniture would only become more pronounced over time as space changes required reconfigurations, and facilities management teams had to creatively repurpose parts and components that were not necessarily designed to fit together.

At Purdue University, the office plans for Freehafer Hall from its first construction as an "office landscape" in 1971 through the 2000s demonstrate the complexity of office redesigns even in a purpose-built open plan. When it was first constructed, Freehafer Hall used simple office landscape furniture with freestanding curving screens, freestanding storage, and freestanding desks. There were many iterations of plans from 1971 to 1986 suggesting that making changes using the original "landscape" furniture (freestanding desks and screens) was fairly common and relatively easy. However, in 1987 and 1988, Freehafer underwent a major redesign (including a building addition) in which the university began integrating more furniture from various lines of systems furniture, some components that were purchased for Freehafer and other pieces that were acquired from other campus buildings. In contrast to the relatively simple office landscape layouts of the past, the plans from 1987 to 1988 include increasingly complex inventories of furniture from eleven different manufacturers. Purdue space planners had to juggle multiple systems furniture lines, specifying the various work surfaces storage elements, and partitions as well as all of the hardware (screws, attachment kits, and brackets) necessary to hook all of the parts together.[53]

This gap between the vision of instant and constant space change as it was portrayed by furniture manufacturers and the reality of implementation at the organizational level illustrates the problem of talking about change only in the abstract, as it was described in systems furniture brochures. Office furniture materials of the period often depicted office design as a hermetically sealed system of perfectly integrated components that easily fit together in any configuration, but real offices often had multiple lines and generations of furniture that they were managing many of which did not go together at all. Changing the design of the office sometimes meant that facilities management teams had to find ways to connect parts and components of furniture that were not designed to fit together. The planning of office change could become increasingly complicated over time as organizations were mixing different lines of systems furniture, different generations of components, and adapting to changing work processes and technologies. Every change, even relatively modest ones, required careful planning, and the implementation of space change was often messy as organizations were negotiating changing organizational structures and changing technologies.

Workers' Perspectives on Change

In 1982, a press statement from a Wisconsin employee union described how a series of recent reorganizations, budget cuts, and layoffs had resulted in continuous shifting of office space. According to the press statement, in the previous year, 125 workers and 5 supervisors in one of the agencies were let go in tandem with a reorganization, which also resulted in an office change, followed by still further budget cuts, additional layoffs, and another reorganization requiring yet another round of office changes; the agency's "beleaguered workers began referring to this process as 'rearranging the deck chairs on the Titanic'."[54] Similarly, a worker at Blue Cross Blue Shield in New York City in 1977 described how their open plan office was like "an Erector set" in that "we could leave one night and come back to find all the cubicles gone. This is *the* modern office space, floating and subject to change. We have to forget that we, too, may be as movable as the office."[55] At the organizational level, change was often conceptualized through new policies, processes, technologies, office spaces, systems, budget cuts, layoffs, and reorganizations, but these diverse changes were not mere abstractions discussed in boardrooms and written on pieces of paper, they were real changes that affected workers' lives in significant ways.

Looking at change through the lens of workers thus offers an altogether different perspective on the nature, meaning, and experience of organizational change in this era. The open plan enabled organizations like the State of Wisconsin and Blue Cross Blue Shield to enact organizational change relatively quickly, but workers had an altogether different experience of change. For those on the ground of these organizations, space changes were a manifestation of a state of continuous upheaval and economic uncertainty in which one's job could change or be eliminated altogether with the shifting of an office partition. For workers, change was underway at every level from large-scale reorganizations to tiny unit-level changes that might only change a single job or a single position, and in some cases these small and large changes were all happening at the same time. In the words of one Wisconsin State worker from 1975: "In the year that I've been in state government: 1) the state planning program has changed; 2) the state planning staff has changed; 3) management in other agencies (with whom we have been developing 'credentials' and positive working relationship) has changed; 4) DOA leadership has changed; 5) DOA is changing; 6) I realize that I've stopped singing in the shower."[56] This ripple of change at all levels of the organization meant that workers were constantly navigating new organizational relationships and new responsibilities, alongside new systems, technologies, and processes.

In their 1978 Steelcase study, Louis Harris and Associates found that the majority of office workers surveyed (including clerical, secretarial, professional, and executive workers) had seen some change including changes to office space (location of workspace or office redesign), organizational changes, and change in the structure of one's job requiring new skills, new tasks, or new responsibilities.[57] These kinds of changes were not neutral from a worker's perspective; they could potentially improve the quality of working life, but they could also make work more stressful. In an overworked, overstretched unit, adding some new workers to help relieve the work flow would certainly be a benefit, but a cut to an already overworked unit could make the work process even more stressful as the remaining workers took on more responsibility to cover the lost labor. In other words, talking in broad general terms about organizational change misses the textures and nuances of change, and the ways in which workers in different divisions and positions within an organization experienced that change.

Perhaps the most significant change in this period was the huge growth in unemployment through the 1970s and early 1980s. From 1973 to 1975, the number of unemployed workers in the United States doubled, and among the unemployed in 1975, 58 percent were individuals who had lost their jobs.[58] It was common at the time for organizations to treat clerical staff as expendable, and as a result workers in those positions were often the most vulnerable to cuts. A 1973 report titled *Work in America* found that low-level, white-collar workers were viewed as nonessential, and were therefore often the first jobs to be cut in an economic downturn.[59] Women and workers of color, even those in professional roles, were frequently among the first to lose their jobs as a result of their low seniority.[60] Meanwhile, as they made drastic cuts to their full-time staff, many organizations increasingly relied on a growing class of contingent labor in the form of part-time and temporary workers.[61]

Layoffs often came in tandem with other changes to the organization, which created additional pressures, challenges, and problems for workers. In their

1984 survey on worker stress, the working women's union 9 to 5 found that nearly 60 percent of respondents had seen some staffing reduction in their offices, 50 percent had seen a "freeze on salaries," 67 percent had experienced some kind of "speed up" in their work, and 60 percent indicated that they had either been promoted or given more responsibility.[62] Among workers who had experienced staff cuts, pay freezes, and speed-ups, there were higher rates of reported health issues including increased headaches, nausea, insomnia, physical pain, and depression.[63] Thus, staffing cuts and layoffs came side-by-side with other efforts to increase efficiency and reduce costs, and the intendant pressure could even manifest through feelings of physical stress.

New technology was another ongoing source of change and disruption in the structure, culture, and process of office work in the 1970s and 1980s. Organizations often characterized "office automation" as a means of increasing operational efficiency, but it often included dramatic changes to the structure of work for clerical staff and frequently brought significant staffing cuts and layoffs in its wake. In 1975 when Citibank implemented a new automated system for their letter of credit division they cut their staff from 142 workers to only 100.[64] Many office automation efforts from the 1960s through the 1980s in both public and private organizations also required a shift of clerical work from individual units, offices, and divisions, into centralized clerical units such as word processing or data processing. It is worth noting that centralizing administrative tasks was not a new idea. Throughout the twentieth century, pools of workers had often been used to staff certain types of clerical divisions such as stenography, typing, and keypunch, but the emphasis on adopting automation in tandem with centralization through the latter part of the twentieth century significantly changed the structure of clerical work.[65]

By plucking the mostly female clerical workers out of their home divisions and placing them in newly re-centralized clerical units, organizations of the 1970s and 1980s treated clerical workers as not only "movable" in a physical sense, but essentially interchangeable within the organizational machinery. Organizations treated low-level workers as a portable unit, whose body and labor could be easily slotted in anywhere it was needed, just like the systems furniture workstation they inhabited. Underneath this way of thinking was the assumption that clerical workers were all doing the same types of work, had the same essential responsibilities, as well as the same knowledge and skills. Yet, as Shoshana Zuboff argues, clerical workers often had specialized knowledge of the work in their particular division, and played important roles in the overall functioning of the division.[66] The adoption of automation often replaced these specialized knowledges and skills with computerized processes that stripped away the variety and complexity of clerical work, including its social aspects. Tasks that formerly required a worker to actually talk to another worker were now often handled through a machine interaction or workflow instead of through a human interaction.[67] In word processing units, workers were socially and spatially isolated, working in windowless rooms far away from the regular staff, and often unknown by the professional workers whose letters and reports they typed. As Anne Machung describes, this approach to word processing "destroys much of the social fabric that formerly wove the office together, undermining bases of loyalty and interaction between clerical and managerial staff, dividing their social worlds from each other, and further segmenting these relationships, all in the name of productivity."[68]

Ironically, even as many companies in this period embraced the ideals of McGregor's Theory Y management in their upper ranks, they implemented automation in their clerical units in ways that reinforced a Theory X approach, controlling and restricting workers instead of giving them autonomy. Technology engineers designed these new automated systems such as word processing and data processing to sharply limit workers' ability to operate within the system, and even monitor workers by tracking and recording strokes. These automated machines constantly tracked the work of their operators, tallying every line, page, and document, and reporting those statistics as direct measurements of productivity. In some cases, these new systems were even set up to "beep" at workers if they were not meeting their productivity quota.[69]

Not surprisingly, clerical workers were sometimes resistant to these organizational and technical changes in the structure of their work. In 1979, as the State of Wisconsin was encouraging more agencies to adopt a centralized structure for clerical tasks like word processing, some workers expressed real concern about this proposed change. One division head in the State of Wisconsin described the reluctance of their clerical staff to be assigned to a centralized word processing unit, writing in a memo: "to a person they have no desire to be in an 'assembly line' production role."[70] Workers frequently viewed these automated word processing units as a factory-like spaces akin to working an assembly line. The work was also stressful, tedious, and alienating, and as a result these newly automated jobs often had very high turnover.[71] In some word processing centers, the turnover was reportedly as high as 100 percent a year as operators sought better working conditions and better pay.[72] Workers in the State of Wisconsin Department of Administration word processing unit in 1985 had such low morale, that the state brought in a faculty member from a local college to work with the staff to help improve the situation. In the evaluations from those sessions, many of the participants described the negative aspects of their work including their feelings of unhappiness in their jobs, high levels of stress and anxiety, a "dehumanizing" work culture, frustration with the way in which they were treated by workers outside of their division, and a general lack of collegiality among workers in the unit.[73] These types of negative experiences in centralized word processing and data processing units were well-documented in both public and private organizations through the 1970s and 1980s.[74]

The physical environment of the office in the 1970s and 1980s was also becoming less comfortable for workers as a result of changing building systems. Concerns about energy consumption and waste beginning in the 1970s meant that many of the new buildings constructed in this period featured building systems designed to minimize energy usage. As Michelle Murphy describes, new ventilation standards released in 1974 sharply reduced the intake of fresh air creating stifling and unhealthy office spaces. The lack of sufficient fresh air in office buildings was only made more problematic by the wide-spread practice of allowing smoking in office spaces in this time period.[75] Toxic and hazardous chemicals and materials in the construction and furnishings of office buildings along with pollutants generated by new machines like copiers created still further potential health hazards for workers.[76] Even temperature levels were increasingly controlled based on energy efficiency standards rather than on worker comfort. In the early 1970s the US federal government established standard temperatures for all government office buildings in order to ensure energy efficiency. Describing this shift in policy in 1973, the General Services Administration (GSA) described how "halls have become a little darker, and working spaces became suddenly warmer in the summer and cooler in the winter" to address concerns about energy consumption.[77] These concerns that were prominent in the 1970s foregrounded the engineering and construction of buildings, and gave little consideration to the comfort and well-being of the human bodies contained within.[78] Through the 1970s, the open plan was often characterized as a tool of increased energy efficiency because it eliminated the need to heat, cool, and light small enclosed spaces, and allowed for a more efficient air handling system.

These details about the ambient air quality in office buildings reveal the inner textures of everyday life in an office building in this period. While the ambient air quality might seem to be a micro-climate (a particular office building in a particular place at a particular time), the basic preconditions of that micro-climate were actually common in office buildings across the United States. This issue of air quality and ambient temperature, which were tied to concerns about cost saving and energy efficiency, were connected to the other changes in the economy, the organization, and technology. The early proponents of the open plan imagined a future of change that was dynamic and progressive ultimately creating a better organization, happier more productive workers, and a more supportive and responsive office, but the changes of the 1970s and early 1980s often produced negative outcomes for workers. The interweaving of organizational change and space change in the open plan meant that space was not just a reflection of organizational change, it was a spatial and material manifestation of change. Workers did not just experience the change in a general sense; they physically inhabited this climate of uncertainty and discomfort.

The Problem of Change

The descriptions of the open plan from its early promotion in the United States read like a love letter to the possibility and potential of radical organizational, social, technological, and spatial change. Architects, designers, and manufacturers saw the open plan as a flexible and nimble solution to the problem of constant change.[79] In the late 1960s, advocates of the open plan saw organizational change not only as inevitable, but also as an intrinsic part of the natural cycle of growth and creative innovation. Underneath this idealistic vision of the open plan was a sincere belief among furniture manufacturers as well as architects and designers that every change in an organization should have a parallel change in office space.

This fantasy of change was central to the design and marketing of systems furniture, which promised that the new furniture could readily adapt to the ever-shifting needs and challenges of organizations and their workers. Despite the marketing claims, in practice, systems furniture was not so much a perfectly integrated and interlocking system of parts, but rather a messy collection of disparate components and hardware that required careful planning to design and assemble and even more careful planning to manage and change. Furthermore, systems furniture became more complicated over time as manufacturers updated and expanded their systems to support new needs. Advocates of the open plan envisioned change as an intrinsic part of the concept and systems furniture was designed as a modular toolkit that would be continuously updated, changed, and augmented to address emerging needs. Yet those changes also made the system itself increasingly complex to manage and use, particularly for facilities managers and their teams who were responsible for managing the furniture and the never-ending space changes.

For workers, this landscape of continuous organizational and space changes in the 1970s and 1980s became an outward manifestation of the instability of their own jobs, which could be changed or eliminated at any moment. Even workers in high level positions within organizations were increasingly vulnerable to cuts and layoffs, but this increasing pressure on workers was not carried by all workers equally. Clerical staff, women, and workers of color were often the most vulnerable to cuts, layoffs, reorganizations, and technology changes that could transform or even eliminate their jobs with little warning or notice. While those promoting the open plan in the 1960s and 1970s often characterized change as an abstract concept, it had real world implications and consequences for workers whose positions, bodies, and needs were often seen as expendable to the needs and goals of the organization.

Chapter 3
Negotiating Privacy and Communication

Seated behind the 5 foot (152 cm) "modules" of their individual open plan workstation at the new McDonald's headquarters in 1972, reporter Andrew Malcolm described how 'an employe [sic] is protected from distraction by pervasive soundproofing, the arrangement of other modules and 400 deftly arranged, leased plants. But when he stands, the worker is instantly part of the entire floor and within easy view of many of the 3,050 bright, cheery windows, and dozens of colleagues."[1] Malcolm's description presents the open office as one in which workers have the benefit of functional privacy, free from distractions or noise, while also remaining a part of a community of other workers who are easily and instantly available for a quick meeting. In this space, the worker can choose to work in isolation, but simply by standing up will feel instantly connected again and accessible to colleagues. This image of the worker standing up to immediately experience a sense of community and connection with colleagues vividly illustrates the ways in which gender norms and assumptions of ability were embedded in the open plan concept and its design. Not only is the worker explicitly gendered as male in the example, he is also tall enough in stature to easily see over a 5-foot partition (unlike his petite female colleagues), and furthermore the worker is able to stand (is not a wheelchair user), and can see (is not blind). The early open plan office was frequently characterized by designers as the best of both worlds, optimally supporting communication and providing modest privacy for workers by screening views and managing sound, but that ideal was not equally accessible or available to all.

For proponents of the open plan, supporting communication was a frequently celebrated benefit of the design concept. Tearing down the walls of private offices would liberate workers from their enclosed offices, support greater interaction among workers, and increase efficiency and procuctivity. Early adopters of the open plan embraced this idea that removing walls would naturally improve communication, particularly for upper level workers previously siloed in private offices. Yet even its most fierce advocates also recognized the need to provide modest visual and acoustic privacy to support thinking and independent work in the open plan interior.

This chapter examines the persistent tension between the goal of supporting communication in the open plan office with the need to provide visual and acoustic privacy. As I argue, these ideas about the open plan office were part of a larger shift in thinking about the social needs of workers in management and organizational theory and the emergence of new theories examining the social uses of space. Champions of the open plan viewed this new office design concept as a critical intervention into postwar organizational culture and as a tool for facilitating communication and interaction. As part of this reimagining of the office through the lens of communication, architects, designers, and furniture manufacturers sought to reframe the value and mechanics of visual and acoustic privacy in the office. As these ideas were becoming mainstream in the 1970s, a new area of research called environment and behavior offered startling evidence that challenged these assumptions about the relationship between communication and privacy and led to a renewed fixation on supporting privacy in open plan office designs of the 1980s and 1990s. The research was widely publicized, but its findings were based on a number of assumptions about workers and their needs, and ignored many attributes of workers' identity including gender, race, and ability that might have influenced workers' experiences and perspectives at work as well as the ways in which organizational culture might influence the social environment of the office.

By examining communication and privacy together, this chapter considers the ways in which these two seemingly antithetical attributes of office design were important to the design of the open plan. For supporters of the open plan, the office was not a bland backdrop of the daily social drama of the workplace, rather they viewed it as a tool for transforming the social life of the organization and the behavior of workers through design. As I argue, these shifting ideas about the relationship between communication and privacy not only had implications regarding the design of the open plan, but it also reflected persistent assumptions and generalizations about workers' behaviors and needs within the open plan.

Supporting Communication

In the mid-twentieth century there was a growing interest in understanding the social relations embedded in all types of work and a parallel desire among many organizations to encourage and support social interactions, teamwork, and collaboration. New research in psychology, management studies, and organizational behavior focused on the social aspects of the workplace particularly issues around worker motivation, interpersonal relationships, and group interactions. For example, in 1945 psychologist Kurt Lewin founded a research center on group dynamics at MIT where he examined the structure and culture of group work.[2] This emphasis on examining the texture of group interactions was also central to the development of sociotechnical systems, a theory introduced by Eric Trist and Ken Bamforth in 1951. In their landmark study of a coal mining operation, Trist and Bamforth revealed how a technological change in the work process was implemented without consideration for the embedded social interactions of coal miners creating negative outcomes for the workers, their productivity, and the quality of their work.[3] There was also an emerging body of research about the social implications of space, most notably the work of anthropologist Edward Hall, who introduced the concept of spatial proxemics.[4] By the 1960s, architectural and design journals also began to feature articles about the social meanings and dynamics of space, and some argued for a new way of approaching design that considered the social interactions and needs of people.[5] As the open plan was gaining significant attention in the American architecture and design press in the late 1960s, it was within the context of this larger discussion about the value of supporting communication in the workplace, and the ways in which the design and use of space could potentially influence worker's behaviors and interactions.

Building on these ideas about the importance of social interactions at work, the Quickborner Team pioneered an approach to design that treated communication as the central function of an office. While conventional American office design of the postwar period had prioritized paperflow as a primary means of office organization, the Quickborner Team looked beyond the physical movement of paper in the office to understand the circulation of information and ideas through the regular interactions between and among different individuals and their larger units. According to Andreas Rumpfhuber, Eberhard and Wolfgang Schnelle viewed the office itself as a sociotechnical system that integrated people and the technology of information circulation. Drawing on the language and theories of cybernetics, the Schnelle brothers foregrounded communication and interactions in the office as a proxy for understanding the movement of information throughout the office from person to person and unit to unit.[6]

In their planning for the new administration building for Purdue University in the late 1960s, the Quickborner Team produced a detailed planning document that outlined their goals for the design process, including improving the speed and process of information exchange, supporting the movement of paper and people, and facilitating communication between people. They describe how this new office concept at Purdue would ultimately "create an environment in which all administrators and office personnel are more closely associated with better evidence of team togetherness."[7] The Quickborner Team also produced a series of planning "maxims" that emphasized the idea that communication was central to the function of the entire building. In their words, the building was "a decisive organizational medium for processing information" and the arrangement of individuals as well as groups and departments should all support the exchange of information above all else.[8] The office landscape treated communication and information processing as two halves of the same underlying principle. The office was a space for processing information and communication was the primary means for sharing and circulating that information. The Quickborner Team imagined the office as a vibrant center for communication and information exchange, and the office landscape was a tool that could support the constant swirl of papers, people, and information.

The Quickborner Team's emphasis on communication as a priority in office design began in their planning process with an intensive survey of each worker's communication patterns in which workers were asked to track all telephone calls, work-related visits, and paperwork for approximately ten days. That survey material was then assessed in a matrix illustrating which workers communicated with each other most frequently and aggregated by division to create a chart reflecting larger unit-level communication patterns. These initial studies were the basis for office planning reflecting the overall office communication patterns. What is notable about these charts is the dynamic way in which they represent the communication network itself. Looking at an example from Purdue's administrative offices, the Quickborner Team represented each division by a box, which varied by size based on the proposed square footage for that division (Figure 13). The boxes connect by a series of dotted and solid lines that each represent different forms of communication (paperwork, phone calls, and visits), with different weights of line reflecting the frequency of communication. The resulting chart shows divisions that have intensive interactions in close proximity—the very heavy black lines linking some divisions together visually signify the strong connections between those divisions, and those divisions are all generally close together in the chart. Lighter weight lines are more profuse throughout, but sometimes stretch great distances across the chart illustrating how the Quickborner Team prioritized high levels of communication above other considerations such as formal organizational relationships. The charts themselves are not only rich with information, but the irregularity of their design (different sized boxes representing different square footage) and the lines zigzagging across the page suggest constant movement, conversation, and circulation of information, paperwork, and people in the office.[9] The chart attempts to visualize that which is generally unseen and largely unknown—the aggregate of individual conversations and communications between staff in different divisions.

The communication charts with their jumble of boxes and lines also mimic the visual chaos of the office landscape itself. Although the arrangement of boxes

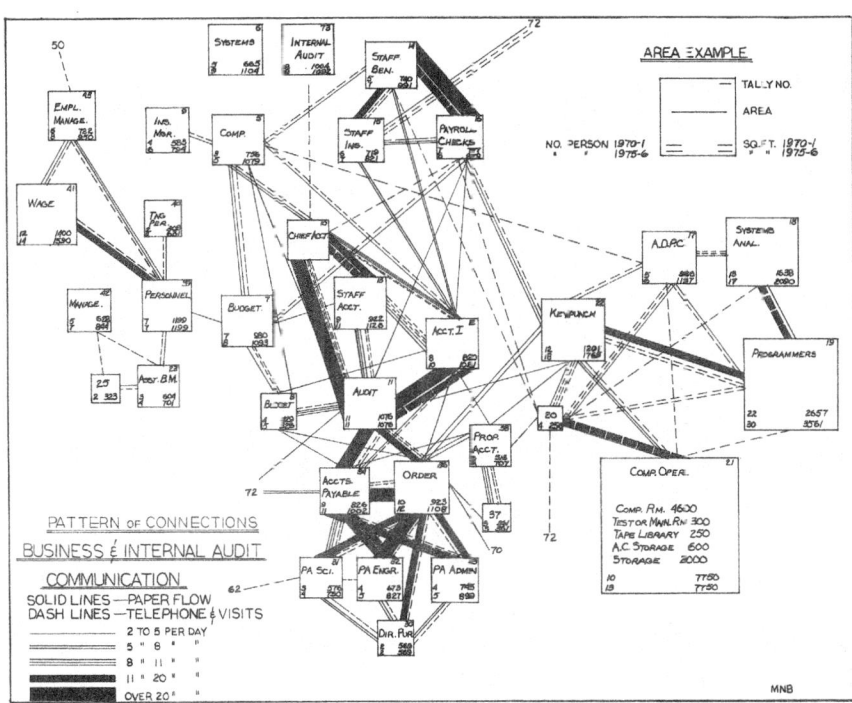

Figure 13 The Quickborner Team's chart depicting the communication patterns of administrative units at Purdue University. In the image, each box represents an individual administrative unit and the connecting lines of different weights symbolize the regular communication activity among individual workers in those units.

Source: Quickborner Team, *Purdue Planning Report*, 1968, p. 50 from Purdue University Special Collections, UA 153, Series 2, Box 1, Folder 8.

and lines in the visualization does not precisely correspond to the final layout, the proximities and general groupings based on the rate of communications between divisions is apparent in the initial arrangement. The final layout, as featured in the visitor's guide for the building, shows an amorphous arrangement of desks and partitions, with solid lines distinguishing full divisions, and dotted lines denoting internal departments (Figure 14). Many of the divisions that showed strong communication links in the survey process were placed in close proximity to one another in the layout for the new administrative building. The loose shapes of the individual divisions suggest the fluid and often dynamic relationships between different areas; the "budget office," for example, is oblong and juts out into the office space surrounded by the comptroller, the chief accountant, and payroll. The irregularity of the shapes thus allows looser groupings and associations between areas that might in a more formal and rectilinear arrangement, be quite rigid and separate.

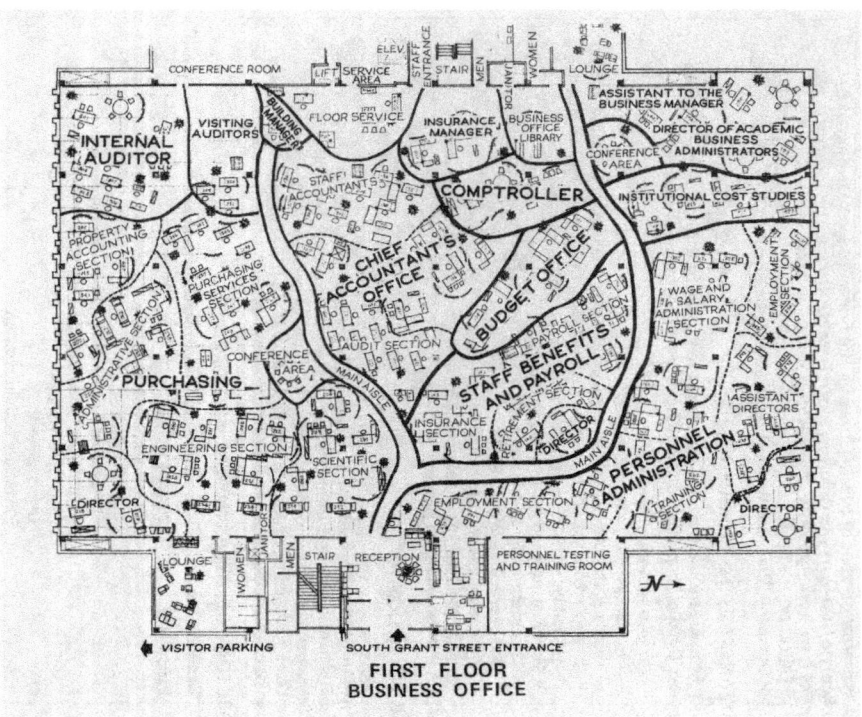

Figure 14 The Quickborner Team's original layout of the first floor of Purdue's administrative offices as shown in the Visitor's Guide with the various divisions identified. The Quickborner Team arranged the units in loose amoeba-like groupings so that the areas that interact frequently are adjacent to one another to support efficient communication.

Source: "Administrative Services Building Information Booklet and Visitor's Guide," n.d. (early 1970s), Purdue University Special Collections: UA 153 Box 1 Folder 3.

As part of this broader interest in facilitating communication, the elimination of private offices was another vital element of the office landscaping concept. Proponents often described the lack of individual enclosure in the office landscape as a means of liberating executives from the formalities and bureaucracy embedded in the design of the conventional office and thereby freeing workers to communicate with each other more freely and easily. To illustrate this idea, they would often use the example of scheduling a meeting or resolving a problem to demonstrate the superiority of the new open plan concept over the conventional office; as Sydney Rodgers describes,

> Mr. A meets a problem requiring coordinating. He calls his secretary and dictates a memo to Mr. B. She types it up, goes off to "report" and gets seven copies (at least!); she comes back and pops some into her outgoing mail tray and files the rest under various headings. Eventually a mail boy arrives and

carries the memo off to the mail room whence, after careful sorting, it returns to the originating floor and lands in Mr. B's office, halfway down the corridor from Mr. A. How much easier if Mr. A could have glanced down the line, seen Mr. B at his desk and strolled over to talk to him in person. He would have had his complete and instant answer with embellishments, not a stated reply by interoffice mail some days later. And no one involved other than the two principals.[10]

This admittedly long-winded description reveals the imagined contrast between a conventional office with its walls and doors that reinforce the traditional bureaucracy, and the open plan which will allow the two men to communicate directly without any mediation or interference. In this narrative, the secretary and the mail boy are part of a larger system that is expressive of the inherent bureaucracy of a conventionally designed office. The circulation of memos is yet another artifact of the entrenched inefficiency created by the office with all of its tedious formalities which are reinforced by the persistence of the walls and doors of private offices. This new ability of professional workers in the open plan to simply "glance" over at their colleague, see if they are present, and immediately engage in a direct conversation about the issue at hand is treated as a miraculous antidote to the formalities of corporate culture that are not only inefficient but also ineffective. The "glance" is also inherently ableist in its assumptions, relying on the presumption of sight as an essential tool in effective and efficient communication. In this way proponents of the office landscape described the new office as a tool of liberation for the executive or manager, freeing him from his private enclave and simultaneously freeing him from the bureaucracy and tedium of formal communication as represented by circulating memos typed by secretaries and delivered by mail boys. This mode of office design tended to prioritize communication over concentration and contemplation, creating spaces that support communication above workers' other needs.

The persistent belief among advocates of the open plan that more communication was inherently good, no matter the context, meant that there was generally very little consideration given to the problem of unwelcome communications and interruptions in the open plan. As the example above demonstrates, the idea of simply looking over and seeing if the other person is free assumes that the resulting interruption is equally welcome and beneficial to both parties. Of course, not all workers are interrupted with equal frequency. Interruptions in general are at least partially tied to a belief that one's own work is more important than the work (and time) of the person being interrupted, and workers in lower positions were often more prone to receiving interruptions at work than people in higher positions. According to organizational psychologist Eric Sundstrom, this is in part an artifact of power in which people in higher positions are afforded more consideration in terms of interruptions than people in lower organizational roles.[11] The manner and method of interruption would likely be quite different depending on the class and position of the worker being interrupted—while someone might simply demand a clerical worker's attention, that same worker might be more cautious, deferential, and polite in their interruption of a manager or executive. Architects and designers often characterized high communication and easy access as a neutral and universal idea in the open plan, but in practice, workers of different classes would have experienced this attribute in very different ways.

The Quickborner Team and other practitioners of open office planning did not generally worry about the problem of interruptions, but they did consider distractions to be a significant concern. To address this problem, and to encourage communication and conversation, the Quickborner Team intentionally included group meeting spaces and dedicated break spaces called *pausenraum* in their design. These areas of the office were included to support the social needs of workers, and to help ensure that conversations in the office did not disrupt other workers at the same time. The formal conference spaces typically featured round tables with chairs, surrounded by low curving acoustic partitions to enclose the group and provide modest sound control.[12] The break room was a more informal space created to allow workers to talk casually away from their desks. Such features were included to ensure that workers had the space and opportunity to socialize formally and informally but could do so without creating significant distractions or disruptions for their neighbors.[13]

Visual Privacy

Even as advocates of the open plan emphasized the value of creating a highly social and interactive office, they also recognized the importance of providing a modicum of privacy for workers to think and process information. The modest partitions of the open plan created individual territories, blocked views of the space, and allowed workers to isolate themselves visually and acoustically from the activity of the office when needed. Of course, the open plan was not designed to provide complete privacy to any worker, but the architects and designers who promoted the open plan recognized that visual and acoustic privacy were essential and sought to support those needs within the open plan context.

Visual privacy, though seemingly antithetical to the open plan concept, was a consideration even in early open plan office designs. In their planning documents for the Purdue building, the Quickborner Team describe how "a constant awareness of the room is to be avoided, it is necessary that there be a certain isolation (privacy, intimacy) for each workplace."[14] As part of planning, advocates described the importance of managing sight-lines at sitting height, ensuring that seated workers would not be inadvertently staring at another worker.[15] The goal was to give workers the feeling of visual privacy without enclosing each worker inside of a box of partitions or walls. To achieve this, workers were carefully positioned in the office landscape to avoid rows of desks all facing one direction, and additionally designers provided low-curving partitions and plants to carefully block views and define groupings giving some sense of enclosure even without fixed walls as can be seen in Figure 15.

The Quickborner Team had used partitions sparingly, but in Action Office panels were key components of the individual workstation and served a double purpose of providing modest enclosure while also creating vertical space for storage. Robert Propst argued that there was a tension between people's desire for enclosure and their desire to stay connected with others. To support these seemingly contradictory goals of "access and enclosure," he argued that three sides of enclosure is optimum in that it provides "a good definition of territory," "privacy is well expressed and the ability to survey or participate is well maintained." By contrast the fully enclosed space left the worker too isolated and insulated, and disrupted the worker's connection to his "organizational family."[16] By balancing these two dimensions for each worker, Propst and his design

Figure 15 Photograph of the interior of Freehafer Hall from 1971. Image illustrates the careful use of partitions to block views and provide modest privacy. See Figure 1 for another view of the original Freehafer interior.
Source: Purdue University Special Collections: UA 153 Box 1 Folder 2.

team sought to create a space that could give workers space for individualized work requiring concentration, and a space that was optimally supportive for communication and collaboration.

Proponents of the open plan office, though recognizing the value of some visual privacy, were deeply suspicious of those workers who were overly concerned about a loss of visual privacy in the open plan. The desire to retain a private office was often characterized as an expression of poor performance and an inherent lack of engagement in work. As Robert Propst warns, "Action Office is indeed not a comfortable environment for those who seek to hide inappropriate or inadequate performance. Over concern of privacy may indicate retreat from responsibility and sagging motivation."[17] Similarly, John Pile, a fierce advocate of open planning, instructed fellow designers that "there seems to be no valid reason why an office worker should feel it necessary to be hidden, truly invisible at normal work."[18] In other words, he insisted that workers should not be afraid to be seen working, and that being seen working was normal and even healthy in a functioning office. Propst also argued that being able to see other people was a beneficial aspect of the office landscape and open plan not only for efficiency of communication, but also for security purposes. He argued that the open environment facilitated a "self implementing supervisory effect" in which people would become more aware of "inappropriate people in territories where they do not belong."[19]

Heightened visibility in the open plan also had gendered implications. Describing the new building at Purdue, a news story in a local paper ran with the headline "New Purdue Building to Be Girl Watchers' Paradise."[20] According to the story, the new office landscape at Purdue with its lack of walls and private offices would make the women workers readily available for men to ogle. Of course, women had long been in open office spaces—the bullpens of the conventional office also put women on display. What made the new open plan office unique was not so much that the women were in the open, but that a greater number of men (particularly professional men) were also in the open. In fact, there is some evidence from the early reporting that workers of both genders felt more self-conscious about their appearance in the new open plan offices of the late 1960s and early 1970s. Descriptions of the open plan and office landscaping designs at the time often noted that workers' sartorial choices changed after the implementation of the new design. One article describes how "employees take a greater pride in the appearance of the office and their own dress has noticeably improved, though in one company the men took a long time to get used to working with their coats off."[21] At McDonald's, a reporter similarly noted that following their move into the new open plan office, workers began dressing in brighter and more fashionable clothing.[22] These kinds of details suggest that some workers experienced a greater self-consciousness in the office after the implementation of the open plan, and imply a sense of discomfort among men as well as women regarding their constant visibility in the open plan.

On the flip side, this same visibility of the office also may have reduced some opportunities for the kinds of aggressive sexual harassment that women often encountered behind closed doors in American offices in this era. Throughout the twentieth century, women working in American offices and other kinds of workplaces had been subjected to unwanted advances from male colleagues, but sexual harassment took on new significance in the 1970s when the issue was brought into the public sphere.[23] A survey conducted by *Redbook* in 1976 found that nearly nine out of ten of their nine thousand respondents reported experiencing various types of harassment including leering, ogling, sexual remarks, teasing, pinching, grabbing, touching, and overt requests for dates and sexual favors. Although 15 percent of women reported finding such attentions flattering, a full 75 percent of the women in the survey indicated that they found the sexual attention demeaning or intimidating.[24] Further, many of these advances happened in enclosed or private spaces with no witnesses.[25] One woman described repeatedly being called into her boss's office where he initiated unwanted physical sexual contact with her, and was told that her job depended on her willing compliance with his sexual demands.[26] Such physical harassment in private offices was fairly common at the time; a follow-up survey of business executives from 1981 by *Harvard Business Review* (conducted jointly with *Redbook*) found that 14 percent of respondents were aware that some female employees in their own company were pinched or patted whenever they entered their boss' office.[27]

The visual privacy afforded by the traditional private office with its four walls and a door thus takes on an altogether different meaning for women at the time, and in the words of an article about the office landscape from *Industrial and Commercial Training*, in the new open plan office "the boss can no longer indulge in bottom pinching."[28] The elimination of these private enclaves would have hindered some types of sexual advances, but certainly not all. Women reported being propositioned, sexually harassed, and sexually assaulted in all types of liminal office spaces including stock rooms, elevators, and partially enclosed areas like filing sections where large filing cabinets could create an isolating alley even in an open plan design.[29] Issues of ogling and jeering remained deeply problematic in the open plan, but the reduction of private offices may have also disrupted or inhibited some other more aggressive forms of sexual harassment and assault that were alarmingly commonplace for working women at the time. As the concept of sexual harassment was just becoming a recognized and named problem in American offices, the increased visibility afforded by the open plan provided women a roomful of potential witnesses to sexual misconduct.

For LGBT men and women, the visual openness of the open plan may have also created increased pressure to more continuously mask their identities through performative heteronormative and heterosexual behaviors and interactions.

In her 1980 article "Compulsory Heterosexuality and Lesbian Experience," Adrienne Rich describes how lesbian women in the workplace were often compelled to participate in heterosexual flirtations and norms of appearance to maintain their position.[30] Building on Rich's work, sociologists Jeff Hearn and Wendy Parkin explore the ways in which this compulsory heterosexuality shaped the experiences of both men and women in the workplace. For example, Hearn describes his observations of male "homosocial" bonding in the workplace where men felt pressured to continuously perform their heterosexual identities not only in the presence of women, but also among other men where jokes and sexual innuendo often served as the lingua franca of organizational interactions. As Hearn and Parkin observe, access to space was an important determiner for many types of sexual interactions in the workplace. They describe the "spaces between spaces" in the workplace that afforded workers the opportunity for covert meetings, intimacy, and sexual interactions as well as the interstitial times (the office Christmas party), when norms of behavior were looser and more frequently and easily transgressed.[31] These examples further illustrate the numerous ways in which the heightened visibility in the open plan office had unforeseen consequences for both men and women.

Acoustic Privacy

Much like visual privacy, acoustic privacy in the open plan office also required careful planning and consideration. It is worth noting that the open bullpens of postwar offices had always been rather noisy spaces with their clattering machines (typewriters, calculators, adding machines, etc.) and the extensive hard reflective surfaces including metal desks, linoleum flooring, and fluorescent light fixtures that only enhanced the noise. When the majority of workers in the open spaces were clerical, technical, and support staff (as was typical in the midcentury American office) there was very little concern about the problems of noise in these open interiors. But with managers, executives, and other professionals in the open plan architects and designers made an effort to consider the technical problems of office acoustics in terms of creating a functional soundscape while controlling noise, and providing workers the psychological perception of privacy to facilitate confidential conversations.

First, advocates often argued that one of the central requirements of an effective open plan design was ensuring the presence of a critical mass of workers in the office at all times. In their plans for Purdue University's new office landscape, the Quickborner Team recommended ensuring a minimum of a hundred workers in the office to provide sufficient and continuous ambient noise.[32] The idea that more workers would be better for managing noise than a small group might seem counterintuitive, but for practitioners of open planning, more people created the necessary background noise that would serve to mask individual conversations and distractions. As Robert Propst and Michael Wodka explain in their acoustic planning manual for Action Office:

> People activity as a source of natural masking tends to be more successful the more people are involved. Thus, larger spaces with many people are better than small spaces with few people. The larger the number of small sound inputs each person provides the better the quality and evenness of the natural masking sound.[33]

Advocates of open planning also emphasized the importance of minimizing reflected sound. Replacing or covering hard surfaces on the ceiling, floor, windows, and walls with sound absorbent materials could dramatically decrease the overall noise of the space. In fact, through the 1970s and 1980s there was a growing cottage industry around providing these kinds of acoustic supplies. Companies such as Owens-Corning, Armstrong, American Seating, United States Gypsum, Columbia Lighting, and Johns-Manville all promoted a range of acoustic products including ceiling tiles, office partitions, wall panels, flooring, and lighting. Ads for these companies and their products in architecture and design magazines frequently featured an open plan office as a common application.

In tandem with managing reflective sound there was also a growing interest in integrating new white noise machines to help manage the clatter of general office sounds. White noise or masking sound machines worked by broadcasting a continuous mix of frequencies over office speakers that together with the ambient noises of the office created a soundscape that masked individual voices and other sounds. Owens-Corning marketed a white noise system for the open plan office, which was designed to provide "unobtrusive" and "uniform" background noise designed to mask unwanted sounds.[34] In the early 1970s, Herman Miller's research group began developing their own integrated sound masking component for the Action Office system. In their evaluation of the problem with sound making systems, Herman Miller's research team noted that most sound masking systems at the time were not only large and complex by design, but they were also very expensive, requiring a large investment in both equipment and installation. Once built, the systems were not easily movable nor very flexible or adjustable to changing acoustic conditions in the office. To address these perceived problems in commercial white noise systems, the research team at Herman Miller developed the Action Office "Acoustic Conditioner," an eight-inch (20 cm) spherical combination speaker and generator that integrated easily with the Action Office system (Figure 16).

Introduced to the market in 1976, Herman Miller's relatively low-cost Acoustic Conditioner was easily movable and required minimal upkeep while providing maximum flexibility and adjustability to the organization and the users. The

Figure 16 Herman Miller's spherical Acoustic Conditioner shown clipped to the top of an Action Office panel from 1976. The Acoustic Conditioner provided localized white noise in the open plan that workers could adjust and "tune" throughout the workday.

Source: Cover from Herman Miller, Ideas (August 1976). Courtesy of Herman Miller Archives.

system was low-wattage, using any standard power outlet, and it worked by providing a mix of high and low frequencies along with a randomizing modulator to ensure that the sound was never monotonous (creating a more natural and less predictable soundscape). While most white noise systems at the time were intentionally hidden away above ceilings, in air ducts, or in another unobtrusive location, the rather small futuristically styled Acoustic Conditioner was kept in plain sight, mounted on top of an Action Office partition, fixed to a wall or ceiling, or even placed upon a filing cabinet using a free-standing base. Unlike conventional sound masking systems at the time, which were carefully planned by acoustic engineers, Herman Miller invited workers to "tune it like a radio" encouraging workers to individually adjust the volume and bass/treble balance of each sphere as needed to meet the particular needs of their work area. Each sphere would cover a twelve-foot (365 cm) diameter space, so most office installations would require multiple units scattered throughout the office space to have sufficient coverage. In their supporting materials, Herman Miller described the Acoustic Conditioner as a useful tool that would act in concert with the other critical sound absorbing elements such as an acoustic ceiling and acoustic partitions to optimally balance the overall sound.[35] Despite the marketing claims, it is not clear how effective the Acoustic Conditioner was, especially when compared with the more robust white noise systems installed and calibrated by professional acoustics engineers, and by the early 1980s it was no longer in production.

Finally, the design of the space and the physical arrangement and orientation of workers within the office was also an important attribute of acoustic management. Propst and Wodka describe the importance of thinking carefully about the groupings of individuals within the office and planning around social distances to ensure that conversations between workers were not disruptive or intelligible to those nearby.[36] In Figure 17, Propst and Wodka illustrate how to strategically utilize acoustic features in the open plan office including acoustic ceilings, carpet, and partitions to reduce sound reflections and provide sound absorption. The arrows in the drawing show the path of sound moving through the office, with solid lines referring to direct sound (e.g., between the typist and the person on the phone) and dotted lines representing the mediation of the sound as it bounces off of various acoustic surfaces. As part of their acoustic planning, designers and architects also had to consider the numerous mechanical sounds that influenced the overall soundscape including office telephones, typewriters, word processors, printers, copiers, keypunch machines, calculators, and teletypes which often produced intermittent noises as well as the elevators, heating, air conditioning, and ventilation elements that produced continuous background noise. Especially noisy office machines such as printers sometimes required special acoustical covers, panels, or hoods that would block their noise.[37] Though some architects and designers recommended grouping office machines (and their operators) together, others indicated that too many machines in one area would produce a level of noise nearly impossible to manage or control, and could actually be very poor for the workers operating the machines as well as serving as a distraction for workers in the vicinity.[38]

Figure 17 Image illustrating the movement of sound in an open plan office from 1975. The drawing is based on the photograph of Action Office shown in Figure 6 and uses arrows to show sound produced by individual workers bouncing off of acoustic surfaces which absorb and reduce the overall sound.
Source: Robert Propst and Michael Wodka, *The Action Office Acoustic Handbook*, 31. Courtesy of Herman Miller Archives.

Each office space was a unique soundscape shaped by the particular work being done, the machines and technologies in use, the architectural space and its materials, the furniture, and the overall layout. Acoustic planning required architects, designers, and acousticians to carefully plan around the particular needs and uses of a given workspace. Despite the numerous products to manage sound issues that were available through the 1970s and 1980s, and the growing body of research about the optimum tools and techniques for managing noise in the office, applied acoustics remained a complicated process often with unanticipated interactions and outcomes.[39]

Of course, the technical aspect of acoustics was only one piece of the larger puzzle. For practitioners of open planning, addressing the social and psychological aspects of sound, and managing workers' expectations about noise and privacy in the open plan was also an important element in acoustic planning. To make the case that functional privacy was entirely possible to achieve in an open plan, designer John Pile often pointed out that private offices were rarely bastions of complete acoustic privacy. The standard partitions between fully enclosed offices were generally thin, frequently made of metal, and porous in terms of sound. Workers would often hear their neighbors' conversations as well as activity and conversations in the hallway just outside their office.[40] Designer Robert Propst argued that the "hush" of the private office even made the inevitable noises and distractions that arose more bothersome because speech became a "high contrast event" instead of just part of the general hum of the office as it would be in an open plan.[41] Propst and Pile both genuinely believed that the ambient noise of the open plan could potentially provide more effective acoustic privacy than a fully enclosed private office. Again this was part of their reframing of the noisy backdrop of the open plan, both Pile and Propst compared the open plan office to a busy restaurant or lively cocktail party where the general ambient noise of the space masked the individual conversations such that one could reasonably have a fairly private conversation despite being surrounded by people.[42] In this way, supporting privacy and strong communication were actually treated as potentially interconnected ideas. By creating a space that supported and encouraged communication and interactivity, the resulting hum of people working would produce an acoustic background that would effectively mask private conversations without requiring the designer to create a cone of silence around each individual worker. Advocates of the open plan also argued that workers would naturally adapt their behavior, their voices, and their modes of interaction to suit the open plan concept. They described how workers' environmental and social awareness would naturally impose a certain level of decorum creating a more hospitable and supportive acoustic environment.[43]

Even as proponents characterized the open plan as perfectly adaptable to each individual's functional privacy needs, and manageable with appropriate acoustic design, workers remained skeptical about the noise issues in the open plan. In fact, the problems related to noise and other distractions were among the most frequently cited issues, even starting with some of the earliest installations in the United States.[44] In their 1978 study, Louis Harris and Associates found that the most frequently cited office space characteristic for getting work done was the ability to concentrate without noise or distractions, but in evaluating their own workspaces in terms of its supportive attributes, the problems of noise, distractions, and lack of visual and conversational privacy were ranked as the very worst aspects of their workspaces.[45] Such findings were consistent in other studies; Eric Sundstrom similarly found that office workers commonly characterized noise as a significant problem, particularly in open plan offices.[46] Yet, as Sundstrom argues "people differ widely in what they define as noise and in the way that they respond to it."[47] One worker's ideal acoustic environment for working, may have been too distracting or too quiet for another worker in the same space. Further, workers' hearing differs significantly as well. Many of the recommendations related to the ambient noise of the office were based on a presumption of normative hearing, and fundamentally failed to consider the ways in which deaf or hard of hearing workers might struggle to hear in the noisy open plan environment. In this way, even as a large number of workers complained about noise, the source, textures and underlying causes of their frustration with noise could vary significantly based on the individual worker's body and hearing, the type of job they had, the type and arrangement of the office, the type of noise (predictable or unpredictable, cacophonous or mellifluous), and even the broader social context of a given workplace. This subjective and individual aspect of sound and noise meant that different workers in the same office space could have significantly different experiences in and reactions to the open plan environment.

Reevaluating Enclosure

Early open plan offices typically used partitions and panels very selectively and modestly, but through the 1970s and 1980s the number and height of furniture partitions grew significantly. In addition to supporting workers' desire for more visual and acoustic privacy, the partitions also served as structural support for the various components of the workspace including work surfaces and storage, and increasingly offered a mechanism for providing power and communication cabling throughout the office. Furniture manufacturers were happy to offer organizations strategies for high levels of enclosure by creating increasingly higher partitions and showcasing layouts in their furniture catalogs featuring workstations surrounded by partitions. Yet, early advocates of the open plan viewed this increasing use of partitions as excessive and even harmful to the more important goal of facilitating communication in the open plan.[48]

Meanwhile, there was also growing interest in the emerging fields of environment and behavior and environmental psychology to assess the claims of open plan proponents, particularly the idea that the open plan naturally increased communication. In fact, these then nascent fields of research cut their teeth on the open plan with numerous studies that were designed to assess the efficacy of the open plan including observational studies, direct surveys, and post-occupancy studies which in turn produced a litany of confusing and often conflicting research on the benefits and failings of the open plan.[49] This concept of measuring the influence of office design on productivity was not new. In the 1930s, management consultant Elton Mayo famously conducted a series of experiments to attempt to prove a causal link between changes in space (lighting in particular) and worker productivity. This research, often referred to as the Hawthorne study, found that no matter how the physical environment changed, productivity increased. Evaluating their results, Mayo and his team determined that the increase in productivity was not because of any of the changes made to the space, but rather was caused by the act of observation itself, and this has since been referred to as "the Hawthorne Effect." Mayo and his researchers found that what was more important than the physical elements of the office in terms of productivity was the social context of the workplace, particularly the relationships of workers to one another and to management. As James Russell notes, the findings of the study, which seemed to prove that the quality of the workplace or its design was not important to work or to the worker, sidelined this type of research for decades.[50]

In the 1960s and 1970s, a number of scholars and writers in organizational behavior and environmental psychology challenged the Hawthorne study and its findings arguing that the problem with it was not just its findings, but that its very hypothesis was based on an overly simple and deterministic relationship between the built environment and human behavior.[51] The new studies of the 1970s and 1980s sought to create a more complex way of understanding the significance of the physical environment on worker behavior. Among the most prominent of these new forays into environment and behavior was a large research project conducted by the research group Buffalo Organization for Social and Technological Innovation (BOSTI) in collaboration with Westinghouse from the late 1970s through the early 1980s.

The BOSTI study, *Using Office Design to Increase Productivity*, had a significant influence on office design practice through the 1980s and 1990s, resulting in major changes in office planning as well as important changes in the manufacture and marketing of office furniture systems, particularly with respect to the use of spatial enclosure in the open plan. While there were many other smaller studies by scholars in a variety of related fields at the time, the BOSTI study was important not only because of its size and scope, but because the results were also shared and discussed in the architecture and design press as well as the business press.[52] Yet, as I argue in this section, these findings and their recommendations reduced workers to broad generic job categories creating prescriptive and even deterministic design solutions for privacy and communication that ignored the ways in which organizational context and worker identity might influence each worker's experiences, needs, and preferences.

The original goal of the BOSTI study was to translate robust empirical data based on the careful study of thousands of workers into real-world design recommendations that would ostensibly improve worker productivity and thereby increase the perceived value of office design. BOSTI surveyed approximately four thousand office workers in different job classifications, different organizations, and in approximately seventy different sites.[53] In the study, all of the participants had experienced a space change and were surveyed some two to four months prior to their move and again eight to ten months after their change and were assessed on a number of different variables related to workspace design.[54]

BOSTI analyzed the results to identify the common patterns, and used those results to provide specific design criteria for office design. The preliminary findings were first published in the early 1980s in a short brochure titled "The Impact of Office Environment on Productivity and Quality of Working Life" and a fuller analysis was then released in 1984 in a two volume set which examined twenty-three different factors related to space including privacy, noise, communication, personalization, attractiveness, comfort, lighting, and integration of technology, while also providing concrete recommendations for design practice, even giving specific suggestions on the optimum workstation designs for different classifications of workers.

Among their major findings, perhaps the most surprising at the time was BOSTI's assertion that workers felt freer to communicate with higher degrees of enclosure. According to the study, "traditional office landscape has got it backwards ... a high degree of physical enclosure provides the climate for high ease of communication while low physical enclosure is a causal factor in low ease of communication."[55] In other words, according to BOSTI, the central claim of open plan proponents, that removing walls would naturally improve communication, was fundamentally incorrect. Explaining this surprising discovery, BOSTI argued that enclosure was a valuable precondition for communication, enabling greater speech privacy, reducing distractions, and allowing workers to more easily and comfortably share sensitive information. In their report, BOSTI argued that privacy was not just an empty status symbol, rather it was a functional necessity for most types of office work, and an important criterion in office design in general. They argued that workers of all types needed support for tasks requiring mental concentration such as producing and analyzing reports and composing documents.[56] According to the study, even a secretary, clerical worker, or receptionist needed some modest or even a high-degree of privacy to support work requiring concentration.[57] Based on their research, BOSTI recommended three to four partitions per workstation that were each at least 65 inches (165 cm) or higher, which was a common partition height at the time.[58] This height recommendation was chosen to minimize the ability for standing men and women of supposedly average height to see over the top of the partition and was often referred to as "standing-height privacy." This height recommendation is yet another example of how the supposedly "average" user was technically built into the design of the open plan, creating environments that were optimal for some users and exclusionary for bodies and individuals that did not conform with the normative and ableist assumptions of ordinary use. While certainly this height would block the views of workers who use wheelchairs or who were shorter than average, it would also create a more claustrophobic environment for those workers whose eye level was well below the partition height, ultimately blocking views not only of the interior of adjacent workstations, but of the space as a whole. This definition of spatial privacy also tended to fixate on managing visual perception as a primary means of achieving privacy, while failing to address the ways in which noise and sound might influence users' feeling of relative privacy.

When the BOSTI study was first released, there was already an emerging trend in design toward increased enclosure in open plan offices, but the BOSTI recommendations solidified that pattern and increased it by providing the justification for its usage. Following the publication of the full report, furniture manufacturers increasingly emphasized privacy as a vital consideration in office planning, sometimes even explicitly referencing the BOSTI recommendations in their marketing. In a planning guide by Kimball for their Artec system from 1985 the BOSTI guidelines for seating and standing height privacy are directly cited in the discussion about optimum partition heights.[53] Even in systems furniture brochures that did not cite the BOSTI study directly, the reference to optimum seating and standing height privacy was common and often used the same height recommendations established by the BOSTI study.[60] While American open plan offices of the early 1970s had deliberately minimized partition usage, by the late 1980s and early 1990s open plan offices used partitions liberally around all types of workstations from executive and managerial workspaces to clerical and support staff.

The widespread adoption of the BOSTI standards was based on a belief among architects, designers, furniture manufacturers, and organizations that the rigorous research methodology used in the study had produced verifiable results. Yet the BOSTI recommendations had some significant flaws. The design recommendations provided by the BOSTI study were based on a statistical fabrication of a supposedly "average" worker, who represented a statistical "majority" opinion within the results. The underlying assumption of this kind of evidence-based design is that design should serve the needs of the majority of workers, yet that approach tends to universalize workers in ways that reinforce the expectations and priorities of those of majority identities (particularly White, abled, cisgender men) often in positions of power, and frequently dismisses the voices, identities, and experiences of those who were outside the statistical majority or in lower organizational positions. Looking more closely at the BOSTI study design as well as its demographic composition illustrates how this new type of design research that became common in this period codified and reinforced the expectations and needs of a dominant group of workers and disregarded or dismissed the needs of those in the statistical minority of the study.

First of all, although the study included workers from a mix of private and public organizations, and a mix of industries (though technology and engineering are dominant among the privately owned companies), the data was not in any way broken out to reflect or examine these differences among organizations.[61] BOSTI's research design tacitly assumed that all workers in a given job category had roughly the same experiences, preferences, and needs no matter their organizational context or industry. Instead, the study sorted workers across all types of workplaces into three broad and very generic groups—managers or administrators, professional or technical, and clerical. BOSTI placed workers into those categories based on the standard occupational codes using the 1970 US Census. For example, a computer technician or programmer was classified as a professional/technical worker in the study and a "machine operator" was classified as a clerical worker.[62] While on the surface this might seem to be a reasonable division between two distinct job titles, historian Mar Hicks's research has shown how the work of a computer "operator" and a programmer in this period were muddy, and in fact the predominantly female "operators" frequently performed similar work to programmers or technicians just without the title or pay.[63] This exemplifies how these kinds of divisions based on job titles and job classifications masked the real labor of workers, creating false, arbitrary, or misleading distinctions within the data, and reproducing structural inequalities tied to differences of gender, race, social class, and ability among different classes of workers at the time.

There were also some significant issues in terms of the demographic makeup of the workers in the study. The managers, professional, and technical workers in the study were predominantly men, while the workers classified as clerical were overwhelmingly comprised of women. In fact, according to BOSTI's own assessment they had a larger proportion of men in their overall sample than the national average at the time, a higher degree of educational attainment, particularly for managers and professionals, and in general more professional and technical workers than the national average (which is not surprising considering the overrepresentation of engineering and technology companies). Further, although gender was documented in the general demographics of the study participants, none of the results were broken out in terms of gender. In other words, there was no effort to consider whether gender was a factor in workers' experiences of the workplace. In addition, there was only a small percentage of workers with disabilities in the sample (3 percent), which BOSTI acknowledges was also well below the national average at the time of 11 percent. The workers with disabilities are also not broken out in the sample so it is unclear what jobs they held, how they were represented among the three major classifications of workers, or even what types of disabilities they had. Race was not addressed at all in the report and it does not appear that demographic information related to race or ethnicity was collected, or if it was, that data was deliberately not included in the reported findings.[64] Based on the available evidence, it is highly likely that the professional and managerial workers in the study were predominantly White men while the largely female clerical workers in the study may have been more racially diverse. The research design, though relying on supposedly neutral job categories, masked some significant structural imbalances related to gender, race, and ability that were embedded in the data and reproduced in the study design from the original sampling of workers used in the study, the collection of the data, the sorting and analysis, and the reporting of the results. By disregarding these types of differences, the BOSTI study codified and reinforced the assumptions, preferences, and priorities of an "average" or "majority" worker, and tended to ignore the perspectives of workers whose bodies, positions, or identities did not conform with that majority experience.

In general, the BOSTI study assumed that workers were more similar to each other than different and used that assumption in their analysis to make larger leaps based on limited evidence. For example, in their findings related to the relationship of enclosure and ease of communication, BOSTI acknowledged that very few of the (predominantly female) clerical and secretarial workers in the study had any enclosure at all making it hard to assess their need for privacy. Yet, they speculated that the findings for the (mostly male) professional and technical staff regarding their preference for higher degrees of enclosure would likely apply to lower level workers in clerical and support positions as well.[35] Of course this recommendation neglects all the structural differences between the working day of a clerical worker literally "trapped" at their desk, and the work of a professional worker who might have significantly more freedom to move around and more autonomy over their work in general. As higher partitions became more common in open plan designs for nearly all classes of workers, some workers in clerical jobs did not see the increasing partitions around their workspace as a source of privacy, but rather viewed them as a tool imposed by management to separate and isolate workers from one another.[66] In other words, the BOSTI study's recommendations failed to meaningfully consider the idea that one worker's private haven in the office might be another worker's jail cell.

By the early 1990s, the ubiquitous cubicle office with its rows and rows of identical workstations surrounded by three to four standing-height partitions had become a standard design in American offices around the country. Although designers had specified higher partition heights in order to provide workers some privacy and a sense of enclosure per the BOSTI recommendations, the office cubicle was increasingly characterized by workers as a dreary and isolating space in which they were constantly subjected to noise, distractions, and a lack of privacy.[67] By the late 1990s, the term "cube farm" came into common use in mainstream media in the United States as a derogatory term for open plan office design of that era with their rows of highly enclosed identical cubicles.[68] The term was likely at least partially a reference to Douglas Coupland's 1991 book *Generation X* in which he snarkily described cubicles as "veal-fattening pens" and characterized the office itself as a "stockyard."[69] In other words, the "farm" reference was not meant to evoke a bucolic rural landscape, but rather was an ironic allusion to an industrialized slaughterhouse, emphasizing the dehumanizing aspects of the design and the space embodied by the flimsy fabric-covered office partitions. Meanwhile, in movies, television shows, commercials, books, and comic strips, cubicles were a frequent source of ironic humor, often riffing on these recurring problems. For example, in the syndicated daily comic strip *Dilbert*, the titular character and his misfit coworkers were frequently seen grousing about the miseries associated with working in an office cubicle particularly the problems of noise, the lack of privacy, a loss of individuality, and feelings of social isolation. The image of the highly enclosed office cubicle became synonymous in popular media with a bored and unhappy white collar worker, trapped in a tedious and unimportant day job.

These complaints and negative images of office cubicles in popular media were a known problem for furniture manufacturers and their designers, who recognized that the cubicle had a very negative image. For example, in the late 1990s, designer William Stumpf, the creator of the Ethospace furniture system for Herman Miller, personally collected popular articles and cartoons describing the negative attitudes toward cubicles and systems furniture.[70] For Stumpf these complaints from workers were serious problems and he even produced a report in 1998 titled "Cubicle Reform: Problems and Solutions," which identified eight significant problems with modern cubicles, including the visual monotony of "cubicle mazes" that convey a sense of impersonal bureaucracy, difficulty with concentration because of noise, interruptions, and distractions and the lack of real privacy, and the stifling or claustrophobic quality of being surrounded by cubicle partitions (a panel just 2 feet or 60 cm from your face).[71]

The Legacy of Environmental Determinism in Office Design

Early proponents of the open plan office imagined the ideal office as a highly social and interactive space in which workers, liberated by the lack of walls, would communicate more freely with one another. Proponents of the open plan sincerely believed in this power of the space to fundamentally transform social behavior and this idea has persisted through multiple iterations and generations of the open plan office concept and remains one of its most significant failures. Again and again, architects, designers, furniture manufacturers, and organizations have imbued office space and the open plan in particular with miraculous powers to change the context and experience of work. Meanwhile, designers also blamed any emerging problems in the design of the open plan on the users themselves. If the open plan was too noisy, it was because workers had failed to adjust their behavior or expectations to the acoustic environment; if workers felt they needed more privacy, it was because they were insecure in their position or lazy and wanting to avoid work. Even the BOSTI study, though challenging some of the assumptions of the open plan concept, focused on establishing a causal link between office design and job performance, not only qualitatively, in terms of workers' perceptions, but also in terms of bottom-line economic measures. Their research design and final design recommendations reinforced the assumption of a deterministic relationship between the design of the office and workers' experiences of the space.

In his 1981 book *Workspace*, organizational ecologist Franklin Becker argued that this represents a kind of "naive environmental determinism" because it failed to account for the complexities and nuances of space, jobs, organizations, and workers. In his analysis, Becker argues that the physical setting is a kind of "social process" that draws together the organization, workers, time, jobs, and technologies creating a complex ecology of interdependent and interactive elements. Further, according to Becker, workers of different identities, positions, and experiences will inevitably understand the space of the office, its usage, and its meaning in different ways.[72] Other scholars have similarly argued that the physical spaces of work must be seen in the context of a larger and more complex system of interaction. Organizational consultant Fred Steele, for example, argued that designers and office planners should consider the "environment" of the office as a series of layers including the geophysical, the technophysical, and the social, which are shaped by culture, and interact with the user at its center.[73] Office space is important to the work process and to the worker, but it can only be fully understood within the context of these other critical elements of the work system as a whole.

While office design may not directly change workers' behavior, it is clear that workers in the 1970s and 1980s believed that their workspace mattered both in terms of their own comfort and well-being, but also in terms of their productivity. Indeed, perhaps the greatest legacy of the original BOSTI study is not the specific findings of how much enclosure workers needed for optimum communication, but rather that it demonstrated just how much workers valued the design of their workspace as an important attribute of their working life. As BOSTI stated in Volume 1 of their study, although they sent painfully long surveys to literally thousands of workers, they had a very high response rate, and often received detailed comments (even with handwritten notes) that suggested just how much workers cared about the quality of their space in general.[74] The Louis and Harris surveys conducted in tandem with Steelcase in the late 1970s and early 1980s similarly found that workers genuinely valued the quality of their workspace, and saw the design of the office as an important attribute in their overall productivity as well as in their overall comfort.[75]

Yet even as these studies affirmed workers' personal investment in the quality and design of their workspace, these same studies often disregarded the ways in which workers' perspectives might vary based on their identities, positions, and experiences. Like the abstract user, enshrined in the planning process of the open plan, the abstract worker in these office design studies was ultimately enshrined and reproduced through data collection and analysis. The average worker, a composite of many workers rendered through rigorous data collection and statistical analysis, is just another abstraction of the worker and the work process modeled on the majority perspective. In the rare instances when categories of difference were built into these kinds of open plan studies, they rarely accounted for the ways in which identities such as race, gender, and ability were inscribed into certain categories of work by way of structural inequalities, and they rarely considered the intersections of identity, which could moderate a workers' individual experience in the workplace. Although measuring social behavior and making recommendations to support users was a common focus in the design research process of this era, social categories of identity were too often treated as noise in the statistical environment that need to be controlled for, rather than as meaningful categories of difference worthy of direct study and individual consideration.

Chapter 4
Personalizing the Workstation

In the conventional American office of the postwar period the essential building block of the office plan was the desk. Far from a simple object, mid-century corporate desks came in an enormous variety of forms and materials. For example, a typical Steelcase desk of this era (3200 or 5200 models) could be specified with multiple sizes and configurations of worksurfaces, various combinations of modular components including different size and style pedestals, various combinations of drawers (box drawers, file drawers, and center drawers), and other interior desk accessories (drawer dividers, file inserts, and reference shelves). Aesthetically, designers could select different materials and colors for the desk including plastic laminate or wood worksurfaces; various styles and colors of enamel finishes for the body of the desk; and even different finishes for the metal frame (polished, brushed, or ember chrome). The desks themselves were not only large in overall size, but they were also quite heavy—a Steelcase double-pedestal desk could weigh anywhere from 200 to 300 pounds (90–136 kg) not including any secondary worksurfaces such as a typing return.[1]

Specifying furniture for an office interior in this era, designers generally created a plan based on a system of standard desk types, styles, and forms, with each position receiving a different size and configuration based on their particular organizational role. These kinds of standardized desks provided visual continuity in the office while also reflecting and supporting the social, technical, and functional needs of each worker based on their place in the organization. Most importantly, desks were not generally selected by individual workers; rather they were prescribed by designers and architects, based on the expectations or assumptions of management. This mode of office design was a means of control over the worker, the workspace, and the work process. In fact, some management manuals of the period even encouraged managers to dictate the exact interior organization of each worker's desks in order to ensure optimum efficiency.[2]

While the essential building block of the iconic postwar office was the desk, the new unit of spatial planning and organization in the open plan was the workstation. The workstation was not just a kind of furniture; advocates described it as a technology, drawing together the essential components (storage, work surfaces, partitions) of the workspace to create a tool for working and an adaptable matrix for the worker and their individual working process. Each worker assigned to a workstation had a place in the open plan office, and the workstation's partitions and components served to define and contain that space. In a conventional office, a worker would sit at (or behind) a desk, but in the new open plan concept of the 1970s, workers would sit "in" the workstation. This notion of creating a furniture-based work environment was not entirely new. In the eighteenth century, the desk and bookcase, a common furniture type in Europe and colonial America, used the vertical form to create an individualized work environment with a fall-front worksurface and integrated storage. In the nineteenth century, the patented Wooton desk from 1874 expanded this idea even further, creating a desk that opened to reveal a complex interior including a fall-front worksurface and an array of cubbyholes and drawers that surrounded the user at its center. The open plan workstation built on some of these prior concepts but reimagined them in a more modular and adaptable form that users could adjust to support their individual working needs. Conceptualized by Robert Propst as a defining feature of Action Office, the workstation represented a critical reimagining of the individual worker's space to support the management of information and to facilitate the thinking process by transforming the interior spaces of the workstation into a kind of interface. The workstation concept also provided a new approach to thinking about storage, moving away from the deep desk drawers of conventional desks and toward a more active storage concept.

As systems furniture became mainstream, architects and designers planning new buildings increasingly used the workstation concept as an essential planning tool for the office. Comprised of a standard combination of partitions, work surfaces, storage elements, and a chair, the workstation served as a basic template for every workspace in the office. Because workstation specification was directly tied to one's organizational position and job, the worker and the workstation became almost synonymous with one another in the planning process.[3] In addition to the functional requirements of each worker, architects and designers also used the visual language of the workstation and its coherent system of finishes and materials as an aesthetic tool.

The planning process imagined the workstation as a generic container for a faceless worker, but in practice each workstation would eventually be a real working space for a real worker. In the last part of the chapter, I focus on the ways in which workers interacted with the workstation in their working lives—particularly the ways in which they populated the interiors with the tools and materials of their work process as well as the ways in which they personalized the space. Some organizations encouraged personalization while others adopted strict rules that were intended to restrict worker's opportunity to make changes, decorate, or bring in persona items. The organizational context and culture could significantly influence the extent to which workers were able to make the space their own.

The Workstation Ideal

In the mid-twentieth century, the workstation concept was more typically associated with a factory or laboratory setting. In a 1951 plant facility guide, the author describes how the "work station" was the "basic space unit" of any plant, defined by "the floor area occupied by the worker and the machine or group of machines which he operates." The workstation, in the context of the factory, needed to encompass all of the equipment and support supplies necessary for an individual worker to do their job.[4] When designer Robert Propst began using the term workstation as part of his development for Action Office 1, he was borrowing a language and concept that, at the time, was more commonly used in a factory setting.

Propst's use of the term workstation was not meant to describe a single workspace, but rather referred to distinct support areas within a workspace that were designed to facilitate different types of activities, encourage different types of interactions, and enable different types of thinking. According to Propst, this new kind of workspace afforded the worker choices and options—they could stand, lean, or perch at a standing-height desk, they could use the "display desk" to interact with their work materials, and they could use the communication station for phone calls. Each workstation within the worker's workspace was intended to serve specific purposes, but their design was flexible to support an evolving array of tasks and needs. For Propst, the workstation concept signified the idea that workers needed some variety in their working environment—they needed constant choices and options and an environment that would respond to their needs and facilitate their individual working process.[5] Writing in 1966, Propst argued that the traditional office with a man stuck behind a desk was too limiting—physically, technically, and socially. To address this conceptual problem, Propst described the new office workspace as an "arena" in which the various furniture units or workstations were placed in a U configuration around the worker allowing them to easily move between different tasks and functional needs throughout the day using different "vectors" as necessary. As Propst describes, "Located in the arena center," the worker is "free to turn and use a suitable work surface, console or conference expression." Propst imagined a typical Action Office arrangement with three workstation components occupying approximately 240° of the "arena" while the remaining 120° would remain open to allow visibility.[6] No longer sitting in a stationary position, the new office worker was at the center of a dynamic system of workspace components that enabled and supported the work process.

Although Propst and the Herman Miller Research Division developed this idea of the workstation in their first iteration of Action Office, they expanded the concept of the workstation significantly in the design of Action Office 2. Even though the design solution was technically different from the first generation of Action Office, its underlying assumptions about the needs of workers remained much the same particularly in terms of affording workers choices about how they work within their respective workspace, encouraging a more physically active worker, and supporting display in the workspace (Figure 18). Action

Figure 18 A worker in an Action Office workstation at JFN Associates office in Chicago from 1968. The workstation includes two different worksurfaces (a standing height drafting table and a regular work surface at sitting height) providing the worker choice in where and how he works.

Source: Courtesy of Herman Miller Archives.

Office 2 was also far more adjustable than the original Action Office design. All of the modular internal components of the Action Office 2 workstation could be moved or changed easily by the user themselves (often without tools)—work surfaces could be raised, lowered, and moved; storage elements could be added or eliminated; and even the supporting partitions were lightweight and easily adjustable. The idea behind all of this interior flexibility was the firm belief that workers should be able to adjust the interior workspace to suit their own individual working needs. Propst envisioned an office full of people standing, sitting, walking, and generally interacting with the space and the furniture. This image of the worker in constant interaction with the workstation arrangement animates the ways in which Propst viewed office work, the office worker, and the office space as actively changing and adjusting throughout the working day. To facilitate this ideal, the new Action Office utilized the partitions to enhance the verticality of the workspace, encouraging workers to stand during the day thus creating a more "kinetic, active, alert, [and] vigorous environment."[7]

Propst was also very interested in the work process itself and sought to create furniture that would optimally facilitate work, and even give workers new ways of engaging with their materials and their space. Among Propst's fixations was the emphasis in many conventionally designed offices on minimizing "clutter" in the workplace. For Propst, the so-called clutter of papers and materials on the work surface and in the workspace were not things to eliminate, but rather vital components of the work process itself. Even the original Action Office design integrated elements that allowed workers to pin and post information in the inner surfaces of their work space, for example the flip-top desk included a tackboard designed for pinning items to its surface.[8] This idea was also central to Action Office 2 in that workers were encouraged to use all of the interior elements, partitions, and storage to display and manage information.[9] Describing his ideas about the importance of display in his 1974 article "Process as Aesthetic," Propst argues that the objects of work, the papers, folders, books, and other materials, are all vital tools in the "feedback structure" of the thinking process. These artifacts, arranged within the workspace, were not messes that needed to be prevented, but critical "signals" and "cueing devices" that were part of the information network of the individual workplace.[10]

In many ways, Propst's vision of the workspace as a tool for information display echoes some of the radical thinking about the meaning and nature of communications, new media, and visual information from the time. Orit Halpern argues that the postwar period saw a new emphasis on visualization and the importance of visual information through the circulation and production of knowledge. Connecting the work of numerous scholars, scientists, writers, artists, and designers including Norbert Wiener, Kevin Lynch, György Kepes, László Moholy-Nagy, and Charles Eames and Ray Eames, Halpern's analysis reveals how vision and visual information were connected to the development of the "interface" concept and became a means of communication and cognition in the postwar period.[11] Action Office was similarly designed to serve as a dynamic interface for paperwork, allowing the material artifacts of the work process to be pinned up, organized, arranged, and rearranged in ways that would ideally facilitate the thinking process. Propst believed that managing visual information was vital to all types of office work, and so he sought to create a workspace that would optimally support and encourage the use of such materials. His vision of the inner surfaces of the work space serving as a tool for manipulating information suggests an analog of the multiscreen computer interface offering multiple and simultaneous streams of information. Sitting at its center, the worker was surrounded by the visual signals of their work. As Ronn Daniel argues, Action Office imagined the workspace as a kind of "cockpit" and the worker at its center was like a "fighter pilot," reading the interior panels of the Action Office workstation for data, information, and rapid decision making.[12]

For Propst, the workstation was not a fixed space prescribed by management, but a nimble, adaptable, and flexible space that could adjust as needed to the preferences and requirements of the worker themselves. The workstation was also conceptually fluid in that it could apply equally to an executive workspace or to a clerical workspace. Although the executive worker would likely have very different spatial needs from a clerical worker, they both would require a similar level of flexibility to make their space useful for their own work. Herman Miller's Action Factory system released in the early 1980s brought this same ideal to the factory floor. Much like their catalogs for Action Office, Herman Miller emphasized how Action Factory was a dynamic and highly flexible system of modular components that could accommodate both the individual worker's ergonomic needs and the changing production requirements of the organization.[13]

From the very beginning, Action Office embraced the ideal of a workspace that was dynamic and permissive and sought to convey this visually through the imagery used in their marketing materials. In contrast to the spartan modernist interiors of postwar corporate office design (such as the image from Knoll shown in Figure 4), Herman Miller portrayed Action Office as inevitably and even joyfully messy with people, paper, and supplies in constant motion. Indeed, many of their brochures featured installations of workstations for corporate clients with workstations filled with a variety of materials, and even the partitions featured items pinned to their walls.[14] This attribute of the marketing of Action Office was picked up by other furniture manufacturers in the marketing of their own systems furniture lines. Many of the major systems furniture manufacturers such as Westinghouse, Haworth, and Steelcase similarly showcased their furniture in use. For example, Figure 19 features a promotional image for the Steelcase 9000+ furniture system showing an office installation that is populated with workers and their work. This aesthetic of the active open plan office, filled with people at work, became a part of the visual language of systems furniture marketing throughout the 1970s.

Figure 19 Image of Steelcase 9000+ furniture installation showing a model office populated with workers. Images like these depicted the open plan office as a naturally lively and bustling space filled with people and their work.

Source: Steelcase, "The Future Just Arrived," NeoCon Brochure, 1980 from the Steelcase Corporate Archives.

Storage Space

Advocates of the open plan often celebrated systems furniture for its high degree of flexibility and capacity for personalization, but as a system, the furniture also sought to impose order and structure on workers and all their work-related possessions. This idea in office design was not new; as Alexandra Lange describes, early twentieth century offices integrated massive systems of storage and filing that housed the various forms and paperwork of the bureaucracy and ultimately ensured that "every paper [had] a place in the chain of record keeping, and there [was] furniture designed especially for each place."[15] This image of perfect containment was tied to an idealized vision of organizational bureaucracy in the early twentieth century in which, as Shannon Mattern has argued, the endless files, papers, and forms along with their requisite indexes were material expressions of a complex system of information management.[16] This fantasy of order and organization was also at the heart of the system furniture concept, which promised its users flexible modular components that would contain all of the material artifacts of office work from equipment and technology to papers and files.

The modular concept of systems furniture also owes a great deal to the emergence of domestic modular storage systems, such as George Nelson's Storagewall, which became popular in the postwar era. According to Lynn Spigel storage systems like the Storagewall were designed to contain, order, and structure the ever-growing array of objects and clutter of the postwar home. As Spigel argues, this image of modular order was also closely tied to the world of corporate management and bureaucracy.[17] In other words, just as postwar storage walls promised to create order out of the chaos of the postwar domestic landscape, systems furniture like Action Office promised to construct a new order out of the inevitable clutter and chaos of office work. In fact, the initial design for Action Office 1 actually used George Nelson's Comprehensive Storage System as its structural foundation to support a new system of office storage elements.[18] As the Action Office system was expanded in the 1960s and 1970s, the seemingly simple storage components of the new furniture offered organizations and users a robust and highly flexible container suitable for any items in the office including office supplies, technologies, and paper. In one 1979 brochure for Action Office, Herman Miller showed a mailroom installation featuring a mix of open shelves, bins, and overhead storage with flipper doors all neatly filled with equipment and supplies (Figure 20). The image of the neatly organized supply area exemplifies the idea that the standard storage components of Action Office could tackle even the challenge of organizing an intensive storage area.[19]

Looking at the workstation through the lens of storage highlights one of the emerging debates regarding the open plan. Designers, architects, and manufacturers, working on new open plan offices and designing systems furniture lines recognized that papers, files, supplies, equipment and the various other detritus of the workplace were inevitable aspects of the working process, but they also viewed these materials, particularly paper, as potential sources of unnecessary mess, clutter, disorder, and even as a reflection of ineffective bureaucracy. Writing in 1978, John Pile described how in the conventional office many workers had large desks with storage pedestals, storage credenzas, and filing cabinets that were all filled with

Personalizing the Workstation

Figure 20 A catalog image showing Action Office in a mailroom space from 1979. This illustrates the flexible storage capacity of Action Office which could not only organize a regular office workspace but could also handle the intensive storage and equipment requirements of a typical corporate mailroom.

Source: Herman Miller, *Managing the Work Environment* (Zeeland, MI: Herman Miller, 1979), 25. Courtesy of Herman Miller Archives.

copies of copies of notes confirming lunch appointments of bygone years. Everyone files a copy of every incoming paper and of every outgoing response and, in addition (especially with the help of the modern copying machine), sends copies of each paper to other staff who might be interested. Those copies are also filed. ... Expensive file cabinets bulge and papers are heaped on top as space runs out. Too much storage space encouraged the growth of personal agglomeration of material, most of it worthless and all of it difficult to retrieve.[20]

For advocates of open planning, all of those copies of copies of copies represented the worst aspects of corporate bureaucracy and were an intrinsic problem in the design and use of conventional office furniture. Most importantly, for architects and designers, the storage itself was often to blame. All those drawers and filing cabinets just encouraged workers to keep copy after copy after copy of the memos and forms they received, and in the new open plan office, architects and designers sought to curb workers' general tendency to keep such old and unnecessary materials. Architects and designers were not alone in blaming the existence of storage for the problem of excess paper. Avis CEO Robert Townsend described the liberating feeling of getting rid of his filing cabinets, and restricting himself to a single file drawer. As he describes, whenever that one desk drawer became too full he would "weed it back to half."[21]

If too much storage was an invitation to clutter one's workspace with unnecessary materials—by limiting storage for the individual worker architects and designers would effectively curb each worker's worst impulses and practices. In their planning documents for the new administration building at Purdue University from 1968, the Quickborner Team insisted that the individual work area should only have active files on hand—all materials in the workspace should be constantly visible and accessible. To this end, the Quickborner Team specified simple tables with no drawers to explicitly inhibit workers' opportunity to hide away material and ensuring high visibility for any papers or files in use. As they argue, "since the files are fully visible, all persons know just what they have in the files and where material is located," and additionally "people will maintain more orderly files when they are visible."[22]

Similarly, Robert Propst explicitly sought to support workers' ability to display materials in their workspace, but he did not want papers to become permanent residents of the workspace. According to Propst, while display was productive and useful as a means of facilitating thinking and creativity, deep storage was a waste because it encouraged workers to hide materials away that should really be in a central file unit rather than an individual's workspace. In fact, this was an idea that was even built into the first version of Action Office; the flip-top and roll-top desks, designed to allow workers to maintain their natural work-related clutter, were deliberately made rather shallow so that they would only allow a stack of papers a few inches high (any higher and the top would no longer close). For Propst, this was intended to ensure that the worker did not give into their worst impulses in terms of filing and keeping materials in their workplace that they no longer needed. In part this was because Propst believed that this tendency to keep materials only inhibited productivity and creativity because it interfered with the worker's ability to see the material and interact with it in a meaningful way. Information needed to be seen, not lost in an overly large pile or hidden away in a file drawer.[23] These ideas remained important in the second iteration of Action Office—as Propst described "the objective of paper management is to keep it alive, limited and tangible." Part of this design concept which limited individual storage was to facilitate and encourage "purging" as a regular activity in the office. As he describes "purging has to become natural for the user as a continuous appropriate process. *HE* must do it. No second person will solve this for him. The office environment has to assist this process, not defeat it. Paper cannot continue to be a permanent overload. It must be used and discarded."[24]

In contrast with Action Office which sought to limit workers' individual storage capacity, other systems furniture lines of the time used a "storage wall" design, which treated storage as core components of the workstation.[25] For example, Steelcase's Mobiles line, which launched in 1968, used cabinet style storage as a workspace defining element that was integrated with their Movable Wall partition system (Figure 21). In an office arrangement, the front side of the

Figure 21 An example of the Steelcase Mobiles storage wall design. The storage cabinets serve as functional storage for individual workstations, display space for workers (supporting a bulletin board on the backside), and as dividers or partitions separating workspaces from each other

Source: Steelcase Corporate Archives.

cabinet would serve as a storage unit for the inhabitant of one workstation, and the back of the cabinet could become a display component for the occupant on the other side. One of the things that made Mobiles' treatment of storage different from Herman Miller's Action Office was its emphasis on providing highly specialized storage for very particular use-scenarios. Even as early as their 1970-brochure for the Mobiles line, Steelcase showed a wide range of interior options and accessories for their cabinets including hanging files, roll-out shelves, index card trays, punch card trays, electronic data processing (EDP) paper storage, tape and disc storage, book shelves, binder storage, blueprint drawers, supply shelves, and even support for office equipment like dictaphones, calculators, and typewriters. The desks of the Mobiles system also included numerous drawer options allowing workers to store a variety of different kinds of materials. Like the cabinets, desk drawers could be specified in a variety of different configurations, for example, file drawers, card trays, stationary trays, reference shelves, and even just simple drawer dividers. Even the center desk drawer in the Mobiles line had 10 different configuration options available.[26] The large storage cabinets and desks of the Mobiles system might appear identical in form, but actually contained a variety of different interior arrangements specified to meet the needs of individual workers.

To make the issue of storage even more complicated, the types of items that required storage in the office were also rapidly evolving as the open plan and systems furniture became popular in the 1970s and 1980s. As some offices were trying to tame the paper dragon of corporate bureaucracy by purging files and adopting new technologies like microfilm, the new "automated office" required a growing array of physical media that also needed to be contained within the office and the workstation. In their book on designing for the automated office, William Pulgram and Richard Stonis describe the numerous accessories required to support the unique storage requirements of the automated office including trays, organizers, binders, dividers, boxes, rotary stands, lazy susans, and other storage devices that could adapt conventional office storage and office space to the specialized storage requirements of these new types of media.[27] Through the 1980s, some systems furniture lines expanded their storage support by integrating more specialized types of storage components and options to reflect the growing array of electronic materials that workers needed for their job. Steelcase's 1985 planning guide offered specialized storage options for a mix of different media, including audio cassettes, disc cartridges, various types of computer print-out paper, floppy discs, magnetic tape reels, microfiche, mag cards, tape cartridges, and disk packs.[28] Thus even as automation offered the promise of a paperless future, the storage needs of the open plan only increased and became more complicated with the growing array of physical media that required specialized storage.

Workstation as Design Process

Through the 1970s as the open plan and systems furniture first became popular, architects and designers began using the workstation idea as a tool in the office design process. The workstation was an organizing concept for the office that represented the integration of the systems furniture components as well as seating (such as task and side chairs) and desk accessories. It was the role of the architect or designer to create an overall system of consistent workstations that reflected the diverse positions of the organization, provided standard configurations that would allow the organization to maintain the space and support their current and future workforce, and offered a coherent visual language through the selection of colors and materials for the various components. The workstation was thus a conceptual tool utilized by architects and designers to identify workspace requirements and create consistent space standards across the organization. It was also a tool for codifying jobs in office space by determining the spatial and functional needs of different job classifications. This process of workstation planning effectively served to conflate workers, the organizational positions that they held, and their workspaces. The workstation was more than just a grouping of furniture; it was the worker-made material through the objects, processes, and space required for their job.

As the open plan and systems furniture became more popular, office space standards increasingly used the workstation as the basis for establishing the standard footprints and components of different classes of workers. This was often directly tied to hierarchy, but it was also connected to some real functional needs that emerged out of particular kinds of jobs. Workstations might need to integrate new technologies, special storage requirements, and distinct configurations that reflected the particular details of a given worker's job or division. There was thus always a negotiation between the goal of standardization, which served to make the space consistent visually and technically, while also meeting the particular needs of different jobs, units, and positions.

For architects and designers, creating the workstation template was a critical part of the design process, often addressed even before selecting the furniture. For example, in July of 1977, the Chicago-based interior design firm Powell/Kleinschmidt was brought on by Prudential to complete the interior planning and design for a new regional office in Merrillville, Indiana. Powell/Kleinschmidt started the project late in the process because they were taking over for another interior design company that had been removed from the project. With a planned occupancy for the following year, the Powell/Kleinschmidt design team had to move quickly to familiarize themselves with Prudential's organization, review the work of their predecessors, and start the planning process in earnest. By September of 1977, just two months into their contract with Prudential, Powell/

Kleinschmidt had already established some recommended workstation layouts that would serve as the basis for planning for the interior of the building, and by October of 1977 Prudential's upper management had approved the preliminary workstation design. After management's approval of the initial workstation standards, Powell/Kleinschmidt arranged a mock-up of the standard workstation types (in December of 1977) using several different furniture options so that Prudential could select an appropriate furniture system for the new building.[29]

For the Prudential project, Powell/Kleinschmidt proposed a standard workstation of 6 feet by 6 feet (182 cm by 182 cm) with a 72-inch (182 cm) work surface and a 42-inch (106 cm) return along with integrated storage. Supervisory staff would have similar equipment, but more space for side chairs and additional storage, and associate managers would receive a larger space still with a small conference table as part of their suite of furniture. The size and basic furniture components were obviously hierarchical, but they were also functional in that they generally reflected the assumed duties and activities of each class of worker. In planning the layout for the office, each workstation represented a generic position or a job, not an individual worker. The abstraction of the workforce into a system of standardized and predictable workstations effectively ignored the ways in which individual workers might have unique spatial or functional needs. Once the initial workstation concepts were established and approved by upper management, divisional managers were invited to comment on the workstations and specify some of the interior components that might be unique to the duties of different units in the organization. Even though the standard had been approved, there were ongoing negotiations and challenges as each organizational unit expressed concerns about the proposed design and asked for amendments to the design for their area. Two different divisions in the new Prudential office reportedly asked for workstation storage that would exceed the space capacity of the planned 6 feet by 6 feet standard. In a series of follow-up meetings, the interior design firm and Prudential managers negotiated some modifications to meet the concerns posed by the divisions while maintaining the basic workstation standard that had been approved.[30] This internal negotiation over the design of the standard workstation illustrates how the standard workstation concept provided consistency but also imposed limits and constraints in the planning process.

Selecting appropriate colors and materials was also a critical consideration in the workstation design process. Workstations were not just a functional system of components designed for work, but designers also conceptualized them aesthetically to ensure a coherent use of materials and colors. In the Prudential office, Powell/Kleinschmidt developed a system of colors and materials to reflect hierarchy and communicate organizational identity. For the designers, the workstation and its intendant components, became aesthetic tools to create visual interest in the overall design, balancing the neutral or standard elements that served as the common aesthetic of the space, but providing accent colors throughout the give greater visual interest. In the Prudential office, Powell/Kleinschmidt specified the standard Steelcase 9000 components in a light-gray tone for panels and drawers, and a slightly darker gray for the work surface. Inside the workstations, chair upholstery and tackable partitions featured bright-accent colors that varied based on location: green chair upholstery and blue partition panels in Section A, red chair upholstery and yellow partition panels in Section C, blue chair upholstery and yellow desk panels in Section D, and green chair upholstery and blue desk panels in Sections E, F, and G. Supervisors were also assigned accent colors for their desks that matched the upholstery colors in each section, but their assigned chairs had black upholstery. Finally, Powell/Kleinschmidt also specified a suite of desk accessories for each classification from elegant black leather and polished aluminum for the vice presidents and other top management positions to the black plastic wastebaskets and white plastic calendars specified for the clerical staff.[31]

The bright primary colors selected by Powell/Kleinschmidt reflected the tendency in offices of the 1970s to use vibrant color palettes, often in bold contrasting combinations to create visual interest. When the open plan and new systems furniture first became popular in office design, office furniture manufacturers often showcased offices awash in vivid colors and graphical elements. In their catalog for the Westinghouse ASD line, the front cover shows an array of partitions with bright jewel-like hues and the inside workspaces feature a miscellany of color and bold graphical elements like brightly colored stripes, circles, and grids.[32] Writing about the importance of visual enrichment in 1978, the Herman Miller Research Corporation described the color and material options as a design "tool" that allowed "the expression of a unique organizational character." They describe the fabrics and finishes of the Action Office system as "a 'wardrobe' for dressing the users' environments."[33]

By the early 1980s, color palettes for workstation components became more muted. In Haworth's "Individually Unique" brochure from 1982, the partitions shown are all soft blues, purples, terra-cotta, and beige.[34] Through the 1980s and early 1990s, neutral palettes became increasingly dominant. Strong color options did not completely disappear, but they were sharply outnumbered by a growing array of neutrals particularly in shades of white, gray, and beige. For example, in the color book for Kimball's "Meridian" series from 1990, there are just a handful of color options paired with some thirty-three different neutral hues in variations of white, gray, blue, black, beige, and brown.[35] As BOSTI described in their 1984 report, "there is a sameness of office interiors both across building and within buildings." Because offices need to house a large number of workers doing similar jobs, the 'problems of facilities management conspire towards uniformity and interchangeability of workspaces and the furniture they contain. Natural variation is suppressed."[36] Open plan offices of the 1980s and 1990s became increasingly monotonous in terms of their color, not because architects and designers necessarily favored such bland palettes, but because for future space management consistent colors and materials made future changes to the office interior easier.

The workstation as a planning tool emphasized standardization of the workspace both functionally in terms of the space and material requirements of each worker, and aesthetically in terms of the strategic use of finishes and colors. The emphasis on uniformity and standardization in workstation design reinforced the idea that workers were not individuals with unique spatial, personal, or technical needs but rather generic positions within an organization system manifest in a set array of components in the office workstation. Obviously, there is a significant conceptual gap between the imaginary worker at the center of this standardized workstation and a real worker with their specific job with diverse responsibilities, and of course all of their intendant personal objects, personal preferences, and their personal needs.

Adapting the Workstation

Once the architect or designer finished their work and the organization moved in, the space of the workstation evolved from a standardized template for an imaginary worker into a personal workspace for a real worker. Although the open plan workstation was often designed for a generic position in the organization it was always eventually inhabited by a person. As part of their interaction with the workstation, workers typically had the opportunity to arrange their own working materials within the provided space. Even a standardized workstation with fixed (inflexible) components had interior spaces that offered each worker some opportunity to customize and personalize. The initially empty drawers, bins, wardrobes, and shelves were soon populated with materials and supplies, and work surfaces were quickly covered by the detritus of the working process. The interior compartments of a workstation's storage elements afforded workers space for containing, organizing, and sorting a variety of objects ranging from common office supplies like pens, pencils, paperclips, pushpins, and staplers to specialized items like computer media and drawing materials. Furniture manufacturers provided a suite of workstation accessories designed to facilitate these various individual needs and enable even quite fixed workstation components to be adapted to different uses and preferences.

The selection and arranging of these organizing things within the working space is itself a design activity. Workers chose which drawers and compartments to use for their working materials, and made decisions on how to organize their files and materials within the workstation. As some likely took pleasure in this process of carefully organizing and arranging the various inner compartments;

others perhaps just dumped their things into their drawers without much concern for order. Nonetheless, both options reflect a choice about how those interior components were used. These decisions about how to arrange and use those interior compartments reflects the worker's unique position and role (the specific things they need to do their job), as well as their individual method of fulfilling that role (the personal way they choose to order materials reflects their usage and their preferences). The drawers and inner spaces were also home to numerous personal items: tampons, makeup, lip balm, brushes or combs, breath mints, umbrellas, extra clothing (a spare set of shoes or a sweater), snacks, tea bags, and even sugar, salt, pepper, and ketchup packets tucked away for future use. The inner life of these workstations was thus very much a reflection of the worker who used it.

In the early 1980s, behavioral consultant Ronald Goodrich conducted a study of several large office buildings to understand how users related to their working environment. In his analysis of individual workspaces, Goodrich identified five distinct criteria that seemed to create marked differences in how workers organized and used their workstations. First, workers who favored visual modes of processing typically had more paper and other physical materials than those who prioritized auditory information. In terms of organization, some workers tended to spread out their work horizontally across multiple work surfaces while others preferred to organize their materials (and their workspace) to accommodate a vertical arrangement. Workers also varied in terms of their neatness, with some "strict organizers" maintaining a carefully ordered space while more "relaxed organizers" tended to have more clutter. In terms of storage, there was a noted difference between so called "pack rats" who save things for a long time because they found older materials often come in handy later and "neat rats" who rarely save anything because they feel uncomfortable with the disorganization associated with too many papers, and feel those old materials are not useful. Finally, the fifth criterion concerns the issue of territory—some workers felt a strong need to mark the space as their own and personalize the space to their individual needs but others seemed to have a more flexible and adaptable sense of their spatial territory.[37]

Similarly, in their book *The Negotiable Environment* first published in 1985, Cecil Williams, David Armstrong, and Clark Malcolm identify four personality types that they argue can inform the way workers use their workspace. According to their model, the "Visionary" tends to have lots of work materials piled in their workspace, the "Catalyst" has a lot of personal items, the "Stabilizer" tends to like high levels of organization, and the "Cooperator" tends to prioritize meeting with people over the presence of stuff in their workspace. For Williams, Armstrong, and Malcolm these differences are not merely aesthetic ones, they map onto distinct working needs for each type of worker.[38] Sitting at the center of a workstation, workers were encouraged to use the components of the workspace as active tools in the working process. The work surfaces supported spreading out papers and materials, while partitions and storage offered a means for displaying, organizing, and containing paperwork and supplies.

Any workstation would over time acquire marks of usage, or what BOSTI called "physical traces."[39] The pristine work surfaces of a brand-new office would soon become scratched perhaps from one worker's careless use of a craft knife or maybe stained from a permanent marker. Inner surfaces might become sticky from old adhesives or old condiments, and dusty from the use of erasers and pencil sharpeners. Usage of any object or space inevitably leaves traces and marks, some accidental and others deliberate as people strive to adapt things to their particular needs. Even an office full of "standardized" and identical workstations carefully planned and arranged by an architect or designer would quickly become nonstandard simply through use, with each over time reflecting the idiosyncrasies of the worker, their job, and their habits of use. Further, workstations were hardly ever used by just one worker over its lifetime of use. More typically, workstations (and their various components) were used and reused by multiple generations of workers, each with their own particular jobs and working styles. The same workstation might eventually serve as the workspace for dozens of workers over its life who each might inflict their own damage or stamp their own preferences into the space through their work.

Jobs too evolve over time as organizations add new tools, tasks, and responsibilities and others become unnecessary. A secretary who used a typewriter in the late 1970s might have had a computer terminal on their desk by the late 1980s. These kinds of changes were inevitable and could create problems as the worker struggled to adapt their workspace to their new needs. Even the assumed work that served as the original basis of the workstation design—the list of responsibilities, tasks, and attendant spatial requirements— were often outmoded by organizational and technological change. This gap between the original design and the changes in the work process could create challenges for workers as they struggled to adapt their space to emerging needs. Work surfaces might be too small to support the new technology, or the position of the installed technology inside of the workstation might be poorly placed relative to the overhead lighting or windows.

Workers' physical bodies also could vary enormously and systems furniture with its various adjustable components created a structure that could adjust to suit the needs of different workers. This flexibility in the design of systems furniture was particularly valuable to supporting the needs of workers with disabilities. As design consultant and disability activist Mary Ann Hiserman described, the modular components of furniture systems were a unique benefit to workers with disabilities by allowing the arrangement of the workstation to be adapted to suit the particular physical needs of its user. Facilities management could easily remove or swap out drawers to improve access, they could raise or lower work surfaces, or they could entirely reconfigure the arrangement to better suit the individual occupant. According to Hiserman, the flexibility also ensured that workers with disabilities would "fit in" with the office—their workstation may have a slightly different arrangement, but it would still be aesthetically unified with the other furniture in the office providing a sense of inclusion.[40] In fact, systems furniture manufacturers recognized this aspect and occasionally featured workstations designed to accommodate workers in wheelchairs in their marketing materials, as shown in a catalog from 1982 by Haworth (Figure 22) and a 1993 catalog for Herman Miller's Ethospace.[41] Unlike conventional furniture which often had a fixed work surface height and fixed storage pedestals, the systems furniture workstation made it possible to adjust the space to, diverse bodies, abilities, and needs. The possibility of adjustment and change to the interior components of a workstation to support diverse bodies was a valuable characteristic of modular systems furniture.

This ideal of workers being able to adjust their space to suit their individual needs was always part of the original idea for systems furniture, but this ideal was sometimes in tension with the practices and policies of offices and their facilities management units. In an article titled "Keeping Blight from the Open Office" from 1974, a facilities engineer working for the Internal Revenue Service describes his own experience managing an open plan facility. According to the author, employees often made "indiscriminate changes" to their workspace. As he describes:

> Employees who were originally assigned a single pedestal desk with a side chair somehow hatched a little typing table (with typewriter), a desktop organizer, a two drawer lateral file, a plant or two, or another screen that seemed to have appeared from out of nowhere. To this day I cannot figure out where some of those screens came from.[42]

As the title of the article suggests, the writer found all of these workstation changes to be incredibly exasperating. From a facilities management viewpoint, these "indiscriminate" changes were problematic not just from an aesthetic perspective, perhaps creating a messy or hodge-podge appearance, but because many of these changes had negative consequences for the overall arrangement in the form of narrowed passageways and the slow attrition of a neighboring workstation (as a worker adjusted their workspace partitions to make their own workstation larger). In other words, these kinds of changes though seemingly benign from the perspective of the individual worker could sometimes have a ripple effect on the rest of the office. The author goes so far as to suggest that any organization adopting the open plan and systems furniture should implement strict rules requiring that workers get permission from the designers or facilities planners before making any changes to their workstation.[43]

Figure 22 A wheelchair user working in an open office workstation featuring Haworth's Unigroup system from 1982. In the image, the worker is using a file sorter mounted to a panel that is at an accessible height for her to reach.

Source: Haworth's *Individually Unique*, 1982. Trade catalog from the Hagley Museum and Library courtesy of Haworth.

For architects, designers, and facilities managers of open plan offices, implementing formal processes for making changes to individual workstations was a way of ensuring that the overall arrangement of the office continued to function as intended. Looking again at John Pile's 1978 handbook on open office planning, he suggests that aside from very modest changes (such as adding a pencil drawer or a bookshelf), any significant change to the interior arrangement of a workstation should involve an office planner or facilities manager who should sketch the change, specify the parts used, and arrange for the change to take place.[44] He therefore describes how organizations needed to achieve a balance between enabling and encouraging some changes that facilitate the needs of the office and the worker while also maintaining some control over how changes are planned and implemented.

Recognizing these enormous constraints and challenges, it is not surprising that some facilities managers would favor systems and policies that ensured their continued control over the arrangement and use of the space. In their 1984 study, BOSTI found that most workers surveyed had never made any changes to the components of their own workspaces, even though more than half wanted to make a change. According to the study workers generally either believed such a change would be too difficult, or would require special permission, in either case workers felt inhibited from making changes to their own workspace. Only 20 percent of workers in the BOSTI study indicated receiving any orientation on how to set up or rearrange their workstations.[45] In their final recommendations, BOSTI provided an overview of a user orientation and user's manual for any new facility that included providing workers information on how to make changes to their workstation (either by themselves or through a formalized request process), and letting them know very specifically what aspects of the workstation they were allowed to change and what aspects they were not permitted to change.[46]

Creating a Personal Space

The ongoing debate regarding control over the arrangement and use of the interior space of the workstation reflects a larger question of ownership and territoriality in the office. In his research, anthropologist Edward Hall described the concept of territoriality as a natural human activity, and he argued that people of all different cultures inhabit space and create ownership through their distinctive uses of space. Hall argues that people have a deeply ingrained sense of personal space, and they inhabit space through expressions of ownership and control.[47] An important dimension of this territoriality in the workplace was not just the worker's ability to tailor the design to their working preferences and needs, but also the opportunity workers had for personalizing the space by bringing in photographs, decorative items, and other personal ephemera.

Research by environmental psychologists and organizational consultants in the 1970s often emphasized the value of allowing workers to express themselves through personal display. Writing in 1974, environmental psychologist Robert Sommer argued, "There is something tragic about an employee who is reprimanded for placing cardboard over her air conditioning vent or a poster on the wall to brighten the otherwise drab office."[48] For Sommer personalization of space was not a frivolous activity, but a vital human need that was often unfairly suppressed by organizational policies. Similarly, writing in their 1977 book *The Feel of the Workplace*, organizational consultant Fritz Steele and management professor Stephen Jenks argued that the "colorless, drab, and lifeless" offices are dull and unpleasant for workers, while conversely the personalized work space could be a source of joy and pleasure.[49]

Among designers and architects, the issue of personalization was often quite contentious. John Pile's handbook described how "some people enjoy bringing personal items into the office to make it seem more homey, and there is no reason why the typical workplace should not make provision for display of family snap-shots, small souvenirs, and similar items, within reason." The "within reason" aspect was an important caveat for Pile; not all personal items were equally welcome. Pile sneers at workers who bring in "ugly plastic plants, tasteless novelties, and pinups" and even references a rather extreme (and extraordinary) example of a worker who kept a cage of live gerbils in their workspace as an instance of taking personalization too far.[50] The perennial horror stories of "tasteless" items and clutter in the open plan were among the reasons some architects and designers favored restrictive policies that expressly limited workers' ability to personalize their space. In the final stages of completing the Merrilleville project, Powell/Kleinschmidt suggested that Prudential implement a policy for the new space specifying that "certificates, awards, etc. be framed in a single style of frame to provide continuity throughout the office." They also recommended that "all desk decorations of any kind should be prohibited," and, that "personal photographs should be limited to approximately 4 inch by 4 inch size [10 cm by 10 cm], again in a single frame style to provide continuity throughout the office."[51] As one reporter from 1977 describes, architects and office designers at the time often had "a mania for uniformity, in space as in furniture, and a horror over how the messy side of human nature clutters up an office landscape that would otherwise be as tidy as a national cemetery."[52]

One of the most frequently cited examples of a restrictive decoration policy was at the CBS building, which opened in 1965 (designed by Eero Saarinen with interiors by Florence Knoll), where the organization restricted workers from having any personal items at all. According to an article from *Life Magazine* about the policy at CBS:

Mementos and gadgets, even family pictures are frowned upon. Potted plants are provided by the company and watered weekly by "monitoring teams." Employes [sic] may not grow their own plants, nor touch or water company plants. Walls must remain bare except for art works selected framed and hung by the company. These may not be moved. No personal art may be hung without specific approval of the director of design.[53]

Florence Knoll derided the haphazard décor of many offices and characterized workers as wayward children whose poor taste in design and aesthetics must be tightly controlled and restrained.[54] Yet even as CBS implemented strict rules in their office space and had an entire staff who were responsible for preserving and enforcing those rules, there was also some outright rebellion from workers, as *Life* sarcastically described, "Epidemics of non regulation art and other individualisms break out like measles."[55] This restrictive approach to space and decor at CBS persisted at least into the late 1970s.[56]

Meanwhile, over at Epic Records (a subsidiary of CBS, and located in the CBS building), the workspaces were highly personalized. According to a 1977 article from *New York Magazine*, the director of Epic had covered the walls and ceiling in music posters, and that permissive attitude toward space was common throughout the Epic offices:

> Even the precise ranks of secretarial desks down the hall have been allowed their quirky personal touches. Rock-star posters and family photographs and Snoopy signs and slogans cover the walls (most at least put up with the proper magnet, but some, like Harris's stuff, stuck up with Scotch tape). Cardboard mobiles dangle from the light modules. And violating the purity of the CBS gray-steel walls, there's a sign in the hall—EPIC IS THE GREATEST RECORD COMPANY IN THE WORLD—spelled out waveringly in masking tape.[57] (Emphasis in original)

The description of Epic Records illustrates how personalization could be a central part of the organizational culture. As a part of CBS, Epic would ordinarily have been held to the same rigorous and inflexible space standards of the rest of the building, but the culture of Epic Records allowed its staff to buck those standards in favor of a more relaxed and playful environment. Of course, this difference between the two offices is also a reflection of the cultural difference between these two industries in general. A broadcast network like CBS needed to maintain a formal image to reflect the gravitas of their national position, and the button-down interior with its rules and regulations embodied that. In contrast, Epic needed to project a more youthful and even countercultural image not only to the public in general who bought the popular rock and roll albums released on the Epic label, but also to recording musicians coming in to the office to negotiate and sign contracts and record albums. The expressive qualities of the workplace at Epic were in keeping with the nature of their own industry.

Beyond these organizational differences, workers regularly viewed their workstations as a kind of personal territory, and they frequently decorated the interior spaces of their workspace to support their own personalities, preferences and even to support their emotional needs. For example, in the introduction to an article featuring a series of profiles of people workspaces in *New York Magazine* from 1977, writer Orde Coombs describes a good friend who had transformed the "impersonal and cavernous" workspace at an insurance company into a "home":

> She'd set up family photographs and, for hating, a poster of a glum Nixon. There were four carnations on her desk, crocheted containers for her pencils and paper clips, a bright red cozy around her teapot. She'd refused to let the workspace—unpromising as it was—stay the company's. For 35 hours a week she lived—not just worked—there.[58]

The description is useful because it animates the multiple ways in which a single worker might "personalize" the space, but also the potential meanings of those objects. On the one hand, there are items like crocheted pencil holders and a cozy for the teapot that suggest pleasure and comfort, but on the other, the poster of Nixon, included "for hating" suggests the complex feelings and attitudes workers might have to the different types of objects found in their workspaces. Whether an exercise of pure whimsy or an emotionally supportive or expressive item, personalization was never an arbitrary or empty activity for workers. In multiple studies on office design, workers often expressed a desire to feel like an individual in the office and personalizing one's workspace was a method for imprinting oneself into the space and into the job.[59]

Research on display has often found differences in the mode and content of displays among different classes of workers as well as differences between men and women. Rosabeth Moss Kanter noted this contrast in her organizational study from 1977, observing that the male professional workspaces were "austere" and uniform in their décor, while the mostly female secretaries' desks provided "splashes of color" and "signs of individuality," including postcards, newspaper cartoons, posters with funny captions, and even "huge computer printouts that formed the names of the secretaries in gothic letters."[60] Similarly, in her research on organizational culture, sociologist Arlie Russel Hochschild found that personal photos were common throughout the organization from the executive suite to the factory, but the types of photographs, the way they were displayed, and the meanings attached to the images varied enormously based on the organizational position of the worker as well as their gender. Top male executives tended to have more formal images (graduation pictures, weddings, etc.) and posed photographs from family vacations, and such pictures were typically in frames and staged behind the worker as a mode of display for visitors. These photographs demonstrated the male executive's commitment to their family as well as their commitment to their jobs. By contrast, the women in clerical positions working in "banks of desks in windowless inner spaces" often had small unframed snapshots of their kids taped to their walls and perched next to their telephones alongside kids' drawings. These images were there to remind the worker of their personal life outside of the office.[61]

Most strikingly, according to Hochschild's research, women managers working in male-dominated divisions and roles in the organization were less likely to display photographs of their family at all, and instead often had their credentials (degrees) framed on the wall. For these women, not showing photographs was a way of signaling their commitment to the organization. As one woman manager explained, "women on a career track make a conscious effort to tell the men they work with, 'I am not a mother and wife. I'm a colleague.'" A woman engineer commented, "If I have my pictures on the desk, the men will think I'm a secretary."[62] In order to be taken seriously in these more elevated positions, these women often felt they could not display images lest they undermine their position in the organization, particularly with their male colleagues. Hochschild's analysis illustrates how even personal photographs could have markedly different meanings for different workers. It reveals another key attribute of such personal items—whatever they mean to the individual worker on a personal level, they are also "read" and interpreted by others.

In his study of corporate culture at a single high-tech company, sociologist Gideon Kunda describes worker personalization as a means of "self-display." According to Kunda, these personal items are deliberately expressive, and, he argues, function as a kind of performance of self. Some of the personal items engineers at the company had in their cubicles were expressive of personal interests and identities, which might include photographs of family, friends, and vacations as well as references to hobbies, religion, and other outside interests. Other items, such as work-related awards, mugs, and other objects with company slogans on them, were part of an "ideological display" meant to convey the worker's relationship to the organization and their commitment to their own work. Still other types of displays might serve to distance the worker from the organization. Kunda found many workstations had humorous cartoon strips, ironic slogans that make fun of the corporate culture, and other types of objects that reflect a form of critique and dissent, which serve to express a worker's distance from the company. These dissenting displays were most common at lower levels of the organization, in workspaces belonging to workers who were spatially and organizationally outside of corporate leadership.[63] In fact, Kunda argues that such dissenting items were not only common among engineers but also in the secretarial areas where poems, comic strips, and sayings often reflected workers' frustrations, annoyances, and grievances.[64] Kunda's description illustrates the layers of meaning and even contradictions that might exist in a worker's personalization, some things conveying commitment to the organization and others suggesting dissent.

Workers also displayed items as a means of managing their feelings at work. In her study on the meaning and purpose of personal display in the office, Susan Scheiberg found that workers used personal items as a means of managing their emotions throughout the workday. One worker's beautiful poster of a forest became a way for that worker to reduce her stress—she periodically looked at the poster to mentally rest and improve her mood. Another employee had humorous cartoons around her workspace to make her laugh or smile, and yet another had hidden a particularly "caustic" cartoon inside of a pull-out typewriter shelf, to glance at when he was feeling frustrated.[65] The hidden cartoon is also an example of the small ways in which individual workers could personalize their workstation in secret (even in offices that did not allow such display).

Liminal Space

The workstation concept has become so synonymous with the office and the open plan in general, it is easy to forget how novel it was. It represented a reimagining of the individual workspace as a system of interchangeable components that served to contain and support the worker and their work. It was also a useful organizing and planning tool for architects and designers creating open plan interiors. The workstation became a container of the worker, work materials, and the work process that the architect or designer could freely arrange in space like a fully contained module. The workstation offered organizations a means of rationally allocating space and amenities within the office and ensuring continuity and coherence across the design of the space. For workers, the open plan workstation was a kind of personal space within the corporate space of the office. Workers populated the interior partitions, work surfaces, and storage with their individual supplies, papers, equipment, and personal items. Although the open plan workstation was not always as flexible and adaptable to individual change as it was advertised in the marketing brochures, it nonetheless gave many workers a sense of individualized space.

Yet the "space" of the cubicle was always ambiguous. The conceptual underpinning of the workstation imagined the interior space of the workstation as inherently fluid and adaptable—a sandbox that would constantly shift and adjust to reflect new needs. Yet even some of the architects and designers who believed in giving workers autonomy and control over their space, sometimes treated the open plan workstation as a tool for restricting workers and their space for example by limiting storage or inhibiting clutter. Some organizations also imposed strict rules limiting workers' ability to adjust or change the space. Those rules, standards, and practices could transform the highly permissive and adjustable workstation into a conceptually rigid and inflexible work environment.

Yet even in a room full of identical cubicles, each workstation, once populated with personal things and one's own work process, would become an inhabited space. The process of personalizing—posting items to partition walls, bringing in plants and other decorative items, or hiding a personal photograph inside of a drawer—served as a means of claiming a sense of ownership over the space. In the words of Ronald Goodrich, the "office environment, as it is used and lived in, becomes animated with memories and meaningful experiences."[66] Sitting inside the office workstation, workers inhabited the organization and the organization's space, but in their use of that interior they were imprinting their own working process into the workstation, and imprinting their own personalities, preferences, bodies, and identities into the office as a whole.

Chapter 5
Supporting Technology

When the open plan concept was in its nascent years in the late 1960s and early 1970s, computers were large hulking machines siloed away in specially built glass rooms.[1] The ordinary office spaces were filled with the conventional office equipment of the period, namely typewriters, telephones, calculators, and Dictaphones. In promoting the open plan, advocates often alluded to the future growth of technology and office automation as part of the broader transformation underway in office work. At the time, there already were enormous changes underway in terms of office technologies from the development of centralized word processing and data processing through the 1970s to the eventual rise of the personal computer through the 1980s.

From our twenty-first-century perspective, the ascendancy of the personal computer as a dominant form of computing in business seems inevitable, but in the 1970s and 1980s it was just one computing model among a number of different competing technologies. The technological uncertainty of the period meant that open plan offices built within this critical phase were often embedding imagined technological futures in their office design choices. Every technology had its own unique design challenges, space requirements, power and cabling needs, as well as organizational structures to support their use. Architects and designers built organizational predictions about the future of office technology into the interior space of the office, and those decisions often had significant repercussions as the technology inevitably changed. Just as organizations were struggling to anticipate their own direction with respect to technology, so too were office furniture manufacturers, who were similarly struggling to accommodate these diverse technologies found in different offices around the country.

There is significant prior scholarship and writing in the history of computing and technology that has unraveled the ways in which engineers and programmers embedded assumptions about labor and managerial priorities in the design and planned use of workplace technologies. Workplace technologies are encoded with power and hierarchy and are often implemented in ways that reinforce structural inequality.[2] Further, issues of identity, particularly related to gender, race, ability, and social class, have long been inscribed into workplace technologies and labor.[3] For example, in her research on the Bell telephone system, Venus Green describes how the changing telephone switchboard technologies and the changing structure of labor were interwoven and had significant implications not only in terms of the organization and structure of work but also in terms of who performed that work, particularly with respect to race and gender.[4] As this diverse scholarship has shown, workplace technologies are not, nor were they ever, neutral technologies. In fact, each new office technology arrived with a significant human cost. The computer promised organizations greater efficiency and productivity, but those gains were often at the expense of the low-level clerical workers whose job it was to feed lines of text and numbers into these systems day in and day out.

In this chapter, I argue that architects and designers built the organizational choices and assumptions about the future of workplace technology into open plan offices in ways that later hampered the adoption of decentralized end-user computers. As new personal computers began appearing on desks throughout the office, organizations struggled to provide enough power and cabling for these new machines, and workers struggled to adapt their bodies to intensive computer usage. Increasingly furniture manufacturers and designers characterized office furniture as both the source of the problem and the ultimate solution. Through the 1980s, systems furniture became a means of filling the gap between the original vision of technology and the new equipment, adapting computers to the space by providing increased power access and cabling, and adapting the user's body and job to the computer through applied ergonomics.

Messy Technological Futures

Throughout the 1960s and 1970s, office automation typically referred to the organizational adoption of large centralized computing and word processing systems. In her article "The Computer Takes over the Office" published in the *Harvard Business Review* in 1960, Ida Russakoff Hoos described all the ways in which these new machines were radically upending organizations and the structure of office work at the time. As Hoos's prescient analysis reveals, the adoption of new computerized systems came with not only grand promises by its champions but also stark consequences, particularly for workers whose jobs were eliminated and restructured in ways that prioritized the technology.[5] It might seem obvious, but it is worth stating that mainframe computers were not purchased on a sudden whim by the organization or its leadership. These machines were expensive to purchase and fussy to install, requiring specially built spaces to support their unique operational needs and often requiring significant organizational change to integrate the machine into operations and support their continued use and maintenance.

The architectural implications of mainframe computing were significant; in the words of a reporter from the *New York Times* writing in 1978, "housing one of the larger computers is still a bit like finding shelter for something as large as a horse and as fragile as a flower.'[6] This description captures the contradiction of these mainframe computers, which were not only large and quite heavy but also very vulnerable to heat, dust, humidity, radio and television frequencies, and even sunlight. These machines required enormous amounts of steady electrical power, coaxial cabling to any connected terminals, floors with sufficient weight capacity, security, and a dedicated air-conditioning system. Organizations had to carefully plan for the construction of purpose-built computer spaces to optimally support their newly acquired equipment. In fact, some computer manufacturers gave very explicit instructions on the spatial and technical requirements for installation of their machines and even threatened that warranties might be invalid if any of the instructions were not followed correctly.[7] To meet these various needs there were entire subsidiary industries producing building materials specially for these mainframe computing systems, including raised flooring to support the weight of the machines and provision of continuous floor access to power and cabling, standby power backups in case of outages, and specialized heating, ventilation, and air-conditioning (HVAC) systems that would maintain the correct temperature and humidity for the new machines.[8]

In designing and constructing new open plan offices, architects generally designed computer spaces for the specific machinery anticipated for the space. As part of their planning for the new addition to their main building in 1978, the John Deere company informed architect Kevin Roche that each of three machine rooms in the new building needed to meet the specialized power and temperature requirements for the planned equipment: one room would have all of the mainframe computing equipment, a second room would have graphics machines, and a third room would have miscellaneous computing equipment for business purposes. Finally, a fourth storage room would serve as copy room. All four of these planned spaces needed extra power access to support the use of the machines as well as cool air to keep the equipment from overheating. John Deere gave their architectural firm a list of all of the anticipated equipment (including makes and models), specific amperage and circuit requirements, as well as estimated heat output for each of the planned machine rooms.[9]

In tandem with these carefully designed spaces for the mainframe computer, there were also spaces designed for operational purposes like data entry. These spaces, and the workers and equipment contained within, were just as much a part of corporate computing in this era as the whirring machine in the carefully calibrated and controlled room that was often nearby. The enclosed rooms, full of glowing cathode ray tube (CRT) screens and keyboards connected by coaxial cable to the mainframe, also needed special planning to physically accommodate the equipment along with the power and cabling requirements of the terminals. These machines, like their mainframe overlord, generated a significant amount of heat—a room full of terminals required additional HVAC to manage the heat load.[10]

Architects and designers generally planned the main work areas of open plan office spaces in the 1960s and 1970s with relatively modest power and cabling access. In the open plan office spaces of the new addition at John Deere, Kevin Roche and his team allocated just a single duplex outlet for most regular workstations in the general office, with one-half of the outlet intended for workstation lighting and the other for equipment (like typewriters).[11] The low number of outlets provided per individual workspace suggests that, in the 1970s, John Deere did not anticipate that their offices would one day have a computer on nearly every desk. This is especially surprising because they actually did plan for a handful of computer terminals in the general office that were connected to the mainframe, and these had special provisions for additional power and coaxial cabling.[12] If they already anticipated some computers in their open office space, why didn't John Deere future proof their new building to allow for additional expansion of computing into their general office spaces? In the mid- to late 1970s, it was not at all clear to organizations like John Deere or to architects like Kevin Roche that there would eventually be a computer on every desk.

There were some legitimate reasons why organizations like John Deere were reluctant to invest too much in potentially unnecessary power and cabling in the 1970s. At that time, the United States had been dealing with an economic downturn and a national energy crisis that together informed the ways in which many buildings were constructed around the United States, particularly in the latter part of the 1970s and early 1980s. Energy saving was seen as an economic necessity, and architects like Kevin Roche sought to help public and private organizations alike to reduce their energy footprint by building energy-efficient office buildings. The John Deere addition used skylights to reduce light usage, and reflective surfaces on the ceiling helped bounce the natural daylight into the working areas. There was no overhead lighting in the work areas; instead, the furniture served as the source of light. According to the project description, these choices were intended to "provide maximum energy efficiency."[13] In light of this effort to reduce power usage in the building overall, it is not surprising that Kevin Roche was economical in his allocation of power and electrical outlets in the main office areas.

For organizations, concerns about long-term energy efficiency along with concerns about the overall building costs reinforced their decision to keep computing equipment spatially isolated from general office areas in newly built open plan offices. This allowed for architects to provide robust HVAC in those new computing spaces that required more careful controls to protect the equipment from overheating and use significantly lower HVAC levels in general office areas. In addition to dedicated HVAC systems, architects also planned computing spaces with more expensive "access" flooring that allowed organizations the ability to rewire and re-cable the space as necessary. By contrast, the general office spaces typically relied on a handful of different strategies for managing power: access via adjacent walls and columns, a "poke-through" system with wiring coming up through holes drilled into the concrete slab, an underfloor distribution system in which integrated channels served as conduit for power, flat wiring that could be run under carpets, and finally power poles that brought power and cabling from the ceiling down to the workstation.[14]

According to a 1988 article from *Progressive Architecture*, the poke-through method which came into wide use in the 1970s was often colloquially called the "swiss cheese" method because it required drilling into the concrete floor to add more outlets or cabling. It was cheaper than the other methods in initial construction and among the most popular ways to handle power distribution in general office spaces in the 1970s. The author of the 1988 article argues that practitioners of this method, "did not anticipate the growing cable requirements of today's office spaces and the fire codes that would limit the number of poke-through fittings used in one space."[15] In other words, just by choosing this mode of allocating power, architects were saving money on the front end but creating future headaches for the organization later on when more computers were required. Because organizations and architects were often negotiating numerous constraints, including cost and logistics, they sometimes made decisions that were good for the short term (saving money, energy, or time) but not for the long term with respect to flexibility and future change.

Through the 1970s and early 1980s, computing technology was rapidly changing. New minicomputers, medium-sized computers that were significantly smaller than mainframes, were first introduced in the 1960s but began to take off in the 1970s, facilitated by the development of integrated circuits and memory chips that featured a novel way of encoding computer memory allowing for more space in a significantly smaller package.[16] In the 1970s, another innovation, the microprocessor, would again allow for the rapid shrinking of computers into yet another form: the personal computer. Though not as powerful as larger minicomputers or mainframe computers, these new personal computers had significantly more flexibility in terms of their design and their potential use. Yet even while these new machines held great promise, they were not very powerful, and large organizations often believed they were poorly suited for enterprise-level computing.[17]

As a result of this tendency of many organizations to dismiss personal computing as viable, the adoption of personal computing in offices often happened in a grassroots process through the late 1970s and early 1980s. In contrast with mainframe computing that was a top-down decision requiring careful planning, personal computers often appeared in offices in a comparatively impromptu manner. Individual units within an organization, and even individual managers, would acquire these new personal computers or microcomputers out of their own operational budgets often to serve specific needs not adequately met by centralized computing and word processing. In her follow-up 1983 article revisiting the impact of the computer on office work, Ida Russakoff Hoos described these executives and managers adopting personal computers on the fly in their offices as "information guerrillas," who were "circumventing their own data processing units in the name of speed and flexibility."[18] In this sense, the gradual adoption of personal computing in some organizations was a workaround to address the frustrations of relying on centralized mainframe computing with its time lags, queued jobs, scheduled batch runs during off-hours, and teams of operators struggling to keep up with the ever-increasing volume of work.

Centralized mainframe computing and decentralized end-user or personal computing were dramatically different approaches to technology, with significant implications for the organization. As personal computers became more common, their selection, installation, and use were idiosyncratic. In many cases each department or division was making its own decisions not only about the type of computers acquired but also in terms of the purposes and uses of those computers.[19] In a 1988 focus group-style study of ninety-six workers in five different cities and from fifty-nine different corporations, including a large number of Fortune 500 companies, computer manufacturer Digital Equipment Corporation (DEC) similarly found that:

> Since systems do not always meet a group's needs, individual managers have purchased low-cost PC's (Apple, IBM clones, etc) which they feel are more helpful. It was not uncommon to hear people citing the daily use of 3-4 terminals—Wang for word processing, IBM for spreadsheets, and DEC for E-Mail. There was little or no understanding that individuals could use just one terminal for all their informational needs.[20]

Most critically, each of these different machines and systems was an independent information island, disconnected from each other as well as from the large mainframe computing systems and the corporate data processing system. This miscellany of computing systems and equipment had significant implications for security because sensitive material was often located on these insecure machines that could be accessed by anyone. These new machines used various internal data-keeping processes that also created gaps in information sharing both internally in the unit itself (where critical information lived on a dedicated machine disconnected from other systems) and with the organization itself whose data on their internal units was sometimes incomplete or out of date.[21]

Although organizations at all levels were attempting to peer into the technological crystal ball and make good strategic choices about the future of technology, they were also trying to address immediate needs and problems. Each technology was an organizational investment and had significant implications for the design and arrangement of office space, as well as the systems and processes of the organization more broadly. Companies that had invested significant organizational resources (time, information, space, furniture, workers, organizational systems, and processes) in one technology were sometimes reluctant to throw their previous investment away for a new system. Adapting to this changing technological environment often required organizations to make difficult choices among competing and contradictory priorities and options. The uncertainty of this period meant that some offices began planning for a personal computer revolution, others were betting on continued centralization, and some were adopting a hybrid model with some mainframe computing and some personal computers. Whichever decision an organization made at this critical juncture had significant repercussions for how they adopted personal computers later, informed the changes required to support the use of these new machines, and of course informed the design and arrangement of open plan offices.

Integrating Technology and Systems Furniture

Because these various technological futures were embedded in office design choices, open plan offices of the 1970s were chronically short on sufficient power and cabling capacity to support the ever-growing array of equipment in the 1980s. Wire management was not just a technical issue and an aesthetic issue (creating an unsightly mess of loose cables), it was also a safety concern as wires and cables running along the floor could become a trip hazard; some offices even relied on electrical tape to secure loose wires to the floor.[22] Early systems furniture had little power support and limited options for computer usage in the 1970s, but through the 1980s most systems furniture manufacturers created a collection of furniture components for the electronic office, specifically designed to support the use of computers in terms of both their power and cabling needs as well as their unique spatial needs.

The integration of wiring and power support in systems furniture was among the most critical changes required for the use of computers in open plan offices. Haworth's development of the new ERA-1 prewired partitions with built-in circuitry in 1975 was primarily driven by their interest in enhancing interior flexibility by eliminating the need to bring in an electrician for office layout changes.[23] Yet very soon after their initial release of a three-wire single-circuit model of ERA-1, Haworth began hearing from users that increased electrical capacity was highly desirable particularly for the growing numbers of word processing and data processing systems, and Haworth quickly began expanding their system to a three-circuit five-wire design.[24] By the early 1980s most of the major furniture manufacturers had their own concept for integrating power, and by the mid-1980s these integrated power systems were increasingly marketed as solutions for the high-tech electronic office, providing at least one dedicated circuit for electronic equipment.[25] The provision of a dedicated circuit in particular was critical for computer usage because any disruption or variation in the electrical current could cause data and power loss for computers.

The arms race for increased power support among furniture manufacturers was on, and each iteration seemed to bring a new capacity for growth and expansion of the power requirements of the office, particularly for use with computers and their many peripheral components. In the late 1980s, Haworth marketed an eight-wire "Power Base" with three separate circuits.[26] Knoll's Morrison Raceway system offered an eight-wire and four-circuit capacity. Their brochure introducing the new "2 + 2" raceway emphasized its value in supporting the growth of computers in the open plan. As the Knoll catalog describes, while two and three circuits were once sufficient, in the modern computer age "additional power is required."[27] Yet the capacity to use these more robust prewired electrical systems was often still contingent on the power of the building itself. In the four-circuit CETRA system by Kimball, the 1988 installation guide specifically states that it is designed for a 120/208-volt, three-phase, four-wire power supply, but in a building that has an older 120/240-volt single-phase power supply only three of CETRA's four circuits could be used.[28] Even the more sophisticated electrical support of the furniture could not change the limits to the building's original power capacity. Offices and their designers also relied on systems furniture to manage the growing numbers of cables required to support computer networks. Raceway systems designed for power also integrated channels to support the expanding number of cables for electronic communication. Figure 23 reveals a cutaway of a raceway in Krueger's Com furniture system from 1988 showing the integration of cables within the panel partition. According to the brochure, the raceway space in the Com furniture partition could accommodate sixty-two 25-pair cables in a nonpowered partition and up to forty in a powered partition.[29] Some systems offered multiple integrated channels in their furniture at the top, bottom, and even middle of the panel to support the array of cables running through the workstations.[30]

Each computer also had distinct spatial requirements that could vary enormously depending on the style and form of equipment in use. Some computer models had a separate central processing unit (CPU), monitor, and keyboard, others had one or more of those elements combined into a single unit. Not only did these form-factor standards vary among different manufacturers but even within a single manufacturer's product line there might be vastly different

Figure 23 Image of the bottom of a Krueger raceway with a cutaway showing communication cables and power inside of an open plan office partition.
Source: Krueger, *Com: Bringing New Distinction to the Workplace* (Green Bay, WI: Krueger, 1988). Trade catalog from the Hagley Museum and Library/Image provided courtesy of KI.

configurations and options. Each of these types of computers had a distinct spatial configuration that required a different type of workspace to optimally support their use. In addition, many computers required spatial support for additional equipment such as disk drives and printers, as well as specialized storage associated with computer media such as disks and tapes, along with the often-oversized dimensions of computer printouts.[31] All of these items took up significant space in the office, crowding open plan workstations.

Conventional desks and workstations of the period were generally ill-suited to the computer. The work surface size of a standard desk extension was often too small for most computer terminals, and even situated on a primary desk surface the computer was often still too large.[32] For example, in Figure 24 a woman is shown working on a computer using a standard desk arrangement

Figure 24 A photograph of a worker using a computer in her open plan workstation at Freehafer Hall from 1991. The computer and its various components are squeezed awkwardly onto the top of a standard-sized work surface.

Source: Photograph from Purdue Special Collections (UA 153 Box 2 Folder 18).

in an open plan workstation at Purdue's Freehafer Hall in 1991—the computer's CPU, monitor, printer, and keyboard are crowded together awkwardly on the narrow desktop. Because low-level clerical workers typically had the smallest workstations in the office, they rarely had enough desk space for the computer and its intendant technologies (monitor, keyboard, CPU, disk drives, and printer) as well as space for their regular work material and for the typewriter, which was often still required. In a study of secretaries conducted by DEC, they found many of their respondents reported having insufficient space. One respondent described having six pieces of equipment in her workspace including a terminal, a screen, a disk drive, a plotter, a printer, and a typewriter. When asked how she moves in her workspace, she said "very carefully. I kind of have to sneak into my office."[33]

The rather awkward fit of these machines on standard-sized desktops led furniture manufacturers to design a new work surface type specifically to handle the depth and width of computers: the visual display terminal (VDT) corner (or 90° corner). As shown in Figure 25, in its basic form, the VDT corner was typically squared (with right angles) on three sides allowing it to wedge into a corner between adjacent rectangular work surfaces, while the front of the desk was flat creating a fifth (front) edge to allow a user to pull up to the equipment. In contrast to the standard L-shaped workstation like the one shown in Figure 24, the new

Figure 25 An installation of Kimball's CETRA furniture showing an office interior with computers positioned on integrated VDT corners.
Source: Image from Kimball International, CETRA (Jasper, IN: Kimball, 1988) tear sheet from the Hagley Museum and Library and used courtesy of Kimball.

five-sided VDT corner took advantage of the extra depth provided by the corner where the two work surfaces of a conventional workstation would ordinarily meet. This wasted space was thus repurposed by furniture manufacturers into a useful corner for supporting this new type of equipment.

The VDT corner assumed a computer in a fixed location, but some organizations wanted computers to be more mobile to allow workers to move the computer between workstations more easily. To support these kinds of uses, furniture and computer manufacturers developed a number of different solutions including rolling computer workstations that allowed workers to wheel the computer around the office, special movable arms that could move a computer terminal between workstations, and spinning surfaces (often called turntables, lazy susans, or carousels) that allowed the computer to "turn" to different workspace (Figure 26). These were all common in all types of furniture and computer equipment catalogs through the 1980s and illustrate again how assumptions regarding computer usage could determine the ways in which architects, designers, and organizations selected and installed furniture and equipment. The expectation that computers would be shared devices, used among multiple workers, meant that even offices built for personal computers

Figure 26 A 1982 promotional image from Herman Miller showing a computer on a spinning turntable designed for sharing. Accessories like these, produced by a number of different furniture and computer equipment manufacturers, were designed to allow a computer to easily move between workspaces to serve multiple adjacent users.
Source: Courtesy of Herman Miller Archives.

were not necessarily designed with the expectation of a computer on every desk. This is another example of how organizational decisions and priorities related to computing could inform the ways in which furniture was specified and the ways in which the office was arranged to support the technology and its particular use scenario.

As part of their planning around the spatial and technical needs of computers, organizations frequently debated whether to acquire all-new furniture or whether to attempt to "retrofit" their existing furniture and office. According to Pulgram and Stonis, retrofitting was typically chosen when purchasing new furniture was seen as "impractical, untimely, or not affordable." As part of this process of retrofitting, designers and facilities managers needed to carefully assess the present needs and make strategic choices about what elements to update and what elements could make-do. Of course, retrofitting had significant technical implications, particularly in terms of managing power. It also could produce a patchy aesthetic in the office, creating a mix of system and stand-alone furniture, and it sometimes used up significantly more office space than a more integrated solution.[34]

Retrofitting was an ongoing practice for facilities managers who spent much of their time in the 1980s adapting their older (or even not so old) systems furniture to the needs of new technologies whether it was retrofitting power and cable runs or adding new types of VDT furniture components. Unless an organization had anticipated a future in which there was a computer literally in every workstation and with fat bundles of cabling running through the inner spaces of most of their partitions, they would eventually have to reconfigure, augment, and even jury-rig their furniture to make it suitable for the spatial and technological needs of the rapidly proliferating equipment. Even in organizations that had planned for the spread of computers in their original open plan design, the changing computing standards, the development of new networking systems, and the technical and material changes in the design of computing equipment required ongoing changes to the design and use of office space and office furniture.

Integrating Technology and People

In the 1970s, low-level clerical workers were the primary users of word processing, data processing, and keypunch systems, and their jobs increasingly revolved around feeding lines of text and numbers into these computer systems day in and day out. Describing these kinds of back-office workspaces for dedicated data and text entry, a US government report on women and computing from 1985 stated:

> These electronic back offices bear names such as "data entry operations" or "system processing centers." The work tends to be factory-like. Scores of workers—usually women—with individual video display terminals, are lined up, row upon row, in huge windowless and fluorescent lit rooms. Amenities such as telephones to call home or private locked space are few.[35]

Beyond the factory-like arrangement of space, automated jobs were often more stressful for workers. Management placed greater pressure on the predominantly female workers to maintain a rapid pace of work, often enforced through electronic monitoring systems and quotas. Workers in these automated units had few opportunities for breaks, which only enhanced their feelings of stress, anxiety, and social isolation. In some offices the rules were so rigid for these workers that even bathroom breaks were very limited and required permission from a supervisor.[36]

At this time, organizations, architects, designers, furniture manufacturers, and equipment manufacturers were increasingly concerned about worker resistance to these new ways of working and expressed a desire to "humanize" the electronic or automated office. In fact, architects, designers, and furniture manufacturers often characterized the new systems furniture and the open plan in general as a means of softening new office technologies, such as word processing systems, and making them more suitable and attractive to users. Figure 27 shows an

Figure 27 Herman Miller's Action Secretary advertisement featuring Paulette Cary and her word processing workstation from 1974. The image depicts Action Office as a humanizing design with attractive decorative elements to make the office more "livable."
Source: Courtesy of Herman Miller Archives.

advertisement for Herman Miller's Action Office from 1974 that featured the "Action Secretary" who used "a great big whirring noise machine" (a word processing system) and had an attractive and brightly colored Action Office workstation with bold graphical stripes, a vase of yellow tulips, and a backdrop of cheerful decorative panels featuring Alexander Girard designs of smiling suns to make her space, and the office in general, more "livable." As the ad copy says, Action Office provided workers "humanity in a world of machines."[37] Similarly, in their advertisements for their word processing workstation, Westinghouse ASD promised that their new furniture would be "more aesthetically pleasing," "reduce fatigue and tedium," and make the worker more comfortable. The accompanying image shows a word processing workstation that easily integrates the components of the system and features a plant on the desk and a spray of dried flowers on a shelf above.[38]

While in the 1970s, furniture advertising described making these new office machines more humane as primarily an aesthetic and psychological exercise, by the early 1980s, humanizing technology increasingly referred to ergonomics. In a perfect world, each new piece of computing equipment purchased by an organization would receive an optimally designed workstation that could perfectly support the technical and spatial needs of the computer and its user. Yet in practice that was rarely the case. As personal computers arrived in dribs and drabs through the early 1980s they were more typically simply crammed onto a desk or table often next to or in place of a typewriter.[39] Not only was this approach to integrating technology ill-suited to the spatial and technical requirements of the computers as noted above, but this setup was also poorly suited to the needs of the computer operator. Many computer operators spent their workdays at conventional desk arrangements with little adjustability and insufficient space for their work-related materials and sitting on low-back secretarial-style chairs or even a regular straight-backed chair that offered little bodily support.[40]

Ergonomic manuals of the early 1980s showed workers sitting in these ill-designed workstations hunched over a low keyboard or stretched awkwardly across a desk, bodies twisted to study source documents as they also tried to type. In other words, workers' bodies were compensating physically for the lack of adjustability in conventional office furniture and computing equipment. For workers with disabilities, the misfit between the worker and their equipment was often even more acute, in some cases rendering the equipment itself mostly or entirely unusable.[41] There were some new developments in computing at the time to support disabled users, for example, new kinds of screen readers for blind users and an array of different devices designed to facilitate usage (particularly input) for workers with limited mobility or motor skills, but these tools and technologies were not widely available.[42]

Uncomfortable and inaccessible computing workstations created significant physical problems for all types of users. As early as the 1970s, intensive computer users began reporting physical issues associated with their equipment including musculoskeletal pain (back, neck, shoulders, legs, arms, and wrists) as well as eye issues (blurred vision, eye strain, and headaches). There were also emerging concerns about the radiation risk associated with computers, and some worry that these new machines were potentially harmful to pregnant women. Various unions, labor activists, researchers, and government agencies like the National Institute for Occupational Safety and Health (NIOSH) and the Occupational Safety and Health Administration (OSHA) began examining these various problems associated with computer usage for workers in VDT-intensive jobs and assessing the potential health hazards associated with this new equipment in the late 1970s and early 1980s.[43] As labor activities and unions demanded regulation and protections for workers for these emerging problems, industry groups including computer and office equipment manufacturers and various trade associations such as the American Newspaper Publishers Association and the National Association of Broadcasters actively challenged such efforts.[44]

Following on preliminary research regarding health concerns among VDT users, Congress held a series of hearings in the early 1980s specifically to consider the potential dangers associated with computer usage and to consider the adoption of ergonomic standards to protect workers. A range of people presented evidence at these hearings including workers, labor activists, union representatives, business leaders, ergonomists, doctors, trade groups, and equipment manufacturers. While labor activists sought regulation of VDT equipment to protect workers, many of the business leaders and manufacturers argued that regulation not only was unnecessary but would be harmful to the industry and to the economy because it would inhibit innovation and create an undue burden. To support their case, labor activists, union representatives, and workers shared their observations, research, and experiences regarding the problems of these new automated workplaces. For example, 9 to 5, National Association for Working Women, submitted a report to the Congressional Subcommittee on Health and Safety of a VDT Operator survey they conducted from May to December of 1983. In addition to providing statistical information about the incidents of reported health issues from the questionnaires, the report also included quotes from workers describing their personal experiences using the VDT. In their comments, workers described difficult working conditions, the stress of computer monitoring and pacing, the poor design of the equipment and their furniture, and the ongoing physical problems they were currently experiencing as a result of intensive computer usage including persistent headaches, eye strain, blurred vision, and backaches.[45]

In response, computer and office equipment manufacturers and their various industry groups pushed back against these complaints from workers, unions, and labor activists. A representative from Business and Institutional Furniture Manufacturers Association (BIFMA) described the problem of regulation as one that would be impossible because "comfort" is so relative; different users would have different needs so any regulations might run counter to the unique needs of individual workers whose bodies and preferences are different.[46] By continuously using the term comfort to describe ergonomic considerations, equipment manufacturers reframed the issue of pain as one of mere discomfort rather than as a serious health or safety concern. In one particularly revealing exchange a representative from the Computer and Business Equipment Manufacturer Association (CBEMA) argued that the adoption of ergonomic regulation

> would force people to sit in special chairs, even if they were satisfied in the present model; mandate covering windows with blinds even if there were no glare problem, or even if the glare problem came from another source. ... They would force employers to pay for meaningless devices and activities, such as metal shielding for terminals and radiation inspections. Channeling funds into useless items simply raises the cost of the products, making U.S. companies less competitive with others around the world.[47]

Instead, the representative from industry argued strongly for a policy of education, which would give people information about the safe uses of VDTs without creating any enforceable regulations. In the end, despite persuasive evidence from workers and activists regarding the real problems associated with computer usage, the congressional committee elected to pursue a voluntary policy that would give businesses greater flexibility and provide no formal protections for workers.[48] Instead of establishing legal protections at the federal level, industry was left to self-regulate. Industry groups like CBEMA established some recommended standards, but those standards were voluntary and not enforced or even enforceable in any meaningful way.[49]

Although Congress neglected to adopt any formal ergonomic regulations, there was a growing body of research in the field of ergonomics in the early and mid-1980s that offered organizations and manufacturers a number of suggestions and guidelines that were intended to improve the interaction between workers' bodies and their computer terminals. Notably, in contrast to activists who fixated on the computer itself as the source of the problem, ergonomic experts increasingly pointed to the context of use as one of the central concerns. In other words, ergonomists argued that it was not the machine that was the source of the problem, it was the poorly designed jobs and poorly designed furniture that were primarily to blame. Ergonomists recommended restructuring VDT work so that workers had greater opportunity for physical movement and task variety in their working day.[50]

They also advocated for rethinking the design and arrangement of the workstation itself to better support the computer user. Ergonomic guidelines conceptually placed the human body and its biomechanical needs at the center of workstation design, with the equipment and furniture arranged adjacent to the body in ways that facilitated VDT work and minimized harm to the operator's body. If one key role of ergonomic furniture and computer accessories was to adapt the computer to the body, then the recommendations needed to be flexible to diverse computer types (and their various form-factors) as well as suitable to diverse human bodies. What was ideal for one specific computer model and its user might be very poor for another computer and another user. This problem was compounded by the fact that workers performing different kinds of operational tasks on the computer also had distinctly different spatial requirements. Ergonomists typically differentiated data and text entry, in which workers were looking at supporting documents while typing (glancing at the screen only occasionally), from more "conversational" tasks in which they looked back and forth between the screen and documents, or data inquiry tasks in which the user needed to read directly from the monitor.[51] These different types of work required a different arrangement of the workstation to optimally position the equipment and support the worker's body.

To address these emerging concerns, furniture manufacturers began developing a slate of specialized furniture components and accessories designed to support the computer operator as well as the equipment. Recognizing that the optimum height for the monitor was different from the optimum height of the keyboard, many furniture manufacturers developed multisurface workstations that allowed the monitor and keyboard to be at different working heights. The ideal ergonomic workstation, like the example from Haworth's UniTek line shown in Figure 28, was one that optimally supported the computer configuration to facilitate comfortable typing and viewing. Haworth offered several different configurations of these dual-height computer workstations with a built-in "keyboard pad" at a fixed height, several inches below the main surface.[52] Like the VDT corner, these types of dual-height work surfaces were available in many different furniture lines, but they also required special planning to integrate into the office, and many lacked adjustability, making them ill-suited to the particular needs of some users and to the unique spatial requirements of some computing systems.

For companies wishing to just adapt their preexisting furniture, many furniture manufacturers also developed specialized accessories that could be used in combination with regular furniture. Herman Miller's Action Office had a number of different accessories specifically for the keyboard including a keyboard drawer, a keyboard extension, and a tilting keyboard tray, each option intended for different classes of users, from the occasional computer user to the intensive user, and for different kinds of installations. Herman Miller also produced a document holder and a machine support tray that allowed users to manipulate the angle or tilt of their monitor.[53] In the 1980s, a number of computer equipment manufacturers also began offering their own accessories to support their own equipment

Figure 28 A catalog image of the Haworth UniTek line showing a worker sitting at an ergonomic computer workstation. The workspace features a lowered typing height surface for the keyboard, a computer monitor at a comfortable viewing height, and an ergonomic task chair.

Source: Image from Haworth, "UniTek: Electronic Support" (Holland, MI: Haworth, n.d. [1980s]), trade catalog from the Hagley Museun and Library and used courtesy of Haworth.

including: monitor stands that allowed height, tilt, and swivel adjustments; document holders that attached to their monitor; and keyboard trays that mounted to work surfaces.[54] These product designs by computer manufacturers for their own equipment were not always usable with computers of other makes and models, making their usefulness somewhat mixed in an office with multiple makes and models of computers in use.

Another persistent ergonomic issue associated with computers in conventional office designs of the period was the persistent glare from overhead lights. The curving monitor of the CRT-style computer screen typically reflected overhead fluorescent lights, making it difficult for users to see the information on the monitor itself. Ergonomic manuals showed images of users fashioning a hood for their monitor out of a cardboard box or paper to better see the screen.[55] While the cardboard box solution was certainly economical, it was obviously not ideal. Some computer equipment manufacturers began producing special filters that attached directly to the front of a monitor to reduce glare. As part of this growing recognition of glare from overhead lighting, there was increased interest in shifting light from an architectural system into a furniture-based system. Furniture-based lighting allowed for a combination of ambient and task lighting that could give users greater control over their individual lighting needs and reduce the risk of glare from overhead lighting. Furniture manufacturers created integrated ambient lighting that architects and designers could specify for the top of workstation partitions, with light fixtures pointing upward to the ceiling creating reflected light that would softly bounce to the workstation below. At the same time, the built-in task lighting gave workers a brighter desk light that made it easier to read supporting materials on the work surface without creating reflective glare on the monitor.[56]

The idealized image of an ergonomic workstation as depicted in the schematic drawings and photographs in ergonomic handbooks often featured the worker sitting on a correctly adjusted ergonomic chair, with the keyboard at an ideal typing height, and the monitor set at an optimum viewing height, but in real offices this kind of setup was actually rather rare. Organizations in the 1980s and 1990s were sometimes reluctant to invest in expensive new adjustable computer furniture to support ergonomic needs and established policies and interventions that deliberately minimized the cost as much as possible.[57] An internal memo from 1980 on the potential market for specially designed computer furniture shows computer manufacturer DEC arguing that few organizations would be willing to simply toss out their perfectly good furniture to purchase new ergonomic computer workstations.[58] At AT&T, workers were offered individual ergonomic assessments and interventions to make their workstations more suitable to their individual needs, but the company still found that retrofitting their older furniture with ergonomic accessories was more cost-effective than buying all-new furniture.⁵⁹ As a result, even for large organizations like AT&T that made a significant investment in adapting the office to the diverse physical needs of workers, cost considerations remained an important factor.

Universal Planning

By the late 1980s and early 1990s, computer design began to consolidate into a fairly standard form factor that used the aesthetics of the IBM PC as the basic template with its separated keyboard, mouse, monitor, and CPU, with each component housed in standard beige plastic.⁶⁰ Aside from a basic tilt and swivel base on the monitor and movable feet on the base of the keyboard to change the typing angle, these standard computers had minimal adjustability in their design, but their greater standardization in terms of their form made them easier to accommodate in office design. Yet, even with greater standardization, it is important to note that older computer models did not disappear overnight—indeed most offices retained a miscellany of computer equipment of different generations for many years even as new computers adopted the more standard design.

As personal computers became more standard in their design and use in offices through the late 1980s and early 1990s, IT departments began trying to bring the growing array of computing equipment, software, and other devices under centralized control by developing local area networks (LANs). Creating these networks was no easy task for IT departments. They were still managing a mix of different makes and models of computers, different operating systems, and different software, and often trying to mediate between different departments and divisions that had invested significant resources themselves in various computing models, operating systems, and software. As management scholar Tim Davis described, companies in the early 1990s were "faced with the formidable task of linking together separate archipelagoes of information and different types of hardware into manageable networks."⁶¹ These networks were not just virtual connections between machines—they were materialized through long runs of cables inside the architecture and tucked inside of systems furniture. Facilities management and IT departments needed to install, manage, and maintain these lengths of cable over time, for example, adding additional cabling to support new computers, updating the system with new types of cables, and adding new connections. The process of moving or changing even a single workstation typically required facilities management or the IT department to unstring the entire run of cabling through multiple workstations in order to accommodate even a relatively modest change.⁶² In this way, the development of office wide networks was no simple matter organizationally, materially, or architecturally.

As a result of this growing complexity of wiring, some companies in the late 1980s and early 1990s began prewiring their entire open plan office with every type of cable that any employee might need in every workstation to reduce the need to update the networks and power with moves and changes.[63] Through "universal planning," a worker could be moved to any workstation in the office and have full access to all of the systems and networks they might need without requiring facilities to make any changes. New virtual phone systems even allowed workers to keep their phone number with each move.[64] While this concept certainly minimized the need for changes to accommodate simple moves, it also meant that the furniture needed to have the capacity to support the maximum amount of cabling and power necessary for the entire system to work, which sometimes required an investment in new furniture or at least new expanded raceways to optimally support this approach.[65]

This emphasis on creating standardized networks and cabling not only reduced the need to make changes to accommodate moves but also limited the capacity to rearrange the office workstation to support diverse users and different types of needs. According to Herman Miller, the standardized cable and power access could determine the work process and workstation arrangement, rather than letting workers' needs determine the setup of the space. By fixing the technology, workers again had to navigate the limits of the space, which might include a persistent glare on their monitor from an overhead light fixture or a nearby window or a left-handed worker having to adapt to a workstation set up with the assumption of a right-handed user.[66] This approach to space prioritized standardization as a means of reducing costs, but it significantly limited the ability of individual users to adapt the space to their particular needs. Designers planned each workstation to be generic and interchangeable to allow the organization maximum flexibility for moving workers, rather than providing workers flexibility to suit the workspace to their individual needs and preferences.

The introduction of personal computing in office work obviously had a significant influence on the design and use of office space and the design of systems furniture. Yet the design of the office also informed the adoption, implementation, and use of computers in offices. In fact, choices about the present and future of office computing that were made by organizations, and the ways in which those choices were implemented spatially by architects and designers in the 1970s and 1980s, had a lasting impact on office design and created limits and challenges later, when the technology inevitably changed. The long life of office furniture and office spaces meant that these vital decisions about the allocation of power, along with the size, shape, and the placement of workspaces and work surfaces, continued to inform the installation and integration of computer equipment for decades beyond the original installation of office furniture. Decisions about the relative adjustability and ergonomic support of the equipment and furniture had a lasting impact on the bodies of workers who spent long hours each day using the equipment. Even today, the legacy of these choices continues to create limits and challenges for architects, designers, manufacturers, organizations, and users as they continue to struggle with office design and furniture that is poorly adapted to their ever-changing technological needs.

Chapter 6
Facilitating Movement

Movement and circulation are important components of any office layout. Decisions regarding the placement of people and furniture within the space, the positioning of work and break amenities, and the specification of interior systems of transportation and circulation (corridors, stairways, elevators, and escalators) facilitate and enable the physical movement of people through the office. As workers circulate the office throughout their workday, their daily movement animates the office, transforming it into a network of interconnected spaces. In this sense, to read the office through the lens of movement is to see the soft connective tissue of ordinary use; the office facilitates a kind of daily performance or dance of workers arriving at work, delivering papers, going to meetings, visiting support spaces to gather information or materials, taking coffee and cigarette breaks, eating lunch, visiting bathrooms, and chatting around water coolers.

Architects' and designers' decisions about the provision and placement of these kinds of spaces and amenities reflect larger ideas about the meanings and uses of movement. Beyond the physical affordances of movement that are embedded in the office architecture and interior design, different classes of workers in different jobs have historically had very different opportunities for movement during the workday. Workers in positions of power have generally had greater freedom of movement than workers in low-level support positions. With the introduction of the open plan in the late 1960s, there was a new interest in facilitating movement as a tool of the working process. Advocates of the new open plan concept viewed movement as a vital means of communication that ultimately supported the circulation of information and ideas, and these architects and designers built these ideas into some early open plan offices by creating circuitous navigational routes to foster interaction. Yet as the open plan became mainstream through the 1970s and 1980s, architects and designers often prioritized efficiency of movement, creating long, straight rows of workstations, each one walled off from the circulation pathways to reduce distractions and interruptions.

In the 1990s and early 2000s, there was a renewed interest in the concept of supporting movement, and architects and designers working on the new "alternative offices" sought to use office design to encourage circulation and interaction during the workday. The term "alternative office" reflects the belief among its supporters that this was an important intervention into office design that would upend conventional norms of the typical open plan of the period. Even as they professed the originality and newness of these new alternative offices, advocates were often echoing some of the same ideas associated with the early open plan. By adopting new portable technologies (laptops and mobile phones), and new organizational policies (telecommuting, hoteling, and teaming), and a new ideal of office design that borrowed the aesthetics and tools of urban design to create more dynamic and interactive offices, these new offices promised to fundamentally change the structure and culture of work. I argue that these new offices did not just encourage movement, but in some cases enforced movement through design choices and policies intended to keep workers on the move during the workday. As with the early open plan concepts, architects and designers connected these ideals of movement to organizational goals and values and to a larger fixation on teamwork and collaboration that was becoming popular at the time.

Freedom of movement and interaction was always a luxury of power in the organization—workers in top-level positions typically had a great deal of freedom (and opportunity) to move about the office during the workday, while workers in support positions were more likely to be stuck in their workspaces with fewer organic opportunities to leave and socialize. This tension between the opportunities of some classes of workers to wander freely around the office and the expectation that others stay in their workspace only became more pronounced in the last decades of the twentieth century as computers became more common (replacing more organic forms of interaction), and as the economy and job market became increasingly precarious creating a large class of underpaid workers whose jobs had less stability, lower pay, and much less flexibility. Indeed, the ability of workers in high-level positions to have so much freedom of movement in these new alternative offices depended on a large class of workers who were stuck in place not only literally (in terms of the workday), but also figuratively in terms of their often insecure position in the job market.

This chapter traces these changing ideas around movement in office design from the early open plan through the alternative office, the evolving uses of movement as a tool in organizational culture and management, and the inequities of movement embedded in the workplace and in the workforce broadly. The various alternative office concepts that became popular in the 1990s and 2000s shared an emphasis on supporting and encouraging movement and mobility in general, but that ideal was always exclusionary. By focusing on the issue of movement, this chapter not only addresses the linkage between the early open plan concepts and the new alternative offices, but also examines the textures, tensions, and contradictions embedded within this ideal of constant movement and mobility in office work.

Wayfinding in the Open Plan

In the office landscape concept, movement was always an important attribute of the space and its design. In laying out the interior, the Quickborner Team carefully considered the pathways of movement through the office in order to ensure circulation.[1] Even their emphasis on using a horizontal building structure over a vertical one (with multiple floors) was intended to encourage workers to physically go to another department rather than send a memo. Pathways in the office landscape were often sinuous and curving, guiding the walker through a series of divisions and departments in a slightly circuitous fashion. Though literature on the office landscape rarely mentions it, these curving pathways were a central part of the design concept. As part of their planning process, the Quickborner Team described the importance of managing traffic through the office. For instance, they describe limiting the total number of "traffic lanes," and differentiating the major pathways (which are wider and more prominent) from the minor routes and pathways intended for local circulation among workspaces of a particular division. For the Quickborner Team, office planning was akin to city planning, requiring a careful evaluation and consideration of the natural movement of workers during the workday.[2]

This emphasis on supporting the circulation of workers through the office was also important in Action Office 2. Robert Propst described the "improved traffic expression" as one of the most attractive aspects of the open office or "free space" concept. In his words, "The process of moving in and out of space should be recognized as a communications act triggering many secondary contacts and involvements."[3] As part of his initial introduction to the new Action Office, Propst gave four different examples of traffic routes through the office to illustrate how the new furniture afforded a more dynamic arrangement of space, particularly in terms of traffic planning. If movement was inherently a communication act for Propst, then supporting movement and planning for circulation was vital to the success of Action Office itself. As part of the planning, Propst advocated for pathways to enable and encourage interaction between related divisions, and "pause or byway" areas where workers could have brief conversations, for example, a small table with a group of chairs positioned like a highway rest area, adjacent to the traffic. In this sense, Propst imagined the traffic circulation pattern itself as a tool for facilitating serendipitous conversations and supporting the social needs embedded in ordinary work processes.[4]

Yet even with its emphasis on movement, one of the persistent challenges in the open plan office in general was the issue of wayfinding.[5] The lack of fixed walls and partitions, and even the lack of doors for signage, meant that signage systems were an important feature in the open plan concept. In 1968, just following the release of Action Office 2, Herman Miller began developing an integrated signage system for Action Office that was designed to aid circulation and movement. The resulting kit of signage included large divisional signage as well as smaller directional and individual workstation signage to aid in navigation.[6] Other manufacturers soon followed with their own signage systems and graphics intended to facilitate spatial navigating. This kind of wayfinding was especially important in the early uses of the open plan when making changes to the arrangement of the space was more common. The high rates of space changes or "churn" in the open plan meant that workers frequently had to learn new spatial arrangements and rediscover the location of colleagues and units with each redesign.

As the open plan became mainstream, American open plan offices increasingly featured a grid-like arrangement of workstations. In the John Deere addition finished in the late 1970s, architect Kevin Roche's open plan featured long tidy rows of workstations, all arranged on a neat grid. The pathways through the John Deere office were evenly spaced, and the workstations adjacent to the traffic areas each have an end partition offering seated workers some screening from the traffic.[7] This arrangement was fairly typical in open plan offices of this period; the major pathways through the office were straight and efficient rows leading to service areas like the copy room, mail room, and bathrooms, and were typically situated along deliberately blank corridors of partitions. They were essentially the office equivalent of an efficient highway overpass allowing users to zoom past large swaths of the office without engaging anyone or even seeing anyone on their route.

Advocates of this model of open plan design often characterized these straight and protected pathways as efficient for both the traveler and their colleagues. For example, in a 1978 edition of their regular magazine *Ideas*, Herman Miller's research division described how studies had shown that workers sitting close to a major traffic area would reflexively look up whenever someone passed. By screening workers off more from those traffic spaces, and orienting workers away from the major office pathways and aisles, designers could reduce workers' distraction.[8] The trend toward increasingly taller partitions around workstations in the 1980s, which were intended of course to improve privacy, support communication, and offer sound control, only increased the enclosure of workspaces and the isolation of walkways through the office. This approach to design reinforced workers' tendency to treat these pathways as utilitarian spaces of movement rather than as spaces of social interaction and communication. BOSTI's 1984 study reported that a majority of workers in their sample favored the most efficient routes through the office rather than taking pathways that would be circuitous to their destination even if the longer route would allow them to interact with people.[9]

Signage took on an entirely new significance in the early 1990s with the passage of the Americans with Disabilities Act (ADA). The new law required organizations to update and retrofit their work places to ensure greater accessibility, which often included significant provisions related to accessible movement and circulation, for example providing stable and level flooring, providing ramps, adding elevators, widening hallways, doorways, and other office pathways for wheelchair access, providing accessible water fountains, and creating accessible bathroom stalls.[10] As part of the ADA, offices were also expected to provide better wayfinding systems that would allow workers of diverse abilities to navigate the space. ADA compliant signage required a high level of legibility as well as support for braille particularly on fixed spaces. Because workers with disabilities often had to navigate alternative routes through the space, sometimes even needing to use different entrances and alternative conveyances (e.g., a ramp or elevator instead of stairs), signage and wayfinding tools needed to support the fact that workers and visitors might be using a variety of different pathways through the space.[11] When it came into effect, a number of organizations and their facilities struggled to make sense of the new law and its various mandates and recommendations for accessibility.[12] Furthermore, as Ruth Colker argues, even after the passage of the ADA, compliance with the new law's mandates for accessibility in public facilities and accommodations remained poor, in part because the legal structures of the law were ill-defined and lacked clear enforcement mechanisms, particularly at the state level.[13] The ADA law illustrates the fundamental tension between the ideals of movement and circulation embedded in the original open plan concept and its practical limitations. The office that was ostensibly designed to support easy movement and constant circulation was often ill-designed and even entirely inaccessible for workers with disabilities.

Techno-mobilities

Designers planning early open plan offices assumed that workers would be physically present in the office every workday, but other changes were underway, particularly the emergence of new mobile technologies and new patterns of work. In the 1980s and 1990s, there was a growing class of workers who were spending less time in their office and more time working from home or on the road. As early as 1980, Alvin Toffler had predicted a future in which a larger number of white-collar and blue-collar workers would work from home. For Toffler, the possibility of this so-called electronic cottage reflected an underlying change in the structure of work itself, which was increasingly abstract in its methods in that it manipulated information rather than physical goods. As more workers in all different sectors of work spent their days "huddled around a computer," their need to be physically located in a fixed location decreased. Toffler predicted that the rising cost of commuting combined with the decreasing cost of computing would enable the growth of telecommuting.[14]

Through the 1980s, some companies were already experimenting with this new approach to organizing work. At the time, so-called telework was a means of employing workers with disabilities or childcare responsibilities that limited their ability to come to an office. These teleworkers, often in low-level and low paid clerical jobs such as word processing, worked from a terminal in their home, and typically sent their work by telephone.[15] Discussions about telecommuting and teleworking were common through the 1980s, but it did not become a common strategy for professional workers until the 1990s. At that time, there was a growing interest among organizations in offering greater flexibility for upper-level workers in terms of their working time and their working space.[16] Notably, while clerical workers of the 1980s were often described as "teleworking," professional workers of the 1990s were more typically described as "telecommuting."[17]

Using the term "telecommuting" implied travel, movement, and presence giving this type of work greater legitimacy in the eyes of the organization. In a broader sense, telecommuting suggests the idea of virtual presence—professional workers were not merely working from home, but rather inhabiting the office through the miracle of technology. In fact, the growth of telecommuting in the 1990s owes a great deal to the increasing use of personal computing in all types of work, as well as the increasing standardization of technology and computer networks in organizations. Thus, in order for telecommuting to be possible, a system of interconnected computers running compatible software on a shared network allowing them to communicate with each other efficiently was a necessary prerequisite.[18] This system of interconnected and standardized computers, software, and networks was a physical system of wires and cables embedded in architecture and connected to a rapidly expanding data and telecommunication infrastructure, stretching from the office to the worker's own home. Telecommuting required a significant investment in equipment for the worker and the company, and the home office was even increasingly conceptualized as a satellite of the corporate office. In 1992, when Bell Atlantic developed a new telecommuting program, they offered cost-sharing to their eligible employees to purchase the necessary equipment to make telecommuting possible including computers, modems, printers, and even an additional telephone line.[19] Some companies even implemented ergonomics policies for home offices to ensure that workers had appropriate furniture to support their work on home computing equipment.[20]

Workers in areas such as consulting and sales were also fast becoming "road warriors," spending significant time traveling to conferences and client offices. In

1995, designer William Stumpf described how this new class of worker relied on portable office technologies and flexible (even "redundant") spaces to facilitate continuous movement. As Stumpf argued, for this "nomadic" worker, the workplace could be anywhere.[21] This of course had significant implications for the design and use of offices in the 1990s, particularly in organizations with large portions of the workforce "on the road" for days or weeks at a time. As these workers were out and about meeting clients and traveling to various locations, corporate offices were ghost towns full of empty offices and vacant workstations, with only support staff consistently present during the week.

Some companies with large parts of their workforce out of pocket for increasing amounts of time sought ways to reduce overhead and unused office space by eliminating permanent workspaces altogether. One of the first experiments with the concept of a non-territorial office was "hoteling," a concept that was first developed in the Chicago offices of management consulting firm Ernst & Young in 1991. Michael Brill of BOSTI organized the Ernst & Young offices like a hotel, where the individual offices (like hotel rooms) could be reserved by workers for use for a few hours to even up to a few weeks. Workers would call in to make a reservation, and a service center would spring into action: assigning their telephone number to their temporary space, sticking a Velcro nameplate by the door, and pulling a trunk of papers and personal materials which were installed in the assigned workspace in advance of the worker's arrival (even placing personal photographs on the desk).[22] A similar hoteling or "just-in-time" office model was also used at the consulting firm Arthur Andersen in San Francisco in the early 1990s.[23]

"Hoteling" implies not only the instability of the space, where workers come and go, checking in and checking out as needed, but also reinforced the ideal of movement as a central value of this new approach to office design. Hotels are places to visit—they are temporary spaces encountered when traveling. In other words, they are brief stopping points on a journey. To refer to this model of office organization as "hoteling" was to reinforce the association with travel, movement, and circulation; it reflected the expectation that workers coming to the office were only visiting for a brief stretch of time.

While the Ernst & Young offices in Chicago and Arthur Andersen's San Francisco branch were modeled on a high-end luxury hotel experience, complete with elegantly appointed spaces and significant personal service (a concierge, housekeeping, etc.), but BM's new hoteling system introduced in the early 1990s in their sales office in New Jersey was modeled on the budget hotel or even motel. Workers would arrive each day and check in at a computer which would then automatically assign them to an "anonymous, empty cubicle" with basic office supplies and a network connection for their laptop.[24] As part of the concept, workers arriving at the office were randomly assigned to a workspace in order to prevent people from squatting in a particular location for too long.

In fact, IBM's somewhat dismal hoteling (or moteling) model was designed to discourage people from coming into the office except for occasional meetings and product demonstrations.[25]

In this case, the drab cube farm was actually an intentional method on the part of IBM to keep workers out of the office and on the road (often telecommuting in from client's office or from home).[26] For IBM this strategy was so successful that while the original ratio of desks was four workers to one workstation, they eventually were able to move to eight workers to one workstation because workers were out of the office so much (which was of course viewed positively by the company). IBM later deployed a similar model at their office in Norfolk, Virginia where their "workplace mobility" program allowed them to condense their workspace to a minimal footprint. Featuring a plain open plan design, this office started with a two person to one workstation ratio, and eventually increased to a 12:1 ratio.[27] Even the more elaborate hoteling examples boasted similar reductions in space and cost requirements. Arthur Andersen's hoteling offices, which provided just thirteen offices for seventy consultants, also created a significant savings in overhead (rent and furniture).[28]

Another model of this non-territorial office concept was the "virtual agency" first developed in the Venice Beach offices of advertising firm Chiat/Day. Like the other hoteling concepts, workers at the new Chiat/Day did not receive a permanent workstation or workspace. Instead, each day workers would arrive, put their personal items away in a locker, and check in at the office "store" to receive a laptop and mobile phone for the day. They were then free to work anywhere in the office. The technology was first-come-first-serve, and workers returned it at the end of each day. Part of the concept assumed that not all workers would be in the office at all times of the day, but unlike the other examples it was not really intended to keep people out of the office. Rather, the intention was to use mobile technology to facilitate greater mobility and circulation within the office. The overall design for the original Chiat/Day, developed by architects Paul Lubowicki and Susan Lanier, was based on the concept of a student union with different types of settings available for different types of work including a "high tech Rathskeller," a media center, and project rooms (a cross between a classroom and a conference room). The office also included some idiosyncratic touches like a "crow's nest" and a "conference womb" that allowed workers to hide away in the office, a "flop" room that allowed workers to lie down while working, as well as spaces and objects for relaxation and fun like a pool table.[29] The "clubhouse" space featured a ceiling covered with artfully crumpled (and epoxy-coated) paper and restored diner booths along with some sculptural elements like an artfully assembled pile of tires, and even garbage can covers as light fixtures.[30] The playful décor was planned to encourage workers to treat the whole office as their workspace. For founder and CEO Jay Chiat, this design embodied his vision for a more dynamic advertising agency in which workers would be liberated by technology and free to be quite mobile throughout the workday.³¹

Very soon after the completion of the California office, Chiat implemented the new "virtual agency" concept in his New York office as well. Created by Italian designer Gaetano Pesce, the redesigned New York branch (opened in 1994) was a visual cacophony of colors, materials, and idiosyncratic objects used as playful decor: a wall of plaster "bricks" molded from remote controls, a conference room wall covered in gooseneck lamps, chairs with springs for feet, and doors with playful collages of found objects like toy cars and electrical plugs.³² As in the California office, workers had a variety of choices in terms of workspaces including small and large project rooms, various nooks and alcoves, a series of wire enclosed workstations, a cafe area, and even small "privacy chambers" that employees jokingly called the outhouse.³³ The whimsical design of the Chiat/Day New York office received significant attention in the architecture and design press for its inventive approach to the space.³⁴ Others were more critical, for example, Michael Brill described the new office as a "vividly colored daycare center," where the highly glossy space was both visually and acoustically noisy, and ill-suited to the needs of the workers who struggled to find comfortable places to work.³⁵ Like the Venice Beach branch of Chiat/Day, the design's whimsical qualities were part of the concept and intended to transform the office into a playground for the itinerant creatives working throughout the space.

Whether providing a tailored luxury executive space (Ernst & Young and Andersen Consulting), a sea of drab cubicles (IBM), or a brightly colored and expressly creative space (Chiat/Day), non-territorial offices depended on the implementation of standardized technology and integrated and accessible networking and cabling as a critical part of the underlying infrastructure. They depended, furthermore, on the assumption that workers could give up their individual workstations and offices because of greater standardization of technology, computer systems, and networking protocols as well as greater portability of technology in the form of laptop computers and mobile phones and portable phone numbers. The image of a highly mobile workforce circulating the office and world was thus enabled, maintained, and reinforced by technologies that were tethered to increasingly fixed systems: runs of cable and wires, corporate networks and databases, and standardized hardware and software.

Paper was also a significant problem in this non-territorial model. Without dedicated workspaces, many of these systems sharply limited the amount of paper and files workers could reasonably keep, and in fact some offices used this as part of a larger effort to go paperless. Advocates often characterized getting rid of old paper and files as a liberating aspect of the alternative office. At Chiat/Day, Jay Chiat described rifling through people's cubicles prior to the implementation of the virtual office concept and finding reams of old and outdated materials that indicated to him a need to upend the practice of individual space.³⁶

By implementing this new model, Chiat imposed a kind paperless ideal, though workers in the new virtual agency were still using plenty of paper and files, they just lacked a place to store them.[37] At other offices, part of the adoption of this kind of model involved significant housecleaning of old papers. At KPMG (a consulting firm), the director of the office held a series of "Pack and Purge Nights" providing pizza and encouraging workers to throw out all their old papers. After their adoption of the new plan, KPMG sought to avoid any new accumulations of old materials by imposing a rule that required workers to change workspaces after thirty days in a row, specifically to prevent "pack-rat habits" from forming again.[38]

Though advocates of non-territorial offices often characterized this change as a benefit to workers because of the increased flexibility and mobility, workers sometimes engaged in tactics that resisted or challenged the underlying model. Michael Brill and Ellen Keable described an array of common "disruptive behaviors" in the hoteling model such as "hogging" a workspace (trying to keep the space even when out of the office), "squatting" at a workspace (bypassing the reservation system), and "pigginess" (leaving messy workstations behind).[39] These kinds of issues were seen at many of the various non-territorial offices including Chiat/Day and Ernst & Young.[40] All of these problems reflect an underlying tension between the ideal of constant mobility and movement, and the real preferences of workers many of whom missed having dedicated and permanent space. In other words, the framing of these as "disruptive" or bad behaviors reflected the assumption of planners and office design advocates that their design vision was superior and more important than workers' own preferences and needs. Some organizations and their designers sought to discourage these habits through the design itself; at the IBM Norfolk office, architectural firm Gensler deliberately eliminated storage elements from the workstations to reduce "squatting."[41]

At other offices, strict codes of behavior reinforced rules and norms necessary for the new hoteling model. Tandem Computer's "Business Center" produced "etiquette" posters to establish new rules and encourage good citizenship at the office. Among the many specifics, workers were told to "WRAP-UP" whenever they were finished in workspaces or common areas by: Wiping down tables, Returning items to their original locations, Addressing accidents (reporting or cleaning up), Pitching out any trash, Updating supplies, and reporting Problems with equipment. Workers at Tandem were asked to be mindful of others in their usage of the space by keeping their voices down in the hallways and common areas, cleaning up after themselves in the breakroom (including washing their own dishes), and keeping spaces tidy.[42] The list of dos and don'ts reflects the numerous challenges and frustrations of this model of office design. Each of these points suggests a trail of bad behaviors that needed correcting. One can easily imagine the empty coffee cups left by the sink (or even in a workspace), the noisy conversations in the hallway, an empty stapler, a missing chair, a sticky surface left behind from a spilled soda, or a broken piece of equipment that was never reported. This also suggests the deeper problems of an office dominated by so many itinerant workers with little investment in the long-term care and upkeep of the space.

Infrastructures of Collaboration and Circulation

Telecommuting and non-territorial office concepts were just two of a whole series of so-called alternative officing ideas circulating in architecture and design, business, and facilities management circles in the 1990s. At the time, there were numerous iterations and terms used to describe these various alternative office concepts including clubs, dens, caves and commons, oasis, hot-desking, and cockpit offices. For designers, architects, furniture manufacturers, space planners, and organizations, these ideas offered a toolkit of strategies that could be used in isolation or in various combinations to create a workplace suited to the needs, priorities, and preferences of a given organizational culture. Each of these concepts were quite flexible and adaptable to different contexts and were frequently adjusted or fine-tuned to the unique culture and needs of a given workplace.

Among the common goals of these various kinds of office strategies was an increasing emphasis on supporting mobility and flexibility of space and time within the office itself, often with the larger goal of encouraging collaboration and communication. As part of these new office strategies, many architects, designers, and space planners began describing the office not as a single space, but as a series of different and distinct settings designed to support a variety of tasks, interactions, and experiences throughout the day and week. In this new kind of office, workers might spend some time at an open plan workstation, but the bulk of their time might be spent sitting in different spaces throughout the office, thus freeing the worker from feeling trapped at a single workspace. It went under a variety of names; Francis Duffy and Marilyn Zelinsky called it a "club" model and Franklin Becker and Fritz Steel describe it as a "total workplace," but they shared a common ideal of creating an office that offered workers greater variety in choice in terms of workspaces and in terms of amenities.[43]

Advocates often compared this type of office to an airline club lounge, where workers in transit might spend a few hours catching up on work while waiting to catch their next flight. Like hoteling, the analogy of this model to an airport lounge again reinforces mobility and movement as central features of the design. Some offices in the club model had individually assigned open plan workstations for workers to use on an ongoing basis, but others were non-territorial, and instead provided a host of different kinds of spaces including temporary workstations, common areas, conference rooms, project rooms, break spaces, eating spaces, and atria. Of course, these so-called club offices were generally open plan by design, often with low partitions around work areas and with few if any private offices. In other words, the "club" concept was really another iteration of the open plan office reimagined as a multifunctional lounge and workspace.

The club concept was appealing in part because advocates saw it as a spatial tool for facilitating teamwork and collaboration. In corporate management circles at the time, teamwork in particular had achieved an almost cult-like status as a means of increasing efficiency and productivity while improving the quality of the work in general.[44] In corporate America, there was a growing interest in the 1990s in the concept of cross-functional teams in which workers from different divisions or areas collaborated together on a project. Proponents argued that this approach to teaming was more efficient in terms of production, and better for problem solving because of the diverse skill sets and expertise that could be brought together.[45]

As a prime example of this club or "total workplace" concept in action, Becker and Steele highlight Steelcase's Corporate Development Center completed in 1989 in Grand Rapids in which teamwork and communication were strategic priorities in the design. Describing the project, Becker and Steele emphasize how Steelcase sought to optimally support teamwork, for example, the small open plan workstations integrated a mix of workers from different divisions to encourage cross-disciplinary communication. The design of the building also encouraged a high degree of mobility and circulation during the workday to support interaction. The Steelcase offices featured a variety of spaces including a commons area, eating spaces, a laboratory, project rooms, conference spaces, a resource center, break areas, outdoor terraces, and an atrium to give workers choices and options for working. Steelcase planned the building for intentional inconvenience—forcing workers to walk a greater distance to get to places and thereby actively enforcing greater movement and circulation. According to Becker and Steele, elevators and stairs were even "hidden" so that workers were encouraged to use escalators to move between floors, facilitating "visual contact" between workers who would pass each other going up and down the escalator and supporting "accidental communication."[46] The space was designed to deliberately increase movement and circulation all with the larger goal of supporting a high degree of collaboration and communication. The Steelcase corporate office, which of course featured their own furniture, was also a kind of working showroom, demonstrating not only the many possible uses of their furniture but also the new alternative officing ideas that the design represented.[47] When companies interested in Steelcase furniture visited the offices, they would see the Steelcase office as a model of this new approach to office design.

Of course, there was a significant emphasis in office design circles on the importance of informal and serendipitous types of communication through circulation, but proponents also believed that dedicated team, project, and meeting spaces were essential amenities in this new kind of office space. Jean Wineman and Margaret Serrato argued that groups needed easy access to a variety of different kinds of well-equipped teaming and collaborative spaces including shared group workspace, meeting rooms, conference rooms, and informal gathering spaces that support different kinds of teams and groups and different kinds of group tasks. Wineman and Serrato described the value of providing display elements and tools for generating ideas (like white boards) in meeting rooms and other collaborative spaces.[48] In prioritizing teamwork and collaboration, the entire office was increasingly oriented toward the ideal of constant interaction.

This club model was based on the assumption that workers would not spend their days sitting in their workstations, but rather would be encouraged to move and circulate throughout the day. Similar to the early open plan concepts, movement through the office was no longer about just getting from place to place, but about facilitating the spontaneous encounters and interactions enabling workers to share information, brainstorm ideas, and stay connected to each other and the organization.[49] For advocates of this club approach, the ideal office was not one in which workers were quietly working at their desks but was one in which workers were up and about, having coffee with a colleague, going to meetings, and so forth. The essential glue of this new kind of office was the constant movement of people and information.[50]

All of these alternative office concepts reinforced an ideal of ability, and often excluded workers with various physical, sensory, and cognitive disabilities through their design. Some organizations, like Steelcase, Alcoa, and Nickelodeon, proudly highlighted their use of stairs or escalators over elevators in their new offices as a tool for encouraging interaction for workers, but, of course, those modes of conveyance were not usable at all for workers who relied on walkers, canes, or wheelchairs to facilitate and support their movement.[51] In other words, the ideal worker imagined in the design of these offices was a person who was able to walk up and down a staircase or comfortably ride an escalator, not someone who required an elevator. The club model also assumed that workers should be able to work anywhere in the office and by extension assumed that every place in the office was equally suitable to every worker, but workers with disabilities were not often considered in the underlying design. Club-style offices frequently featured tables and chairs that were too low (lounge seating) or too high (bar height), spaces with low or dim lighting, and with poor noise control, all of which could create inaccessible, uncomfortable, or unusable spaces for older workers or workers with sensory and physical disabilities. Visibility (both seeing and being seen) was also central to the design of these new alternative offices, but that attribute privileged sighted workers. Even the obsession with supporting constant interaction, communication, and teamwork through design reflected the assumption that all workers naturally benefit from constant talking and are comfortable engaging with others all the time. This too was exclusionary, disregarding workers for whom socializing and talking were uncomfortable, difficult, overwhelming, or distracting for example workers who were introverted or neurodivergent (including those with autism or a form of attention deficit disorder). Many of the key attributes of this new idealized office space prioritized workers with certain abilities, and marginalized or excluded workers whose bodies, personalities, or identities did not conform to those ableist assumptions.

The Office as Urban Playground

As this new style of office was becoming popular, architects, designers, and organizations increasingly adopted urban aesthetics and urban language to describe their office spaces. In the late 1990s the newly merged advertising agency TBWA/Chiat/Day moved their LA offices. In their new offices, designed by Clive Wilkinson Architects, there was a mix of urban-inspired environments to give workers a sense of place and to convey the idea of a bustling and dynamic office culture (Figure 29). The large warehouse space included a wide "main street," an espresso bar made of surfboards, a park-like area called "Central Park" with rows of ficus trees, and a basketball court, all provided to encourage mingling, interaction, and movement among staff. Perhaps the biggest change in these new offices, particularly as compared to their previous "virtual office" design was the inclusion of permanent (assigned) open plan workspaces called Nice Environment for Sitting and Thinking (NESTs) and "cliff dwellings," shared office spaces housed in stacked yellow shipping containers for teams of copywriters and art directors. All of the workspaces were grouped in "neighborhoods" to promote and encourage greater collaboration and teamwork. Describing the new office, *New York Times* reporter Frances Anderton called it "a playful version of Fritz Lang's *Metropolis*," and a reporter from the *LA Times* similarly described it as an "ersatz city" evoking Disneyland in its "doe-eyed sentimentalism."[52]

This use of urban language and iconography was not just a metaphor for the design, but was also a literal model for office planning. In his 2004 book, Franklin Becker explicitly connected the ideals of urban design at the time, particularly the increasing emphasis on increased social density and walkability, as a valuable model for office design.[53] As part of this transformation, some offices were reimagined as consumer spaces that aimed to strategically attract workers to various office amenities. Becker and Steele even describe the importance of creating a "town square" and other types of social spaces like break areas, coffee

Figure 29 The TBWA/Chiat/Day Los Angeles offices designed by Clive Wilkinson Architects in 1999. The photograph shows the urban inspired space with "cliff dwellings" in stacked yellow shipping containers, the central park area with ficus trees, and a basketball court in the background.
Source: ©Fotoworks/Benny Chan.

shops, and atria as "activity generators," which act like "magnets" drawing people to them.[54] Similarly architect Frank Duffy argued for clustering collaborative and social spaces like training rooms, coffee areas, restaurants, and meeting rooms in ways that maximize and support contact.[55] At Apple Computer's offices in Cupertino, café-style break areas providing high-quality free coffee and food were scattered throughout the office on major circulation routes to encourage workers to stop and talk. Another example highlighted by Becker and Steele was the 1987 Scandinavian Airline Systems headquarters in Stockholm, designed by Norwegian architect Niels Torp, where the interior "street" that served as the main passage through the building was lined with real shops and cafes, where workers could buy food, coffee, and even a card or gift. According to Becker and Steele, the effect, is of a "bustling center of a market town."[56]

This ideal of the urban-inspired workplace reimagined the office worker as a workplace flâneur, enjoying the sights and pleasures of the office. Workers were invited to stroll the "main street" of the office, visit "neighborhoods" of workstations, have a casual chat in the "town square," browse in the office store, and grab a bite to eat or a cup of coffee at the cafe.[57] In this sense, this new kind of office, with its urban-inspired topography, deliberately muddied the lines between work and leisure for workers. In some of these offices, the design even became akin to a kind of play space. At Taylor + Smith, an advertising agency in Houston, the space included playful sculptures like a large pencil, and a lounge space with a punching bag, basketball hoop, and a dartboard, all to give workers an "escape from corporate structure or work their way out of a creative block."[58] These amenities are actually quite modest relative to those provided by some of the major tech companies in the 1990s and 2000s, where gourmet meals, ping-pong tables, elaborate gyms complete with pools, yoga and step classes, regular corporate events featuring star comedians and musicians, and dog-friendly policies became common, and even necessary to attract and keep the best workers. Some reportedly even offered massage, dry cleaning services, and car detailing all as a way of competing to get and keep the best talent.[59]

There is a long history of offices and even factories providing exercise and leisure spaces, even dating back to the late nineteenth and early twentieth centuries.[60] From the postwar period through the 1980s, providing on-campus food and coffee as well as lounge spaces for breaks was also quite common on the major corporate campuses. For example, in his work for various corporate clients from the late 1960s through the early 1980s, architect Kevin Roche often planned elaborate eating spaces including cafeterias, executive dining rooms, and provision for coffee-access during the workday as well as fitness centers with exercise equipment. Some of these corporate offices also included such amenities as a shoeshine stand, a company store with various convenience items, and a barber shop.[61] At Union Carbide's new office completed in the early 1980s, the grounds included elaborate walking and jogging trails that were available for use by workers from 7:00 a.m. to 8:30 a.m., 11:00 a.m. to 1:30 p.m., and 4:30 p.m. to 6:00 p.m.[62] The times are notable because they reflect the assumption that such recreational spaces like walking trails were for nonworking hours (specifically before and after work or during a lunch break).

While these older buildings treated such amenities as coffee, food, and recreational spaces as somewhat tangential (and in some cases unrelated) to the work process, these new office of the 1990s increasingly treated such spaces as extensions of the workspace, and as a means of keeping workers at work throughout the day. Describing the benefit of providing an elaborate food court with free food for his workers, Michael Bloomberg explained, 'I want people to be well fed and satisfied. I want them to be able to grab a cup of coffee with a colleague and hash things out. But most of all I want them to stay here. I don't want them leaving."[63] Instead of leaving the office to grab a snack, lunch, or dinner, workers could simply walk to the office restaurant or cafe and have a free or heavily subsidized meal or cup of coffee; instead of leaving the office to go the gym, workers could just head to the office fitness center for a quick workout during the day. Organizations provided these amenities to explicitly encourage longer working hours from their staff.

In these elaborate offices, designed to support creative thinking and collaboration, the expectation was of a high level of commitment from the worker. Each worker's time was "flexible," but they were also frequently working long hours and these office amenities helped to keep workers at the office. The urban playground model might seem to provide an escape from work, but management deployed these amenities as strategic tools of the work process. A visit to the office gym might be an opportunity to take a break, but that time might also generate fresh energy, new ideas, and even spontaneous connections with other workers. A game of pool, table football, or basketball with colleagues might start as a break from work (or an escape from the workspace), but might, over the course of the game, evolve into a brainstorming or problem-solving session.

The spatial and temporal flexibility afforded by these new offices was thus a kind of double-edged sword in that it came with expectation of a high degree of commitment to the company and the work. In fact, many of these elaborate corporate offices with their great amenities also had an intense work culture. Tech industry workers frequently worked through the night and over weekends. One engineer at Electronic Arts, a gaming company, reported spending 179 out of 180 days working for nearly eighty-five to ninety hours a week in order to get a new game to market as quickly as possible.[64] Although the Electronic Arts office in Redwood, California was a self-consciously funky place with many of the amenities associated with a cool tech campus, the playful corporate office design masked an intense work culture with long hours and expectations of a high-level of commitment to the work.[65] Another software engineer at a major tech company in the 1990s similarly described frequently being asked to work seventy-five hours a week to get a piece of software out the door.[66] Such long hours were not only a hallmark of the tech industry in Silicon Valley but also common in other industries; famously at Chiat/Day long working nights were so common that the workers designed a t-shirt with the slogan "Chiat/Day and Night" in reference to their exceptionally long working hours.[67] In her 1991 study, *The Overworked American* sociologist Juliet Schor describes how workers in nearly every industry and in every job category were experiencing longer working hours and a parallel loss of leisure and personal time.[68] In some offices the culture of overwork and strain had a significant toll on worker's mental health. In his study, Gideon Kunda found that a number of the engineers reported working 17 to 18 hours a day and as a result experienced burnout, which manifest in a number of ways including depression, emotional breakdowns, alcoholism, and even suicide.[69]

While the image of the urban-inspired office offered a vision of the workplace as a leisure space, the goal of that design was ultimately to keep workers at work. Even the amenities that were designed to allow workers to unwind were strategically used to facilitate and encourage more work that was merely disguised as play. This blurring of the boundaries between home-life and work-life, between leisure and labor, was a feature of the design, not a bug, but it had real consequences for the well-being of workers who were often compelled to demonstrate their commitment to the organization sometimes at the expense of their own well-being.

Precarious Stagnation

In the literature about these new alternative office concepts, descriptions typically paint a picture of a space full of full-time permanently employed knowledge workers whose jobs and responsibilities afford workers infinite flexibility and autonomy over their time and space. Architects and designers described these workers as thinkers, creators, decision makers, and problem solvers who needed a highly supportive and flexible environment to support their critical and highly valuable work. Some advocates of these new ideas, like architect Frank Duffy, even imagined a future in which clerks and clericals workers would become obsolete or shifted to far removed off-site locations "away from the creative teams and decision makers."[70] Yet, many of these alternative office concepts depended on a system of labor for the ongoing maintenance of the space. At the high-end hoteling offices there was an entire system of office administration responsible for managing the reservations and coordinating the set up and maintenance of offices throughout the week.[71] At Chiat/Day's original virtual offices in Los Angeles and New York, staff were similarly required to manage the technology check-out process, receive visitors, answer the phone, and to track down workers in the office whenever necessary.[72] There were also a large number of staff required to maintain and clean offices, maintain the grounds, staff the food services areas, and provide security.

The design of the alternative office depended on the stasis and exploitation of a large class of support, service, temporary, and contract workers to enable the freedom of movement of a privileged professional class. As Saskia Sassen has argued in her book *Globalization and Its Discontents*, highly paid professional workers relied on legions of low-paid and precarious service workers, temps, and other support staff, sometimes working in the same space as the creative and knowledge workers, and other times laboring in far flung locations.[73] This in turn perpetuated a growing economic gap between those in the high paid permanent jobs, and the ever-growing class of contingent and contract labor on the margins and edges of those highly paid workers and their cool offices. Further, this gap between workers in top positions and those in more precarious or low-wage roles underscored inequities of opportunity and access that in turn reflected differences of identity particularly in terms of race, gender, ability, social class, and education. This group of workers, though providing essential services and critical labor are often overlooked or ignored by architects and designers who focus almost entirely on the needs of professional workers at the expense of the large class of administrative, service, temporary, and contract workers whose spaces, experiences, and needs are rarely considered. Looking at the office through the lens of these ignored workers illustrates the chasm between the idealized vision of the alternative office and the reality of its inner life.

All office buildings require some basic operational support for ongoing maintenance and use, and this critical though low paid work was often performed by men and women of color. Larger and more elaborate offices with eating spaces, recreational spaces, and other amenities common in the flagship tech office of Silicon Valley, for example, had even larger numbers of service staff required for day-to-day operations. A significant portion of these essential building support roles were increasingly provided by outside vendors in the 1990s and 2000s.[74] In 1998, a survey of facilities managers found that 47 percent of those surveyed were already spending more than one million dollars per year on outsourced services, particularly in custodial work, food service, landscaping, and security.[75] The same survey conducted again in 2000 found continued growth of outsourcing in those same areas.[76] By outsourcing these classes of work in the organization, companies reduced their operational costs and avoided paying expensive benefits packages to full-time workers.[77] These workers were sometimes treated as fully outside of the organization; in Kunda's research, workers in housekeeping, security, and other such support roles were essentially ignored by professional workers, and were rarely acknowledged even when they were a daily presence in the office. Kunda describes how workers in these classifications were often treated as "nonpersons," structurally and culturally excluded from the organization and its benefits.[78] Contract-based service workers were also sometimes regarded with suspicion by other full-time workers. For example, in the State of Wisconsin office buildings in the early 1990s, workers complained about the use of contract services for cleaning, and even accused the cleaning staff of stealing from and harassing state workers. The head of the Department of Administration at the State of Wisconsin at the time so distrusted the contract cleaners employed in state offices that he reportedly insisted that his own office be cleaned exclusively by state-employed janitors, and kept his office doors locked so that the contract janitors would not enter his office.[79] Such behavior illustrate the kinds of discriminatory actions toward these diverse contract workers, who labored in the same offices as full-time workers and whose jobs provided necessary services for full-time staff.

Most organizations also had significant clerical and administrative support staff including receptionists, secretaries, billing administrators, HR workers, payroll specialists, switchboard operators, accountants, IT support, customer service representatives, and so forth. The idealized image of an office exclusively comprised of knowledge workers, "decision makers," professional workers, and creatives thus dismisses an entire infrastructure of bureaucratic labor whose work underpinned the organization and its operations. This large class of workers rarely had the freedom of movement afforded to workers in more elevated organizational roles. In fact, they regularly spent their days trapped at their desks, while their colleagues in professional roles were able to come and go at will. In her study of work-life balance, Arlie Hochschild interviewed a secretary who described the enormous double standard applied to workers in administrative and technical positions at her organization. When a manager left their desk, it was assumed they were away for a business purpose, but if a secretary stepped away (e.g., to make photocopies) their supervisor would suspect the worker of slacking off or stepping away for a personal (or even frivolous) reason. Despite a family-friendly corporate policy, the manager in charge of the secretarial staff did not believe that the workers in those positions should have the same degree of flexibility in their schedules as those in more advanced positions and thus denied requests for flexible schedules from administrative workers.[80]

Working side by side with professional and clerical staff in offices in this era were also many temporary workers, "permatemps," or contract workers. Organizations' increasing dependence on temporary or contract labor reflected a larger organizational shift that began in the 1980s and 1990s toward downsizing and so-called rightsizing. Corporate leaders like "Chainsaw Al" Dunlap and Jack Welch made their names and reputations by brutally and dramatically cutting positions to create "lean and mean" organizations.[81] By trimming their permanent staff down to a very low number, the company would then rely on temporary or contract labor to create a cushion that ultimately served to insulate the remaining full-time permanent workers from layoffs.[82] What is perhaps most surprising about this growing use of temporary labor is how even very successful companies in the 1990s and 2000s relied heavily on temporary workers. At the height of the tech boom in the 1990s, companies like HP and Microsoft used a huge number of contract and temporary workers in all types of jobs including administrative, technical, managerial, and even professional positions.[83] At Microsoft, in the 1990s as much as a quarter of their workforce in their Seattle based office were reportedly temporary workers.[84]

These temporary workers, though sometimes working for months and even years for the same organization, received lower pay and none of the benefits (such as health insurance, stock options, etc.) of full-time permanent work at these high performing companies.[85] Their job was always at risk—their position could be cut at any time without notice—creating a deeply unstable economic position for those workers. Though they often worked in the same spaces as their full-time peers, they too were often treated as outsiders. As Gideon Kunda and Stephen Barley document, "knowledge economy" contract workers at major tech companies generally received different colored badges (visibly marking them as outsiders), and worked in the least desirable spaces within the office, sometimes in shared cubicles, hallways, cafeterias, and in one case, even a first aid room. These kinds of liminal spaces in the office, which the organization viewed as undesirable or even unusable for full-time staff, were readily repurposed for these marginalized workers who were seen as unimportant. This large class of contract workers was frequently given older technologies and even forbidden access to certain tools, equipment, and passwords necessary for their work. They were also excluded socially, left out of team-building activities (even when they were part of the team) and celebrations, and even prevented from using any of the corporate recreational facilities (fitness centers and so forth) and other office amenities (like the free bikes made available for full employees to quickly go between buildings).[86] Again this illustrates how the amenities of the elaborate high-tech office and the ideals of this new kind of alternative work environment were not universally available to all workers in the space. Even in the most elaborate corporate offices, there were large swaths of workers present in the space with very different working conditions and experiences than their full-time professional colleagues. To read the idealized playground office exclusively through the experience of the full-time professional staff is to dismiss a large class of workers in diverse jobs laboring in their midst, but under very different conditions.

As some administrative support workers, permatemps, and contract workers were working within the same buildings and even the same spaces as permanent professional staff, there were also large off-site offices providing core administrative and 'back office" support services. In this era a number of companies in a variety of industries had call centers that provided a wide range of services including telemarketing, tech assistance, banking, nursing, insurance information, and other types of customer service.[87] Call centers were typically located far away from the main offices of the company, often in different states and sometimes in rural, suburban, or exurban areas rather than urban neighborhoods, due to the need for large amounts of inexpensive space.[88] The growing geographic distance between call centers and the flagship corporate campuses is significant because it illustrates how call centers were treated as entirely separate divisions from other parts of the corporate culture. Yet as call centers became more common, and more important to a company's bottom line, there were emerging concerns about attrition of workers in call centers as well as the quality of work performed in call centers.

As a result of these persistent issues with hiring and retention, some companies began investing more resources in the design of call centers to improve the culture and the quality of work. In 1996, the architecture firm Gensler designed a call center in Bedford, Texas, that used an abandoned Walmart store to create a new facility designed to house 313 agent workstations (staffed for multiple shifts) along with some administrative offices and conference areas. In their design, Gensler reportedly not only sought to "maximize employee time and avoid unnecessary movement" for the call center workers, but also tried to create a humanizing space that would reduce employee turnover. The open plan areas of the new call center featured gray cubicles with low partitions grouped in clusters of four workstations throughout the space to encourage a sense of community and teamwork. While the space featured a breakroom (notably in a former loading dock of the Walmart), it was a rather spartan affair with no windows, a few pendant lights, a single ficus tree, and a lunchroom arrangement of tables and chairs (no cozy lounge furniture).[89]

In contrast to the urban inspired flagship campuses, which architectural firms like Gensler designed to explicitly promote and encourage movement and interaction, the call center was designed to keep people in place and on task. Perhaps even more than clerical staff at the flagship offices, call center workers spent their days tethered to their open plan workstations, often constantly surveilled by supervisors and by a system of technology that tracked their actions and communications throughout the day. Time away from the workstation was time lost from answering calls, and so some call centers were strict about breaks, even mandating the number or timing of breaks, and in some cases penalizing workers for every minute spent in the bathroom while on their shift.[90] These workers were stuck at their desks throughout the day, with very few opportunities to move, take breaks, or even just stretch their legs. The high-level of control imposed over workers' time and bodies is obviously completely counter to the image of the liberated workers described in the alternative office concepts.

Because of their geographic isolation, workers in these call center jobs generally had far fewer opportunities for growth or upward mobility within the organization; they were thus both spatially and structurally trapped at the call center. Through the late 1990s and early 2000s, this geographic distance and isolation of call center workers only became larger as a number of companies began moving call centers out of the United States to Canada, India, and the Philippines. It is important to recognize that these classes of workers laboring in locations far removed from their employers, whether in a small town in the United States or a city in India, were not irrelevant or disconnected from the work being done in corporate offices in major US cities with all of their amenities and benefits. As Doreen Massey has argued, these various classes of workers working all around the world were inherently interconnected and interdependent within the organization and within the broader system of production, creating what she terms a "spatial division of labor."[91]

All of these workers, including service workers, administrative support staff, temporary and contract workers, and off-site back-office workers (like call center staff), were necessary to support the high mobility and flexibility that professional staff had. The highly mobile professional worker who spent their day schmoozing at the corporate office drinking endless cups of coffee and brainstorming on white boards, needed an entire system of workers to answer phones, coordinate meetings, run payroll, handle billing, clean offices, provide security, make and serve coffee and food, address customer enquiries and complaints, and so much more. The physical stasis and economic stagnation of one class of workers ultimately enabled and supported the high mobility and flexibility of time and space for another class of workers.

Fantastic Mobilities and Exclusionary Systems

In 2001, the Museum of Modern Art (MoMA) in New York held an exhibition titled *Workspheres* that explored the emerging ideas in office design, technology, and work of the 1990s and early 2000s. In the press release for the exhibition, curator Paola Antonelli described how

> Work has become transportable and ubiquitous, almost a state of mind ... Like a bubble of pure concentration that one can turn on and off with or without the help of tangible tools, work is where you are. The title of the exhibition comes from the concept of the individual workspace as a halo, a private and personal space, that better defines and enables interaction among people with work tools.[92]

Featuring furniture that supported movement and mobility such as movable tables and storage alongside new technologies like personal digital assistants and mobile phones, the emerging work culture depicted by the MoMA exhibit was one in which all the materials and objects of work were mechanisms of movement, circulation, and mobility.[93]

The MoMA show presented museum goers with a fantasy of office work in which work was simultaneously everywhere and nowhere. The interactions and connections among workers and their organizations were transmuted into a digital network of connected devices that would facilitate constant mobility and constant interaction following the worker from home to work and even to an airport or a hotel. Of course, the imaginary worker at the center of this fantasy was a knowledge worker with a high degree of autonomy and flexibility. The seamless mobility and interactions embedded in the office were expressions of an idealized worker as much as they were reflections of an idealized workspace. In the words of architect Francis Duffy, the explosive change in technology and the structure of office work itself created a "new fantastic mobility" in which the rules of location and time in the workplace have been entirely rewritten.[94]

By treating mobility as universally good and beneficial, these offices essentialized the needs of a highly privileged class of creative and knowledge workers, and often ignored the differences that inevitably exist among workers, even as it claimed to provide workers "choice" through its fixation on supporting constant circulation and movement. As noted, these alternative offices which emphasized mobility were deeply ableist in their design and use, and they also reinforced structural racism and sexism by continuing to prioritize and fetishize the White cisgender (often male) knowledge worker at its center. The ideal embedded in these offices of a large class of universally mobile, autonomous, and flexible knowledge workers also ignored enormous number of workers whose jobs had much less flexibility in terms of their use of time and space. Whether working in the corporate flagship office, or in a cube farm hundreds or even thousands of miles away, these various workers held jobs that were tightly limited in terms of their opportunities for movement and interaction, and more controlled in terms of the structure of the work itself. The spaces, furniture, technologies, and corporate systems that afforded freedom and flexibility for professional staff became tools of control, oversight, and surveillance for many others.

Conclusion

Early advocates of the open plan office frequently described it as a transformative solution to the thorny problems of contemporary organizations, a solution that would upend organizational hierarchy, support communication, and facilitate rapid change. According to architects and designers, walls and doors were barriers to communication, change, and egalitarianism, and simply eliminating those partitions would fundamentally change the way people worked. In exchange for giving up the enclosure of private offices, architects and designers promised workers a liberating office space in which they would have more control over their work process and their workstation and have the freedom to move and interact with each other as necessary. As I have argued, the ideals of the open plan office emerged out of a particular organizational, social, political, and economic context. These ideals reflected an entire set of assumptions about organizational culture; the meaning, purpose, and use of office space, the needs and behaviors of workers; and even the structure and future of office work and office technology. These assumptions, embedded in the design of the open plan and systems furniture, have been continually reproduced and reinforced materially and spatially through the use of the open plan in American offices.

The ideals of the open plan concept have remained remarkably persistent from its origins to today. Like its predecessors, the modern open plan embodies a kind of magical thinking about the possibilities of space to transform the culture of the organization, the behavior of workers, and the structure of work itself. In 2015, Facebook opened its new offices in Menlo Park, California. News stories described the new headquarters designed by architect Frank Gehry as the largest open plan office in the world, covering over 1 million square feet and containing not a single enclosed office space. In the descriptions of the interior design, reports emphasized how the arrangement was intended to facilitate a high degree of interaction and collaboration among workers, encourage movement, support organizational change, and reflect an egalitarian organizational culture in which even the founder and CEO Mark Zuckerberg worked at an open plan desk "just like everyone else."[1] The open plan office design at Facebook was meant to serve as an idealized manifestation of the company's philosophy, culture, and product, according to the architectural firm Gensler: "It's open, mobile, socially connected, dimensionally aware, culturally relevant, and personally sustaining."[2] As Shannon Mattern argues, the modern open plan of tech companies like Facebook is a "material manifestation" of the organization's "ideal virtual self," but that image produced by the office is a kind of candy-coating exterior on the real culture and coding underneath.[3] In the case of Facebook, while their large open plan office may have been designed to project an image of egalitarianism, inclusivity, and openness, their technology, their culture, and their own internal practices were anything but inclusive, open, and egalitarian. A report from 2017 found that women comprised only 33 percent of Facebook's workforce, including 27 percent of leadership positions and only 17 percent of technical roles.[4] Workers of color were also significantly under-represented at Facebook; a 2013 diversity report found only 2 percent of workers were Black at Facebook and only 4 percent were Hispanic.[5] There have also been reports of racial discrimination, particularly experienced by Black employees who have encountered persistent harassment by security and hostility from coworkers.[6] The internal workings of Facebook have remained a closely held secret, even as there have been concerns about inappropriate targeting of information (like job and housing advertisements on the platform) based on gender and racial identities, issues concerning the exploitation of users' data, the propagation of hate speech, the sharing of harmful stories and images, and broader questions about the process, politics, and labor of content moderation.[7] This gap between the idealized organization as embodied by the open plan office and the real organizations shaped by an exclusionary, discriminatory, and highly secretive corporate culture is not new, but it reflects the ways in which the supposed "openness" of the open plan was at best aspirational.

What is most surprising is not that the open plan was a contradictory concept that has never lived up to its ideals, but rather that the underlying concept and ideals of the open plan have persisted through so many generations of architects, designers, furniture manufacturers, and organizational leadership. The open plan has been repeatedly offered as a miraculous solution to various social, organizational, architectural, and technological problems. Lessons learned in earlier iterations of the open plan are quickly forgotten while the latest version is offered as an antidote to the most immediate concerns and problems. Thus, every few years, the open plan is reborn as a "new" idea that promises to change the design of the office. Sometimes, it seems as though the open plan is perpetually new, like a phoenix forever rising out of its own ashes, but other times it seems more like a zombie crawling out of its own grave. Articles in the popular, business, and architectural press regularly declare the imminent demise of the open plan office, but it is not going anywhere. It has remained popular over so many decades of office design not because it is so effective or beneficial for workers or worker productivity, but rather because it is an inexpensive office design solution that allows companies to fit more workers into less space.

When I started this project on the history of the open plan office back in 2005, the pop-culture cubicle ennui was in full swing. While at parties chatting with strangers about my research, they would inevitably ask if I had ever seen the 1999 movie *Office Space*, which mines the comedic potential of the cubicle. At the time, negative images of cubicles remained common in movies, television shows, comic strips, cartoons, commercials, novels, and even news stories. In the 2008 Pixar animation *The Incredibles*, for example, Mr. Incredible spends his days working for a bureaucratic insurance company in a dreary cube farm. In the film, the image of Mr. Incredible, trapped inside of his grey cubicle, his large body squeezed next to a giant column in his small workstation, was used to visually signify the tedium of Mr. Incredible's day job and to indicate that he was literally trapped in his job and in his life in general. For many, the cubicle seemed to symbolize the worst aspects of modern working life.

Just in the last few years or so, as the "new" open plans with their bright and airy interiors and no partitions have become more common in offices around the country, there has been an emerging nostalgia for cubicles.[8] In 2015, the *New York Times* ran a debate with the title, "Are Cubicles Preferable to the Open Layout?" in which several experts discussed the various problems associated with the modern open plan office and proposed their own solutions. In response to the "debate," some readers wrote in to say that they much preferred the cubicle with its higher partitions over their new open plan workspace.[9] In a 2017 article in *Fortune* titled "It's Time to Bring Back the Office Cubicle" the author argues that the cubicle, which reduced distractions and cut overall noise, "made it easier to perform better at your job." As the author points out, despite its drab popular image, the cubicle existed for a reason—it was a response to the very problems that remain endemic to the open plan particularly the noise, distractions, and lack of privacy.[10] In light of this history, it is perhaps not at all surprising that the cubicle is starting to look rather appealing to some, particularly when compared with the aggressive openness of so many contemporary open plans such as the spartan "benching" offices in which workers sit elbow-to-elbow at long open tables. Some office equipment manufacturers have recently begun producing a new kind of cubicle—a fully enclosed and soundproof "phone booth"—where workers can retreat for private conversations. The coronavirus pandemic has only fueled further speculation about the supposed end of the new open plan and the possible return of the cubicle.[11] The story of the open plan is thus one of repeated recycling of the same ideals, the same solutions, and even the same failures over and over again. Why does the idealism of the open plan persist even as decades of research along with the perennial complaints from workers continue to reveal its limitations?

One answer to this conundrum is the nebulous quality of the open plan concept itself. Though often described and marketed as though it were a singular idea, it was never really one thing but rather a layout, an office design process, and a furniture concept that were all loosely but only vaguely connected. The open plan's fluidity has allowed it to evolve and shift over time in response to various social, economic, technological, architectural, and organizational changes. Its ambiguity has made it a kind of tabula rasa—the open plan's utility, purpose, and value have always been in the eye of its beholder. For organizations seeking managerial enlightenment, it represented a progressive ideal that would help to remake the culture of the organization through the design of the space. Other organizations with little interest in the progressive idealism of the open plan could adopt this new kind of office as a practical solution to the persistent problems of shrinking space and shrinking budgets.

Even the term "open plan" embodies this Janus-like quality. On the one hand, the "open" aspect offers the possibility of unlimited and open-ended change unfettered by the material, spatial, social, or technological aspects of the space, the organization, or its workers. Indeed, advocates often treated the professed "openness" as a kind of metaphor for a nonhierarchical and transparent culture in which the inner workings and social systems of the organization are rendered both visible and accessible through the design of the space. Yet on the other hand, the "plan" aspect offers a system of order, control, and power that disciplines, contains, and restricts the space, the organization, and the worker. The planning process with its system of standards was in fact an expression and reproduction of the very organizational authority and bureaucracy that the open plan promised to upend through its design. These tensions and contradictions were embedded in the open plan concept from its origins and continue to define and shape the open plan office, its usage, and its meaning even today.

More than a fantasy about office design, the open plan remains primarily a fantasy about the future of office work and the idealized knowledge worker. From its early usage in the 1960s, proponents viewed the open plan as a spatial counterpart to the knowledge worker whose needs, ways of working, and organizational position ostensibly required a new kind of office space. According to Renyi Hong, the persistent fantasy of knowledge work fetishizes "serendipitous connections," fosters "synergies," and facilitates innovation. In her words, workers become "blimps of information sponges whose capacity for value relates to the degree of communicativeness." As Hong argues, success in this emergent organizational culture was always contingent on workers' ability to adapt to the compulsory socializing of the open plan environment.[12] The open plan was the knowledge worker's vital spatial support, offering a frictionless space in which workers were liberated from their dreary enclosures and given the freedom to circulate and interact without the burdens of walls or corporate bureaucracy.

The architectural ideal of the open plan as a neutral space filled with abstract workers, disregarded the many ways in which individual workers' needs or preferences might run counter to this ideal. This idealized knowledge worker in the idealized open plan office is never uncomfortable or self-conscious in the open interior; never bothered by noise or distractions; never awkward or uncomfortable in compelled interactions with their colleagues; never cranky, upset, overworked, or irritated; never subject to any form of harassment or discrimination from colleagues or supervisors based on their race, social class, age, gender, sexuality, nationality, or ability; and never excluded from the full use of the space and its amenities. In imagining an abstract worker in an idealized workspace, the open plan concept thus elides the differences of experience and perspective that relate to a worker's incividual identity or their organizational position.

As a setting and expression of the organization and its culture, the open plan office is a space in which numerous workers regularly encounter racism, sexism, ageism, ableism, and other forms of discrimination and exclusion.[13] Sociologist Victor Ray argues that contemporary organizations (and the offices they inhabit) remain overwhelmingly White, and for workers of color in particular the workplace is often full of codes, rules, and expectations that reproduce and reinforce Whiteness as an "unstated credential." As Ray notes, "grooming codes" in organizations frequently target Black hairstyles, which reinforce "white normativity."[14] A recent study on the gender dynamics of the open plan has shown that women also feel significant pressure to manage their appearance in an open plan design and often feel continuously watched by their male colleagues.[15] The open plan is deeply problematic in its design for workers with disabilities as well. The contemporary open plan office design's tendency to encourage constant mobility, its use of stairs as a primary tool of circulation and communication, and the ubiquitous low lounge furniture and bar height tables and stools all enforce the assumption of a young nondisabled worker who can easily lounge, perch, and lean on any surface. The open space creates a noisy backdrop that is problematic for workers who are deaf or hard of hearing, the emphasis on visuality is challenging for workers who are blind or have low vision, and the compelled social interaction and general activity of the open plan is uncomfortable for many workers who identify as neurodivergent (such as those with autism or ADHD). The space that is designed to facilitate comfort and a high degree of access for one group of workers remains uncomfortable or inaccessible for many others. In their fixation on supporting the imagined needs of knowledge workers in the open plan, architects, designers, and organizations have also frequently disregarded or ignored the needs and experiences of workers who are not classified as knowledge workers or who do not have full membership within the organization, which includes administrative support and temporary, contract, and service workers in security, food service, and building maintenance.

As this research illustrates, the exclusionary aspects of the open plan office begin in the design process itself, which has too often failed to meaningfully include a variety of viewpoints and perspectives. Office design as a process has historically treated low-level clerical, support, and service workers as generic abstractions (a job or position within the corporate hierarchy), materialized as a predictable set of tasks and technologies, a network of relationships, and finally as a workstation in an office layout. When lower-level workers and workers of diverse identities are included in the process, it is too often in a perfunctory manner, typically through generic surveys that are designed to essentially affirm the choices that have already been made by those in positions of power or that represent the preferences of the majority of workers. Yet who is that majority? The workers who think the same ways and have the same needs, frequently identify similarly in terms of race, age, class, gender, and ability. The tendency to prioritize the views, requirements, and preferences of the majority worker often codifies and reinforces systems of inequality. The parallel failure to include a variety of perspectives and views in the design process means that an office may be ideal for a certain group of workers and very poor, inaccessible, or unusable for another.

How can architects and designers intentionally include and accommodate more diverse needs in office planning and design? For example, in an organization dominated by cis-gender men, a nursing woman or a trans man might identify the need for a lactation room. In the open plan, where there are so few enclosed and private spaces, such a room is arguably essential for people who are nursing. A majority perspective would treat that worker's individual request as an unnecessary accommodation that does not reflect the needs of most workers in the space. Since the one nursing worker will likely no longer be nursing by the time the office is complete, why should architects, designers, and organizations reserve valuable space for such a request? In fact, by including the lactation space in the design, architects, designers, and organizations produce a more supportive space overall that will be more inclusive not only for that one worker but for future nursing workers. This is just one example of how an underrepresented viewpoint may draw attention to a critical resource in the office that the majority of workers in a given workplace might be unaware of or might not even recognize as useful or important.

Of course, office design is always a process of negotiation among competing and sometimes contradictory economic, material, technological, spatial, organizational, and temporal constraints. Architects, designers, and organizations need to think more consciously and deliberately about how they are negotiating those contradictory needs among different classes and types of workers (with diverse jobs, bodies, and identities), and how they are deciding whose needs matter when making decisions about office space and its usage. While the conventional design process often reproduces and reinforces power relations by prioritizing the views of organizational leadership over those of workers, a participatory design process strives to engage and include the diverse and sometimes contradictory voices, perspectives, and experiences of stakeholders in a more intentional way.[16] Genuine participation is not simply passing out a survey to workers; it should be an interactive process that invites and includes different voices and perspectives at every stage of design starting from the initial planning stage.[17] Such a process is inconvenient because it takes time and inevitably brings up difficult questions, reveals new problems, creates conflicts, and frequently leads to new requirements, restrictions, or needs for the workplace as a whole. This approach also requires practitioners to recognize and acknowledge the real problems of discrimination and inequality that are embedded in organizational culture and reinforced and reproduced in office design.

Despite its well documented problems, or perhaps because of them, the history of the open plan reveals the extent to which workers have placed value in the design of their workplace. Over many iterations, and through many decades of use, workers have characterized the open plan as the primary source of numerous irritations and annoyances, but the very fact that so many workers complain about the space is itself a reflection of its perceived significance. Just like the architects and designers who so avidly promoted the open plan over so many decades, workers too are sometimes guilty of a kind of magical thinking or environmental determinism about office space, blaming the design of the office for problems that are actually organizational, technological, or social in nature. Yet, even if the open plan is not solely to blame for all of the problems of modern working life, the open plan remains a vital component of workers' daily lives, an occasionally frustrating tool for their work process, a backdrop of their workplace interactions, a manifestation of the organizational culture, and in some cases, an outward expression of systemic discrimination, hierarchy, and unequal power. These meanings and associations, embedded in the daily experience and use of the open plan for workers, are as much a part of the history, legacy, and ongoing use of its design as the idealism espoused by its most vocal advocates.

Notes

Archive and Library abbreviations used in notes:

DEC	DEC collection at the Computer History Museum Archive
DOA	Department of Administration Secretary Subject Files at the Wisconsin Historical Society
HAU	Hauserman papers at the Western Reserve Historical Society Library
HMCA	Herman Miller Corporate Archives
HML	Hagley Museum and Library
KRJDA	Kevin Roche and John Dinkeloo Associates Records (MS 1884). Manuscripts and Archives at Yale University Library
MWCR	Montgomery Ward and Corporate Records at the Chicago Public History Research Center
PK	Powell/Kleinschmidt Records at the Art Institute of Chicago, Ryerson and Burnham Libraries
PUSC	Purdue University Special Collections
RP	Robert Propst Papers at the Benson Ford Research Center
WP	William Pahlmann Papers in Manuscripts and Archives at the Hagley Museum and Library
WS	William Stumpf Papers at the Benson Ford Research Center

Introduction

1 Purdue University, Board of Trustee minutes, November 6–7, 1967, http://earchives.lib.purdue.edu/cdm/ref/collection/bot/id/25751 from PUSC.
2 For example, "Burolandschaft USA." *Progressive Architecture*, May 1968, 174–6; William Robbins, "'Radicals' Offer New Office Plan," *New York Times*, July 4, 1968; Robert Shiff, "The Changing Office Scene: Fewer Walls, Better Services," *Management Review* (December 1968): 2–10; P. G. Twitchell, "The Office Landscape: What It Is; How It Works," *Skyscraper Management* 53 (December 1968): 5–12; "From Grid to Growth," *Progressive Architecture*, November 1969, 100–9; "Office Landscape, No Walls, No Halls," *Design* 70, no. 4 (1969): 14–18; "More Controversy over Office Landscaping at IBD, BEMA Seminars in New York

and Chicago," *Contract* 9, no. 12 (December 1968): 80–3; "Office Landscape: Pro and Con," *Contract* 9, no. 4 (April 1968): 80–5.
3   Louis Harris and Associates, *Office Environments: Do They Work* (Grand Rapids, MI: Steelcase, 1978), 28–9.
4   "Cubicle, n." OED Online, March 2020, Oxford University Press.
5   For an example of the postwar usage of cubicle to refer to small private offices, see: Alan Harrington, *Life in the Crystal Palace* (New York: Alfred A. Knopf, 1959), 52, 106; for an example of the postwar cubicle seen as distinct from the open plan design see John Pile, "The Open Office: Does It Work?," *Progressive Architecture* (June 1977): 70.
6   For a 1970s example of the term cubicle used in relation to the open plan workstation, see Susan Seliger, "Tempo: Are Cubicles an Answer or Just an Open Invitation to a Hard Day at the Office," *Chicago Tribune*, August 9, 1979. For a later example from the 1980s, see June Lemen, "Cubicle Blues," *Ms* (January 1988): 18.
7   James Russell, "Form Follows Fad: The Troubled Love Affair of Architectural Style and Management Ideal," in *On the Job: Design and the American Office*, ed. Donald Albrecht and Chrysanthe Broikos (New York: Princeton Architectural Press, 2000), 49–73.
8   Anna Andrzejewski, *Building Power: Architecture and Surveillance in Victorian America* (Knoxville: University of Tennessee Press, 2008), 68–70. Oliver Zunz, *Making America Corporate, 1870-1920* (Chicago: University of Chicago Press, 1990), 110–21; Angel Kwolek-Folland, *Engendering Business: Men and Women in the Corporate Office, 1870-1930* (Baltimore: Johns Hopkins University Press, 1994), 105–28.
9   Jonathan Lipman, *Frank Lloyd Wright and the Johnson Wax Buildings* (New York: Rizzoli, 1986), 93–4.
10 Iñaki Ábalos and Juan Herreros, *Tower and Office: From Modernist Theory to Contemporary Practice* (Cambridge, MA: MIT Press, 2003), 190; Russell, "Form Follows Fad," 50–3.
11 Gail Cooper, *Air-Conditioning America: Engineers and the Controlled Environment, 1900-1960* (Baltimore: Johns Hopkins University Press, 1998), 160–2; Russell, "Form Follows Fad," 56; Ábalos and Herreros, *Tower and Office*, 193–6.
12 Frank Duffy, *Office Landscaping: A New Approach to Office Planning* (London: Anbar, 1969); John Pile, "The Nature of Office Landscape," *AIA Journal* (July 1969): 40–8; "Office Landscape," 80–5.
13 Howard Brick, *Transcending Capitalism: Visions of a New Society in Modern American Thought* (Ithaca, NY: Cornell University Press, 2006), 268–9.
14 For example, Daniel Bell, *The Coming of Post-Industrial Society: A Venture in Social Forecasting* (New York: Basic Books, 1976); Nils Gilman, "The Prophet of Post-Fordism: Peter Drucker and the Legitimation of the Corporation," in *American Capitalism: Social Thought and Political Economy in the Twentieth Century*, ed. Nelson Lichtenstein (Philadelphia: University of Pennsylvania Press, 2007), 119–31; Paddy Riley, "Clark Kerr: From the Industrial to the Knowledge Economy," in *American Capitalism*: *Social Thought and Political Economy in the Twentieth Century*, ed. Nelson Lichtenstein (Philadelphia: University of Pennsylvania Press, 2007), 86.
15 Judith Stein, *Pivotal Decade: How the United States Traded Factories for Finance in the Seventies*, Kindle ed. (New Haven, CT: Yale University Press, 2010).
16 Ábalos and Herreros, *Tower and Office*, 190–209.
17 Andreas Rumpfhuber, "Space of Information Flow: The Schenelle Brothers' Office Landscape 'Buch Und Ton'," in *Experiments: Architektur Zwischen Wissenschaft*

Und Kunst = Architecture between Sciences and the Arts, ed. Ákos Moravánszky and Albert Kirchengast (Berlin: Verlag GmbH, 2011); Olga Pantelidou, "Designing for the Workflow," in Kevin Roche: Architecture as Environment, ed. Eeva-Liisa Pelkonen (New Haven, CT: Yale University Press, 2011), 100–21.

18 Lucinda Kaukas Havehand, "A View from the Margin: Interior Design," Design Issues 20, no. 4 (2004), 41.
19 John Pile in particular was an active promoter of the open plan office concept in the United States—he wrote regular articles for the major architecture and design journals and published a prominent handbook on open office planning for architects and designers which I reference throughout this book: John F. Pile, Open Office Planning: A Handbook for Interior Designers and Architects (New York: Whitney Library of Design, 1978).
20 Thomas Carter and Elizabeth Collins Cromley, Invitation to Vernacular Architecture: A Guide to the Study of Ordinary Buildings and Landscapes (Knoxville: University of Tennessee Press, 2005), 16.
21 David Edgerton, The Shock of the Old: Technology and Global History since 1900 (London: Profile Books, 2008), ix–xviii.
22 Nikil Saval, Cubed: A Secret History of the Workplace, Kindle ed. (New York: Doubelday, 2014).
23 Michael J. Smith and Pascale C. Sainfort, "A Balance Theory of Job Design for Stress Reduction," International Journal of Industrial Ergonomics 4, no. 1 (1989), 74–6; M. J. Smith and F. Carayon, "Balance Theory of Job Design," in The International Encyclopedia of Ergonomics and Human Factors, ed. W. Karwowski (London: Taylor & Francis, 2001), 1181–3.

Chapter 1

1 Russell, "Form Follows Fad," 56–9.
2 Louise Mozingo, Pastoral Capitalism: A History of Corporate Landscapes (Cambridge, MA: MIT Press, 2011), 102.
3 Alexandra Lange, "This Year's Model: Representing Modernism to the Post-War American Corporation," Journal of Design History 19, no. 3 (Autumn 2006): 237–8.
4 For examples of this conventional office design and its design process see: National Stationery and Office Equipment Association, How to Plan Your Office Layout: A Guide for Planning a Modern, Efficient Office (Washington, DC: National Stationery and Office Equipment Association, 1953); Michael Saphier, Office Planning and Design (New York: McGraw Hill, 1968); Lois Wagner Green, Interiors Book of Offices (New York: Whitney Library of Design, 1959).
5 Rosabeth Moss Kanter, Men and Women of the Corporation (New York: Basic Books, 1977) 35.
6 Vance Packard, The Status Seekers (New York: David McKay, 1959), 116–17; Kanter, Men and Women of the Corporation, 34–5.
7 Bobbye Tigerman, "'I Am Not a Decorator': Florence Knoll, the Knoll Planning Unit, and the Making of the Modern Office," Journal of Design History 20, no. 1 (2007): 65–7.
8 C. Wright Mills, White Collar: The American Middle Classes (New York: Oxford University Press, 1953), 189.

9 For example, National Stationery and Office Equipment Association, *How to Plan Your Office Layout*, 20.
10 Alexandra Lange, "White Collar Corbusier: From the Casier to the Cités d'affaires," *Grey Room*, no. 9 (Autumn 2002): 66.
11 Michael Zakim, *Accounting for Capitalism: The World the Clerk Made* (Chicago: University of Chicago Press, 2018), 9–20.
12 Aimi Hamraie, *Building Access: Universal Design and the Politics of Disability* (Minneapolis: University of Minnesota Press, 2017), 19–40.
13 William H. Whyte, *The Organization Man* (New York: Simon & Schuster, 1956), 171–201.
14 Dianne Harris, *Little White Houses: How the Postwar Home Constructed Race in America* (Minneapolis: University of Minnesota Press, 2013), 31–2; Saval, *Cubed*, Chapter 5, section 2, Kindle.
15 Joan Acker, "Theorizing Gender, Race, and Class in Organizations," in *Handbook of Gender, Work, and Organization*, ed. Emma Jeanes (New York: John Wiley and Sons, 2011), 65–80.
16 Vance Packard, *The Pyramid Climbers* (New York: McGraw Hill, 1962), 30–2; Kanter, *Men and Women of the Corporation,* 25–7; Katherine Turk, *Equality on Trial: Gender and Rights in the Modern American Workplace* (Philadelphia: University of Pennsylvania Press, 2016), 3–4.
17 For more on this see for example, Margery Davies, *Woman's Place Is at the Typewriter: Office Work and Office Workers, 1870–1930* (Philadelphia: Temple University Press, 1982); Kwolek-Folland, *Engendering Business*; Zunz, *Making America Corporate*; Sharon Hartman Strom, *Beyond the Typewriter: Gender, Class, and the Origins of Modern American Office Work, 1900-1930* (Chicago: University of Illinois Press, 1992).
18 Michelle Murphy, *Sick Building Syndrome and the Problem of Uncertainty* (Durham: Duke University Press, 2006), 46. Teresa Amott and Julie Matthaei, *Race, Gender, and Work: A Multicultural Economic History of Women in the United States* (Boston, MA: South End Press, 1991), 335–6.
19 Julie Berebitsky, *Sex and the Office: A History of Gender, Power, and Desire* (New Haven, CT: Yale University Press, 2012), 143–5; Kanter, *Women and Men of the Corporation*, 76.
20 Patricia Hill Collins, *Black Feminist Thought: Knowledge, Consciousness, and the Politics of Empowerment* (New York: Taylor and Francis, 2002), 58–66.
21 For a detailed analysis of these various efforts to challenge discrimination in the workplace among different racial and ethnic groups in the United States see: Amott and Matthaei, *Race, Gender, and Work* and Nancy MacLean, *Freedom Is Not Enough: The Opening of the American Workplace* (Cambridge: Harvard University Press, 2006).
22 The original report identifies Black Americans as "Negroes," Asian Americans as "Orientals," and Hispanic or Latino individuals as "Spanish Surnamed workers." Equal Opportunity Employment Commission, *Minorities and Women in Private Industry* (Washington, DC: EEOC, 1966), 2–3, 10.
23 Amott and Matthaei, *Race, Gender, and Work*, 180.
24 Audra Jennings, *Out of the Horrors of War: Disability Politics in World War II America* (Philadelphia: University of Pennsylvania Press, 2016), 1–4, 94–5.
25 Bess Williamson, *Accessible America: A History of Disability and Design* (New York: New York University Press, 2019), 17–42, 43–65.

26 For example, see: Kimberlé Crenshaw, "Demarginalizing the Intersection of Race and Sex: A Black Feminist Critique of Antidiscrimination Doctrine, Feminist Theory, and Antiracist Politics," in *Feminism and Politics*, ed. Anne Phillips (Oxford: Oxford University Press, 2009), 314–343; Hamraie, *Building Access*, 65–94.
27 Jennifer Kaufmann-Buhler, "If the Chair Fits: Sexism in Office Furniture Design," *Journal of Design History* 32, no. 4 (2019): 376–91; Caroline Criado Perez *Invisible Women: Data Bias in a World Designed for Men* (New York: Abrams Press, 2019), 113; Boris Kingma and Wouter Van Marken Lichtenbelt, "Energy Consumption in Buildings and Female Thermal Demand," *Nature Climate Change* 5, no. 12 (2015): 1054–6.
28 Amott and Matthaei, *Race, Gender, and Work*, 341–5; Victor Ray, "A Theory of Racialized Organizations " *American Sociological Review* 84, no. 1 (2019): 34–5; Collins, *Black Feminist Thought*, 59–66; Sharon M. Collins, *Black Corporate Executives: The Making and Breaking of a Black Middle Class* (Philadelphia, PA: Temple University, 1997), 3–7, 73–7.
29 Thomas Frank, *The Conquest of Cool: Business Culture, Counterculture, and the Rise of Hip Consumerism* (Chicago: University of Chicago Press, 1997), 6–9, 152–6; Susannah Walker, *Style and Status: Selling Beauty to African American Women, 1920-1975* (Lexington: University Press of Kentucky, 2007), 169–204.
30 Art Kleiner, *The Age of Heretics: Heroes, Outlaws, and the Forerunners of Corporate Change* (New York: Currency, 1996), 12–18.
31 Douglas Murray McGregor, "The Human Side of Enterprise," *Management Review* 46, no. 11 (November 1957): 23, 88–9.
32 See for example, Peter Drucker, "Worker and Work in the Metropolis," *Daedalus* 97, no. 4 (Fall 1968): 1243–62; Peter Drucker, *The Essential Drucker*, Kindle ed. (New York: Harper Collins, 2001), 69–94, 112–26.
33 Robert Townsend, *Up the Organization: How to Stop the Corporation from Stifling People and Strangling Profits* (London: Michael Joseph, 1970), 25, 127–33.
34 James O'Toole, *Work in America* (Cambridge: MIT Press, [1973] 1981), 43–51.
35 Jay M. Sahfritz and J. Steven Ott, *Classics of Organization Theory* (Pacific Grove, CA: Brooks/Cole, 1992) 263–8.
36 Reinhold Martin, *The Organizational Complex: Architecture, Media, and Corporate Space* (Cambridge, MA: MIT Press, 2003), 13.
37 Rumpfhuber, "Space of Information Flow," 201–11.
38 "Office Landscape," *Progressive Architecture*, September 1964, 201–3; "Introduction," *Office Landscaping: An Open Plan Concept of Office Design* (Elmhurst, IL: Business Press, 1969); Carroll Cihlar, "No More Walls or Halls," *Office Appliances* (June 1967): 62–70.
39 "Burolandschaft USA," 174–6.
40 For examples of the heads of the US Quickborner Team, Hans Lorenzen and Dieter Jaeger discussing the office landscape as a rejection of hierarchy see: William Robbins, "'Radicals' Offer New Office Plan," *New York Times*, July 4, 1968; P. G. Twitchell, "The Office Landscape: What It Is; How It Works," *Skyscraper Management* (December 1968): 5–12; Hans Lorenzen, "The Economic Reasons Behind Landscaping," *Office Landscaping* (Elmhurst, IL: Business Press, 1968): 38–41.
41 "From Grid to Growth," 100–4.
42 For a more detailed history of Robert Propst's work with Herman Miller and the development of Action Office at Herman Miller see: Hugh De Pree, *Business as*

Usual: The People and Principles at Herman Miller (Zeeland, MI: Herman Miller, 1992), 81–103.
43 Robert Propst, "The Landscape Is Based on Thorough and Technical Data," *Office Landscaping: An Open Plan Concept of Office Design* (Elmhurst, IL: Business Press, 1969), 26–30; Robert Propst, "Commanding Information Equals Office," *Office Landscaping: An Open Plan Concept of Office Design* (Elmhurst, IL: Business Press, 1969), 34–8.
44 For example, John Pile, "The Nature of Office Landscape," *AIA Journal*, July 1969, 40–8; "Chaos as a System," *Progressive Architecture*, October 1968, 160–9; "From Grid to Growth," 100–9.
45 Robert Propst, *The Office: A Facility Based on Change* (Zeeland, MI: Herman Miller, 1968), 17–18; Propst, "Landscape Is Based on Thorough and Technical Data," 27.
46 "A Democratic Landscape … in a Natural Setting," *Office Design*, March 1969, 27–32; Ronald Beckman, "Designer's Statement," *Office Design*, March 1969, 33.
47 "Chaos as a System," 164.
48 Franklin D. Becker, *Workspace: Creating Environments in Organizations* (New York: Praeger, 1981), 141.
49 Francis Duffy, Colin Cave, and John Worthington, eds., *Planning Office Space* (New York: Nichols, 1976), 72.
50 Andrew H. Malcolm, "McDonald's Sold on Its 'Think Tank' Office," *New York Times*, January 31, 1972.
51 The use of the term "cubicle" in this quote refers to the small enclosed offices in conventional offices, not to open plan workstations. Malcolm, "McDonald's Sold on Its 'Think Tank' Office."
52 John F. Pile, *Open Office Planning: A Handbook for Interior Designers and Architects* (New York: Whitney Library of Design, 1978), 34.
53 William Pulgram, "Office Landscape System for Furniture Connoisseurs," *Interiors*, August 1971, 94.
54 "Share the Wealth Open Plan," *Interiors*, October 1971, 88–91.
55 "Share the Wealth Open Plan," 88–91; Robert Cross, "Inside Hamburger Central," *Chicago Tribune Magazine*, January 9, 1972, 18–21; Dennis Chase, "You Deserve a Break on the Employee Waterbed," *Management Review* 61, no. 9 (1972): 61–2.
56 Memo from Jack Schoop to Harry Schmidt, August 15, 1972, DOA: Box 11 Folder 18.
57 Letter from Fred Hiestand to Wayne McGown, February 2, 1973, Letter from John Short to Wayne McGown, February 6, 1973, Letter from Wayne F. McGown to Fred Hiestand, February 13, 1973, DOA: Box 14 Folder 12.
58 "Guidelines and Standards for Effective Space Management," December 1978, DOA: Box 33 Folder 22.
59 Various units in Wisconsin State Government contacted the DOA with concerns about the adoption and implementation of the new open plan concept for State Government buildings including the Department of Revenue (DOA: Box 32 Folder 30), The Department of Public Instruction (DOA: Box 34 Folder 13), and the Department of Health and Social Services (DOA: Box 39 Folder 27).
60 For examples of agencies at the State negotiating for more private offices in the State of Wisconsin see: Letters between Barbara Thompson and Kenneth Lindner, July 6, 1979 and July 25, 1979, DOA: Box 34 Folder 13. Letters between Mark Musolf and Kenneth Lindner, July 9 and 13, 1979, DOA: Box 32 Folder 30 and

Letters between Donald Percy and Kenneth Lindner September 25 and October 16, 1981, DOA: Box 39 Folder 27. Letters exchanged between Donald Percy and Kenneth Lindner, September 25, October 16 and 19, November 30, 1981, DOA: Box 39 Folder 27.
61 Louis Harris and Associates, *Office Environments*, 108–9.
62 Jeffrey Prince, "Getting the Holdouts to Accept the Open Plan," *Administrative Management* (1979): 32.
63 Montgomery Ward, Montgomery Ward Plaza Corporate Headquarters building brochures and sheet information sheet, 1973. MWCR: Series 10, Box 110 Folder 10 "Plaza Topping Out Ceremony."
64 "From Grid to Growth," 104–5; Maurice Mogulescu, *Profit through Design: Rx for Effective Office Space Planning* (New York: American Management Association, 1970), 104–7.
65 Pile, *Open Office Planning*, 57–8, 144.
66 Cynthia Froggatt, "Correll Workspace Study," June 1985, KRJDA: Box 424 Folder "Workspace Study"; Andrea Dean, "Corporate Contrast in the Suburbs: Kevin Roche's Union Carbide and General Foods Headquarters," *Architecture*, February 1985, 62.
67 Union Carbide Project Statements, KRJDA: Box 424 Folder "Project Statements." Secretarial and clerical workstation mock-up responses, KRJDA: Box 427 Folder "Workstation Review."
68 Louis Harris and Associates, *Office Environments*, 86–95.
69 Eric Sundstrom, *Work Places: The Psychology of the Physical Environment in Offices and Factories* (New York: Cambridge University Press, 1986), 229–31.
70 Lila Shoshkes, *Space Planning: Designing the Office Environment* (New York: Architectural Record Books, 1976), 24–7, 44.
71 Ronald Goodrich, "The Perceived Office: The Office Environment as Experienced by Users," in *Behavioral Issues in Office Design*, ed. Jean Wineman (New York: Van Norstrand Reinhold, 1986), 130–1.
72 Karen Dale and Gibson Burrell, *The Spaces of Organisation & the Organisation of Space: Power, Identity and Materiality at Work* (New York: Palgrave, 2008), 27.

Chapter 2

1 Hauserman, *Modern Monoliths Subdivide with Hauserman Movable Steel Partitions* (Cleveland: Hauserman, 1932). Trade literature from archive.org: https://archive.org/details/Sweet1932hauserman150001.
2 Hauserman, *The Inside Story of Building Economy* (Cleveland: Hauserman, 1950–8 [exact date unknown]). Trade literature from HAU: MS 5361 Box 7 Folder 22.
3 Hauserman, *Ten Factors in Buying Movable Walls* (Cleveland: Hauserman, n.d.). Trade literature from HAU: MS 5361 Box 7 Folder 23; Hauserman, *Inside Story of Building Economy*.
4 Martin, *The Organizational Complex*, 95–8.
5 Martin, *The Organizational Complex*, 98–9.
6 Martin, *The Organizational Complex*, 105.
7 "Manufacturers' Design Process," *Progressive Architecture* (June 1964), 183; Martin, *The Organizational Complex*, 120.
8 Shoshkes, *Space Planning*, 4.
9 Project Statements, Union Carbide, Box 424 Folder "Project statements" KRJDA.

10 Interview with General Services in the Chemical and Plastics Division, October 27, 1976, Box 426 Folder "Interviews" KRJDA; standard office sizes might range from 100 to 375 square feet according to a Union Carbide Programming Survey, Box 428 Folder "Programming Survey," KRJDA.
11 Duffy, Cave, and Worthington, *Planning Office Space*, 5–7.
12 Ábalos and Herreros, *Tower and Office*, 198.
13 Hauserman, *A New Concept to Manage Change in Business Interiors* (Cleveland: Hauserman, 1969). Trade literature from HAU: MS 5361 Box 8 Folder 5.
14 Hauserman, *A New Concept to Manage Change in Business Interiors*.
15 "Manufacturing Engineering Preliminary Objective Setting Meeting 69/70" March 25–26, 1968, HAU: MS 5361 Box 16 Folder 6.
16 Hauserman, "Hauserman Annual Report," 1970. HAU: MS 5361 Box 18 Folder 1.
17 Michael Brill, Terry Collison, and Eileen Harvard, *The Management of Change & Productive Interiors* (Cleveland: Hauserman, 1972), 1.
18 Michael Brill et al., "Performance May Be a Great Idea (but Will Anybody Really Pay for It?)," *Progressive Architecture*, November 1974; Brill, Collison, and Harvard, *Management of Change & Productive Interiors*.
19 John Pile, *Open Office Space* (New York: Quarto Marketing, 1984), 18.
20 Hugh Keiser, "Open Plan Furniture: An Investigation and Analysis," *Progressive Architecture*, November 1974, 94–5.
21 Knoll, "Component Guide," in *Stephens Office Systems Binder* (East Greenville, PA: Knoll, 1970s [undated]). Trade catalog from HML.
22 Pile, "The Open Office," 74.
23 Pile, *Open Office Space*, 18–19.
24 Andrea O. Dean, "The Pros and Cons of Affixing Lighting to the Furniture," *AIA Journal*, October 1977, 52–5.
25 Steelcase, *Lite-Savers* (Grand Rapids, MI: Steelcase, 1977). Trade catalog from HML.
26 Donald Canty, "Landscaping: Idea to Industry in Ten Years," *AIA Journal*, October 1974, 43.
27 "Energy Distribution in the Open Plan," *Environment*, May/June 1970, 36–40.
28 Steelcase, *Mobiles* (Grand Rapids, MI: Steelcase, 1975) and *Steelcase Series 9000: Case Study of a Steelcase Installation by John Tilton* (Grand Rapids, MI: Steelcase, 1977). Trade catalogs from HML.
29 Pile, "The Open Office," 76.
30 Driscoll, "Movable Divider Panels with Electrical Wiring," US Patent 4135775, January 23, 1979 (filed June 20, 1977).
31 Haworth, "Wall Panel with Prewired Power System," US Patent 4060294, November 29, 1977 (filed September 22, 1975).
32 Haworth, "ERA-1 Advertisement," *Progressive Architecture*, September 1976, 2.
33 Kimball, *CETRA Planning Guide* (Jasper, IN: Kimball, 1988). Trade catalog from HML.
34 Herman Miller, "Herman Miller Introduces Ethospace Interiors, Interior Architecture," Press Release dated October 1984 from HMCA.
35 Walter Kleeman, *Interior Design of the Electronic Office: The Comfort and Productivity Payoff* (New York: Van Nostrand Reinhold, 1991), 163–5; Haworth, *Places* (Holland, MI: Haworth, 1989). Trade catalog from HML.
36 Dwayne Meisner, "Work Stations Move into the Mainstream," *Administrative Management*, October 1973, 23–5.

37 Neal Steinhoff, "History of DOA Organization," January 1, 1979, DOA: Box 33 Folder 20. Reorganization Proposals State agencies, DOA: Box 62 Folder 6. Reorganizations, DCA: Box 67 Folder 39. Press Release, July 25, 1979, DOA: Box 33, Folder 15. Memo from Neal Steinhoff to James Klausner, November 21, 1989, DOA: Box 73 Folder 38. Memo from David Ward to Stan Vigne, June 16, 1978, DOA: Box 31 Folder 38. Memo from Paul Brown to Ken Lindner, August 6, 1982, DOA: Box 41 Folder 7. Agency Request for Building Commission Action, September 1982, DOA: Box 41 Folder 40. Memo from Veronica Luster to Kenneth Lindner January 2, 1980, DOA: Box 35 Folder 29.
38 Letter to Governor Patrick J. Lucey, from Joe E. Nussbaum, March 19, 1971, subject: Department of Administration Organization, Responsibilities and Status, DOA: Box 6 Folder 5.
39 Louis Harris and Associates, *Office Environments*, 103.
40 Donald Canty, "Evaluation of an Open Office Landscape: Weyerhaeuser Co.," *AIA Journal*, July 1977, 43.
41 Pile, "The Open Office," 79.
42 Andrea O. Dean, "Workplaces: The Open Office Revisited," *AIA Journal*, July 1980, 51–2.
43 "Space Consolidation Effort Underway in GEF #2," *DOA Today*, May 1982, 1, Wisconsin Historical Society.
44 Memo from Veronica Luster to Eileen Polizzotto, February 1, 1982, DOA: Box 40 Folder 29.
45 Susan Seliger, "Tempo: Are Cubicles an Answer or Just an Open Invitation to a Hard Day at the Office," *Chicago Tribune*, August 9, 1979.
46 "Backtalk: 'Open Plan office are designed for fast re-positioning as office procedures change. How often are you called to re-arrange clients' Open Plan Systems," *Interiors*, January 1979, 104.
47 IFMA, "Brief History of IFMA," https://www.ifma.org/about/about-ifma/history, accessed on June 24, 2019.
48 "Hallmark: A Study in Facilities Management," *Ideas*, October 1978, 4–5, HMCA.
49 Pile, *Open Office Planning*, 149–51.
50 Stephen Binder, *Corporate Facility Planning: An Inside View for Designers and Managers* (New York: McGraw Hill, 1989), 160–8.
51 Binder, *Corporate Facility Planning*, 207–11.
52 Claudia Propst, David Armstrong, and Robert Propst, "Growing into Facility Systems Management," Research report (Ann Arbor, MI: Facility Management Institute), 9–13, RP: Box 120.
53 Various generations of office plans and layouts for Freehafer Hall from 1971 to 2000, Purdue University Physical Facilities.
54 Press Statement from the Madison Area Fightback Committee, September 23, 1982 (WSEU-Wisconsin State Employees Union), DOA: Box 40 Folder 40
55 Orde Coombs, "The True Tales of the New York Workplace," *New York Magazine*, October 31, 1977, 69.
56 Letter from Steve Born to Tony Earl, February 15, 1975, DOA: Box 23 Folder 15.
57 Louis Harris and Associates, *Office Environments*, 40–1.
58 United States Commission on Civil Rights, "Last Hired, First Fired: Layoffs and Civil Rights" (Washington, DC, 1977), 11–12.
59 O'Toole, *Work in America*, 40.
60 United States Commission on Civil Rights, "Last Hired; First Fired," 22–7. Kimberlé Crenshaw, "Demarginalizing the Intersection of Race and Sex," 316–17.

61 Murphy, *Sick Building Syndrome*, 51; Erin Hatton, *The Temp Economy: From Kelly Girls to Permatemps in Postwar America* (Philadelphia: Temple University, 2011), 82.
62 National Association of Working Women, *The 9 to 5 National Survey on Women and Stress* (Cleveland: 9 to 5 National Association of Working Women, 1984), 35.
63 National Association of Working Women, *The 9 to 5 National Survey*, 37–8.
64 Karen Nussbaum and Judith Gregory, "Race Against Time: Automation of the Office: An Analysis of the Trends in Office Automation and the Impact on the Office Workforce," *Office Technology and People* 1, no. 2/3 (1982): 200.
65 Shoshana Zuboff, *In the Age of the Smart Machine* (New York: Basic Books, 1988); Thomas Haigh, "Remembering the Origins of Word Processing and Office Automation," *IEEE Annals of the History of Computing* 28, no. 4 (2006).
66 Zuboff, *In the Age of the Smart Machine*, 136–7.
67 Zuboff, *In the Age of the Smart Machine*, 136–59.
68 Anne Machung, "Word Processing: Forward for Business, Backward for Women," in *My Troubles Are Going to Have Trouble with Me: Everyday Trials and Triumphs of Women Workers*, ed. Karen Brodkin Sack and Dorothy Remy (New Brunswick: Rutgers University Press, 1984), 129.
69 Sandra Salmans, "The Debate over the Electronic Office," *New York Times*, 1982; Paul Attewell, "Big Brother and the Sweatshop: Computer Surveillance in the Automated Office," *Sociological Theory* 5, no. 1 (1987): 95; Office of Technology Assessment U.S. Congress, *Automation of America's Offices* (Washington, DC: U.S. Government Printing Office, 1985), 127–9; Machung, "Word Processing," 131.
70 Memo from Victoria Potter to Ken Lindner, 1979, DOA: Box 33 Folder 12.
71 Nussbaum and Gregory, "Race Against Time," 222–8.
72 Machung, "Word Processing," 131–2.
73 "Seminar Evaluation," December 1985, DOA: Box 52 Folder 9.
74 For example, Nussbaum and Gregory, "Race Against Time"; Machung, "Word Processing," 124–39; Evelyn Nakano Glenn and Roslyn L. Feidberg, "Degraded and Deskilled: The Proletarianization of Clerical Work," *Social Problems* 15, no. 1 (October 1977): 52–64; Janine Morgall, "Typing Our Way to Freedom: Is It True That New Office Technology Can Liberate Women?" *Feminist Review* 9 (Autumn 1981): 87–101; Mary Murphree, "Brave New Office: The Changing World of the Legal Secretary," in *My Troubles Are Going to Have Trouble with Me: Everyday Trials and Triumphs of Women Workers*, ed. Karen Brodkin Sack and Dorothy Remy (New Brunswick: Rutgers University Press, 1984), 153–6.
75 Murphy, *Sick Building Syndrome*, 34.
76 Murphy, *Sick Building Syndrome*, 81–4.
77 General Services Administration, *General Services Administration Annual Report* (Washington, DC: General Services Association, 1973), 26.
78 Murphy, *Sick Building Syndrome*, 34.
79 Duffy, Cave, and Worthington, *Planning Office Space*, 74.

Chapter 3

1 Malcolm, "McDonald's Sold on Its 'Think Tank' Office."
2 Kurt Lewin, "Frontiers in Group Dynamics: Concept Method and Reality in Social Science; Social Equilibria and Social Change," *Human Relations* 1, no. 1 (1947).

3   E. L. Trist and K. W. Bamforth, "Some Social and Psychological Consequences of the Longwall Method of Coal-Getting," *Human Relations* 4, no. 1 (1951).
4   Edward Hall, *The Silent Language* (New York: Anchor Books, [1959] 1990), 162–85; Edward Hall, *The Hidden Dimension* (New York: Anchor Books, [1966] 1990), 101–25.
5   C. M. Deasy, "When a Sociologist Gets in the Act," *AIA Journal*, January 1968, 72–6. *Office Design* ran an article on the concept of proxemics in 1964: "An Anthropological View of Space," *Office Appliances* 120, no. 1 (July 1964): 114. This citation is a reprint of the original article featured in a sister publication produced by the same publisher in Elmhurst, Illinois.
6   Rumpfhuber, "Space of Information Flow," 209–16.
7   Quickborner Team, "1.3 General Planning Goals," *Purdue Planning Report*, 1968, 2, PUSC: UA 153, Series 2 Box 1 Folder 8.
8   Quickborner Team, "10 General Maxims," *Purdue Planning Report*, 1968, 141, PUSC: UA 153, Series 2 Box 1 Folder 8.
9   Quickborner Team, "5 Communication Survey," *Purdue Planning Report*, 1968, 48, PUSC: UA 153, Series 2 Box 1 Folder 8.
10 Sydney Rodgers, "Modularity versus Free-Form Clustering," in *New Concepts in Office Design* (Elmhurst, IL: Business Press, 1968), 13.
11 Sundstrom, *Work Places*, 308–9.
12 Quickborner Team, office layouts for Purdue University administrative building, 1968, Purdue University Office of Physical Facilities.
13 "Chaos as a System," 157.
14 Quickborner Team, "10 General Maxims."
15 Pile, *Open Office Planning*, 133.
16 Propst, *The Office*, 43.
17 Propst, *The Office*, 62.
18 Pile, *Open Office Planning*, 133.
19 Propst, *The Office*, 62.
20 "New Purdue Building to be Girl Watchers' Paradise," undated and unidentified newspaper article clipped in a scrapbook (1970–1), PUSC: UA 153 Series 1, Box 1 Folder 3.
21 "Living in an Office Landscape," *Industrial and Commercial Training* 3, no. 11 (1971): 531.
22 Malcolm, "McDonald's Sold on Its 'Think Tank' Office."
23 Julie Berebitsky, *Sex and the Office: A History of Gender, Power, and Desire* (New Haven, CT: Yale University Press, 2012), 206–27; Catharine MacKinnon, *Sexual Harassment of Working Women: A Case of Sex Discrimination* (New Haven, CT: Yale University Press, 1979), 1–55.
24 Claire Safran, "What Men Do to Women on the Job: A Shocking Look at Sexual Harassment," *Redbook*, November 1976, 217.
25 Safran, "What Men Do to Women on the Job," 224; Yia Eason, "When the Boss Wants Sex: How to Handle the Harasser," *Essence*, March 1981, 114; Suzanne C. Carothers and Peggy Crull, "Contrasting Sexual Harassment in Female- and Male-Dominated Occupations," in *My Troubles Are Going to Have Trouble with Me: Everyday Trials and Triumphs of Women Workers*, ed. Karen Brodkin Sack and Dorothy Remy (New Brunswick: Rutgers University Press, 1984), 222; Peggy Crull, "Stress Effects of Sexual Harassment on the Job: Implications for Counseling," *American Journal of Orthopsychiatry* 52, no. 3 (July 1982), 540–1.
26 MacKinnon, *Sexual Harassment of Working Women*, 45.

27 Eliza Collins and Timoth Blodgett, "Sexual Harassment: Some See It … Some Won't," *Harvard Business Review*, March–April 1981; "The Joint Redbook–Harvard Business Review Report," *Redbook*, March 1981, 48.
28 "Living in an Office Landscape," 531.
29 Eason, "How to Handle the Harasser," 82; Safran, "What Men Do to Women on the Job," 149.
30 Adrienne Rich, "Compulsory Heterosexuality and Lesbian Experience," *Signs* 5, no. 4 (Summer 1980): 640–3.
31 Jeff Hearn and Wendy Parkin, *'Sex' at 'Work': The Power and Paradox of Organisation Sexuality* (New York: St Martin's Press, [1987] 1995), 96, 156–60.
32 Quickborner Team, "11 Special Environment Maxims," *Purdue Planning Report*, 1968, 144, PUSC: UA 153, Series 2, Box 1 Folder 8.
33 Robert Propst and Michael Wodka, *The Action Office Acoustic Handbook: A Guide for the Open Plan Facility Manager, Planner and Designer* (Ann Arbor: Herman Miller Research Corp, 1975), 23.
34 Owens-Corning, "Owens-Corning Tells You Why You Should Remember this Unusual Picture Next Time You Design an Open Office," *AIA Journal*, May 1976, 2–3.
35 Herman Miller Research Corporation, "The Action Office Acoustic Area Conditioner," Research Report undated (early 1970s), RP: Box 43 Folder "Action Office Acoustic Conditioner." Herman Miller Research Corporation, "The Action Office Acoustic Conditioner," Systems Product Statement, 1974, RP: Box 44 Folder "Action Office Acoustic Conditioner Sys. Product Report." Herman Miller, "Action Office by Herman Miller: Sound Solutions for Office Privacy," 1976, and Acoustic Conditioner informational material, 1976 RP: Box 60 Folder "Product Literature Misc."
36 Propst and Wodka, *The Action Office Acoustic Handbook*, 17–21.
37 For example, see: Herman Miller, *Machine Integration and the Action Office System* (Zeeland, MI: Herman Miller, 1985). Trade catalog part of an Action Office System Binder from HML.
38 Duffy, Cave, and Worthington, *Planning Office Space,* 139; Propst and Wodka, *Action Office Acoustic Handbook*, 42.
39 Sundstrom, *Work Places*, 166.
40 Pile, *Open Office Planning*, 132–3.
41 Propst, *The Office*, 62.
42 Pile, "Nature of Office Landscape," 48; Propst, *The Office*, 62.
43 Ranger Farrell, "Sounds of the Open Plan," *Office Design*, July/August 1970, 32.
44 "Burolandschaft USA," 176.
45 Louis Harris and Associates, *Office Environments*, 50, 52.
46 Sundstrom, *Work Places*, 132–4.
47 Sundstrom, *Work Places*, 165.
48 Pile, *Open Office Space*, 16.
49 For example, Becker, *Workspace*, 104–11; Malcolm Brookes, "Office Landscape: Does It Work?," *Applied Ergonomics* 3, no. 4 (1972); Eric Sundstrom, R. Kring Herbert, and David W. Brown, "Privacy and Communication in an Open-Plan Office: A Case Study," *Environment and Behavior* 14, no. 3 (May 1, 1982): 379–92; Greg R. Oldham and Daniel J. Brass, "Employee Reactions to an Open-Plan Office: A Naturally Occurring Quasi-Experiment," *Administrative Science Quarterly* 24, no. 2 (1979): 267–84.
50 Russell, "Form Follows Fad," 55.
51 Fred Steele, *Physical Settings and Organization Development* (Reading, MA: Addison-Wesley, 1973), 12–14; Becker, *Workspace*, 14–18.

Notes   **185**

52 "Using Office Design to Increase Productivity," *Progressive Architecture*, January 1985, 154–5; "Using Office Design to Improve Productivity," *Office Administration and Automation*, February 1985, 26–9, 77–8.
53 Exact numbers of participants in the study are unclear. An early report BOSTI, "The Impact of Office Environment on Productivity and Quality of Working Life," 1983 (from the Hagley Museum and Library) gives the general number of 4,000 that is referenced in the text, but the final report does not provide a total number of people in the study, though they do describe the number of workers in various research databases (some of which seem to have duplication for cross referencing) and list the specific research sites Michael Brill, Stephen T. Margulis, and Ellen Konar, *Using Office Design to Increase Productivity*, vol. 1 (Buffalo, NY: Workplace Design and Productivity, 1984), 53, 389–91.
54 Brill, Margulis and Konar, *Using Office Design to Increase Productivity*, vol. 1, 42–5.
55 Michael Brill, Stephen T. Margulis, and Ellen Konar, *Using Office Design to Increase Productivity*, vol. 2 (Buffalo, NY: Workplace Design and Productivity, 1984), 54.
56 Brill, Margulis and Konar, *Using Office Design to Increase Productivity*, vol. 2, 88.
57 Brill, Margulis and Konar, *Using Office Design to Increase Productivity*, vol. 2, 100.
58 Brill, Margulis and Konar, *Using Office Design to Increase Productivity*, vol. 2, 35–6.
59 Kimball, *CETRA Planning Guide*, 4–6. Trade catalog from HML.
60 For example, Knoll, *Morrison Planning Guide* (East Greenville, PA: Knoll, 1988), 10–11; Hauserman, *Privacy Panel System* (Cleveland: Hauserman, 1985). Both trade catalogs from HML.
61 Brill, Margulis, and Konar, *Using Office Design to Increase Productivity*, vol. 1, 389–91.
62 Brill, Margulis, and Konar, *Using Office Design to Increase Productivity*, vol. 1, 71–2.
63 Mar Hicks, *Programmed Inequality: How Britain Discarded Women Technologists and Lost Its Edge in Computing* (Cambridge, MA: MIT Press, 2017), 16–17.
64 Brill, Margulis, and Konar, *Using Office Design to Increase Productivity*, vol. 1, 73–7.
65 Brill, Margulis, and Konar, *Using Office Design to Increase Productivity*, vol. 2, 37, 96–104.
66 Zuboff, *In the Age of the Smart Machine*, 125, 38–50; Murphy, *Sick Building Syndrome*, 52; Nussbaum and Gregory, "Race Against Time," 207–8.
67 For example, Francy Blackwood, "Office Designers Show Employees Way Out of Cubicle Hell," *San Francisco Business Times*, August 2, 1996.
Dorothy B. Atcheson, "Learning to Live, Love, and Work in a Cubicle," *Cosmopolitan* 222, no. 1 (1997), 82–3; David Molpus, *Employees Say No to Cubicles*, All Things Considered (Washington, DC: National Public Radio, 1997); Carol Hymowitz, "If the Walls Had Ears You Wouldn't Have Any Less Privacy," *Wall Street Journal*, 1998; Karin Rives, "In Cubicle-Filled Workplace, Walls Really Do Have Ears," *McClatchy Tribune Business News*, 2003.
68 For example, "Wired for Slang in the Online Age," *Los Angeles Times*, June 5, 1997.
69 Douglas Coupland, *Generation X: Tales for an Accelerated Culture* (New York: St. Martin's Press, 1991), 19–20.
70 See WS: Box 43 Folder "Critiques of Office."
71 William Stumpf and Associates, "Cubicle Reform Problems and Proposed Solutions," October 1998. WS: Box 21 Folder "Ethos and Ethospace 1986."
72 Becker, *Workspace*, 14–39.
73 Steele, *Physical Settings and Organization Development*, 7–9.
74 Brill, Margulis, and Konar, *Using Office Design to Increase Productivity*, vol 1, 65.

75 Louis Harris and Associates, *Office Environments*, IV; Louis Harris and Associates, *Comfort and Productivity in the Office of the 80s* (Grand Rapids, MI: Steelcase, 1980), III–V.

Chapter 4

1. Steelcase *Mobiles Price List: Desks, Cabinets, Service Modules, Accessories* (Grand Rapids, MI: Steelcase, 1973). Trade catalog from WP: Series 25, Box 46.
2. George Terry, *Office Management and Control*, third ed. (Homewood, IL: Richard D. Irwin, 1959), 242.
3. Shoshkes, *Space Planning*, 39.
4. Randolph W. Mallick, *Plant Layout: Planning and Practice* (New York: Wiley, 1951), 43–4.
5. Robert Propst, "The Action Office," *Human Factors* (August 1966): 299.
6. Robert Propst, "The Action Office Work Arena Concept," March 14, 1966. RP: Box 42 Folder "Action Office undated."
7. Propst, *The Office*, 24, 49.
8. Herman Miller, *The Action Office* (Zeeland, MI: Herman Miller, 1960s [n.d.]). Trade catalog from the HMCA.
9. Propst, *The Office*, 57.
10. Robert Propst, "Process Aesthetic: Some Thoughts on the Thinking Process," *Progressive Architecture* (November 1974): 79.
11. Orit Halpern, *Beautiful Data: A History of Vision and Reason since 1945* (Durham: Duke University Press, 2015), 79–85.
12. Ronn M. Daniel, "Herman Miller's Action Office: Corporate Interiors in the Cold War," *Interiors* 6, no. 1 (2015): 15–16.
13. For example, Herman Miller, *Production Work Stations: The Action Factory System* (Zeeland, MI: Herman Miller, 1982), 5–6; Herman Miller, *The Integrated Facility System* (Zeeland, MI: Herman Miller, 1981), 6. Trade catalogs from RP: Box 60, Folders "Production Work Stations" and "Integrated Facility."
14. For example, Herman Miller, *AT&T: Long Lines* (Zeeland, MI: Herman Miller, 1973); Herman Miller, *Bloom Agency* (Zeeland, MI: Herman Miller 1973); Herman Miller, *Caudill Rowlett Scott* (Zeeland, MI: Herman Miller, 1973); Herman Miller, *Hallmark Cards* (Zeeland, MI: Herman Miller, 1973). Trade catalogs from an Action Office Binder held at HML.
15. Lange, "White Collar Corbusier," 67.
16. Shannon Mattern, "Indexing the World of Tomorrow," *Places Journal* (February 2, 2016), available at https://doi.org/10.22269/160202.
17. Lynn Spigel, "Object Lessons for the Media Home: From Storagewall to Invisible Design," *Public Culture* 24, no. 3 68 (September 1, 2012): 546, 559.
18. Herman Miller, *The Action Office* (Zeeland, MI: Herman Miller, 1964). Trade catalog from the HMCA.
19. Herman Miller, *Managing the Work Environment* (Zeeland, MI: Herman Miller, 1979). Trade catalog from HML.
20. Pile, *Open Office Planning*, 22.
21. Townsend, *Up the Organization*, 159.
22. Quickborner Team, "4.5: Furniture" *Purdue Planning Report*, 1968, 23, PUSC: UA 153, Series 2 Box 1 Folder 8.

23 William Zinsser, "But Where Will I Keep My Movie Magazines?," *Saturday Evening Post*, January 16, 1965
24 Propst, *The Office*, 59 (emphasis in original).
25 Pile, "The Open Office," 73.
26 Steelcase, *Mobiles* (Grand Rapids, MI: Steelcase, 1970), 26–37. Trade catalog from HML.
27 William Pulgram and Richard Stonis, *Designing the Automated Office: A Guide for Architects, Interior Designers, Space Planners, and Facility Managers* (New York: Whitney Library of Design, 1984), 140–1.
28 Steelcase, *Filing and Storage Guide* (Grand Rapids, MI: Steelcase, 1985), 3–20. Trade catalog from HML.
29 Minutes of meeting-Interior Design, MARI building, July 28, 1977, PK: Box 7 Folder 10. Minutes of weekly meeting with Powell/Kleinschmidt, September 13, 1977, PK: Box 7 Folder 10. Minutes of Meeting, MARI building, September 21, 1977, PS: Box 7 Folder 10. Minutes of weekly meeting with Powell/Kleinschmidt, October 11, 1977, PK: Box 7 Folder 10. Minutes of Meeting-Presentation by Powell/Kleinschmidt of Interior Design Concept for MARI building, October 26, 1977, PK: Box 7 Folder 10. Meeting with Corporate Building Department, representatives of Mid-America Home Office and Powell/ Kleinschmidt, December 14, 1977, PK: Box 8, Folder 1.
30 Interior Design Presentation, December 16, 1977, PK: Box 8 Folder 1. Memo (draft), January 26, 1978, PK: Box 8 Folder 1.
31 Minutes of Meeting, October 26, 1977, PK: Box 7 Folder 10. Interior Design Presentation, December 16, 1977, PK: Box 8 Folder 1.
32 Westinghouse, *ASD Group* (Grand Rapids, MI: Westinghouse, 1975). Trade catalog from HML.
33 Herman Miller Research Corporation, "Visual Enrichment in System Environments," May 1979, RP: Box 43 Folder "Visual Enrichment."
34 Haworth, *Individually Unique* (Holland, MI: Haworth, 1982), trade catalog from HML.
35 Kimball, *Meridian* (Jasper, IN: Kimball, 1990). Trade catalog from HML.
36 Brill, Margulis, and Konar, *Using Office Design to Increase Productivity*, vol. 2, 21.
37 Goodrich, "The Perceived Office," 117–18.
38 Cecil Williams, David L. Armstrong, and Clark Malcolm, *The Negotiable Environment: People, White-Collar Work, and the Office* (Zeeland, MI: Herman Miller, 1992), 29–33.
39 Brill, Margulis, and Konar, *Using Office Design to Increase Productivity*, vol. 2, 231–3.
40 Mary Ann Hiserman, "Design for Disabled People in the Electronic Office," in *The Ergonomics Payoff: Designing the Electronic Office*, ed. Rani Lueder (New York: Nicholas, 1986), 345–6.
41 Haworth, *Individually Unique*; Herman Miller, *Ethospace Interiors* (Zeeland MI: Herman Miller, 1993), trade catalog from WS: Box 21, Folder 5.
42 Al Schumann, "Keeping Blight from the Open Office," *Administrative Management*, October 1974, 27.
43 Schumann, "Keeping Blight from the Open Office," 28, 80.
44 Pile, *Open Office Planning*, 148–9.
45 Brill, Margulis, and Konar, *Using Office Design to Increase Productivity*, vol. 2, 69.
46 Brill, Margulis, and Konar, *Using Office Design to Increase Productivity*, vol. 2, 273.

47 Edward T. Hall, *Silent Language*, 162–85; Edward T. Hall, *The Hidden Dimension*, 52–4, 101–12.
48 Robert Sommer, *Tight Spaces: Hard Architecture and How to Humanite It* (Englewood Cliffs, NJ: Prentice-Hall, 1974), 112–13.
49 Fritz Steele and Stephen Jenks, *The Feel of the Work Place: Understanding and Improving Organizational Climate* (Reading, MA: Addison Wesley, 1977), 111–12.
50 Pile, *Open Office Planning*, 145.
51 Memo (meeting notes), June 13, 1978, PK: Box 8 Folder 1.
52 George Harris, "Psychology of the New York Work Space," *New York Magazine*, October 31, 1977, 51.
53 Chris Welles, "How It Feels to Live in a Total Design," *Life*, April 29, 1966, 59.
54 Welles, " How It Feels to Live in a Total Design," 59.
55 Welles, "How It Feels to Live in a Total Design," 60A.
56 Harris, "New York Work Space," 52.
57 Orde Coombs, "The Human Touch at Black Rock," *New York Magazine*, October 31, 1977, 53.
58 Orde Coombs, "True Tales of the New York Workplace," 69.
59 Sundstrom, *Work Places*, 217–51.
60 Kanter, *Men and Women of the Corporation*, 69.
61 Arlie Russell Hochschild, *The Time Bind: When Work Becomes Home and Home Becomes Work* (New York: Metropolitan Books, 1997), 85–6.
62 Hochschild, *The Time Bind*, 86–7.
63 Gideon Kunda, *Engineering Culture: Control and Commitment in a High Tech Corporation* (Philadelphia: Temple University Press, 1992), 192–7.
64 Kunda, *Engineering Culture*, 206.
65 Susan Scheiberg, "Emotions on Display: The Personal Decoration of Work Space," *American Behavioral Scientist* 33, no. 3 (1990): 334.
66 Goodrich, "The Perceived Office," 131.

Chapter 5

1 Paul Atkinson, "Room with a VDU: The Development of the 'Glass House' in the Corporate Workplace," *Interiors: Design, Architecture and Culture* 5, no. 1 (2014): 89–116.
2 David Noble, *Forces of Production: A Social History of Industrial Automation* (New Brunswick: Transaction, 2011), 144–92; Joan Greenbaum, *Windows on the Workplace: Technology, Jobs, and the Organization of Office Work* (New York: Monthly Review Press, 2004), 46–80; Zuboff, *In the Age of the Smart Machine*, 126–50; Marco Diani, "The Social Design of Office Automation," *Design Issues* 3, no. 2 (1986): 73–82.
3 Strom, *Beyond the Typewriter*, 172–226; Haigh, "Origins of Word Processing," 11–12; Hicks, *Programmed Inequality*, 5–7; Sally Hacker, *Pleasure, Power, and Technology* (Boston: UNWIN Hyman, 1989), 44–57; Paul Atkinson, "The Best Laid Plans of Mice and Men: The Computer Mouse in the History of Computing," *Design Issues* 23, no. 3 (2007): 59–60; P. Atkinson, "Man in a Briefcase: The Social Construction of the Laptop Computer and the Emergence of a Type Form," *Journal of Design History* 18, no. 2 (2005): 191–205; Elizabeth Petrick, *Making Computers*

Accessible: Disability Right and Digital Technology (Baltimore: Johns Hopkins University Press, 2015), 36–8.
4   Venus Green, *Race on the Line: Gender, Labor, and Technology in the Bell System, 1880–1980* (Durham: Duke University Press, 2001).
5   Ida Russakoff Hoos, "When the Computer Takes over the Office," *Harvard Business Review* 38, no. 4 (1960): 102–12.
6   Dee Wedemeyer, "Adapting the Workplace to Computers," *New York Times*, April 23, 1978.
7   Elaine Cohen and Aaron Cohen, *Planning the Electronic Office* (New York: McGraw-Hill, 1983), 51.
8   Atkinson, "Room with a VDU," 106–11.
9   Memo from R. C. Lance to Robert H. Bolt, John Deere Company, December 15, 1978, KRJDA: Box 325 Folder "Client Materials 1."
10 Office of Technology Assessment, *Automation of America's Offices* (Washington, DC: U.S. Government Printing Office, 1985), 151–2; Pulgram and Stonis, *Designing the Automated Office*, 66–8; Don Korrell, "Planning for the Future Office—Today," *Behaviour & Information Technology* 3, no. 4 (1984): 334.
11 John Deere West Office Building floor outlet plans, KRJDA: Box 336.
12 John Deere West Office Building coaxial cable plans, KRJDA: Box 336.
13 "The West Office Building," John Deere project statement, p3, KRJDA: Box 325 Folder "Project Statements."
14 Pulgram and Stonis, *Designing the Automated Office*, 72–3; Walter Kleeman, *Interior Design of the Electronic Office: The Comfort and Productivity Payoff* (New York: Van Nostrand Reinhold, 1991), 90–3.
15 Stevens Anderson, "Open Office Systems Gain Flexibility," *AIA Journal* (1988): 121.
16 Paul Ceruzzi, William Aspray, and Thomas Misa, *A History of Modern Computing* (Cambridge: MIT Press, 2014), 177–8, 95.
17 Ceruzzi, Aspray, Misa, *History of Modern Computing*, 221–4, 265–6.
18 Ida R. Hoos, "'When the Computer Takes over the Office'—Update," *Office Technology and People* 2, no. 1 (1983): 74.
19 Information Resources Management Service, *End User Microcomputing: A Federal Survey Report and Guide* (Washington, DC: General Services Administration, 1986), 6, 17, 18.
20 DEC Human Factors Department, "Ergonomic Office Focus Group," July 1988, 9. DEC: Box 450 Folder 21.
21 Tim Davis, "Information Technology and White-Collar Productivity," *The Executive* 5, no. 1 (1991): 58.
22 Pulgram and Stonis, *Designing the Automated Office*, 70.
23 Richard G. Haworth, Charles J. Taylor, Harold R. Wilson, Wall Panel with Prewired Power System, US Patent 4060294 filed on September 22, 1975 and issued on November 29, 1977.
24 *Haworth Inc. v. Steelcase Inc.*, opinion from the United States District Court, W.D. Michigan S.D., May 17, 1988. No K85–256.
25 Kleeman, *Interior Design of the Electronic Office*, 98.
26 Haworth, *Unigroup* (Holland, MI: Haworth, 1989). Trade catalog from HML.
27 Knoll Binder, *Knoll Introduces 2 + 2 Raceway* (East Greenville, PA: Knoll, 1987–1990). Trade catalog from HML.
28 Kimball, *Artec Planning Guide* (Jasper, IN: Kimball, 1988), 34. Trade catalog from HML.
29 Krueger, *Com: Bringing New Distinction to the Workplace* (Green Bay, WI: Krueger, 1988). Trade catalog from HML.

30 Pilar Vilades, "Panel Discussion," *Progressive Architecture*, May 1982, 195.
31 E. Cohen and A. Cohen, *Planning the Electronic Office*, 183.
32 Pulgram and Stonis, *Designing the Automated Office*, 134.
33 DEC, "Tactics and Strategies for Improved Office Productivity," January 1987, A-5 to A-6, DEC: Box 450.
34 Pulgram and Stonis, *Designing the Automated Office*, 112–13.
35 Women's Bureau, *Women and Office Automation: Issues for the Decade* (Washington, DC: Department of Labor, 1985), 5.
36 Women's Bureau, *Women and Office Automation*, 5; National Association of Working Women 9 to 5, *Computer Monitoring and Other Dirty Tricks* (Cleveland: 9 to 5, National Association of Working Women, 1986), 3.
37 Herman Miller, Action Office Secretary: Paulette Cary, late 1970s. Advertisement from HMCA. A similar "humanizing" ideal is depicted in Herman Miller's promotional film "Machine Army" from 1980 in the Hagley Digital collection, https://digital.hagley.org/FILM_2018222_FC93.
38 Westinghouse ASD Group, *Maximum Flexibility* (Grand Rapids, MI: Westinghouse, 1970). Trade catalog from HML.
39 Office of Technology Assessment, *Automation of America's Offices*, 152.
40 Office of Technology Assesssment, *Automation of America's Offices*, 152–3; Steven Sauter, L. John Chapman, and Sheri J. Knutson, *Improving VDT Work: Causes and Control of Health Concerns in VDT Use* (Madison: Department of Preventative Medicine, University of Wisconsin, 1985), 14–19.
41 Mary Ann Hiserman, "Design for Disabled People in the Electronic Office," in *The Ergonomics Payoff: Designing the Electronic Office*, ed. Rani Lueder (New York: Nicholas, 1986), 347–8.
42 For a detailed description of the development of accessible programs and tools for personal computers, see: Petrick, *Making Computers Accessible*, 39–47.
43 William Murray, *Potential Health Hazards of Video Display Terminals* (Cincinnati, Oh: National Institute for Occupational Safety and Health, 1981); Steven Sauter, L. John Chapman, and Sheri J. Knutson, *Ergonomic Evaluation of VDT Workplaces in New York State Departments of Taxation and Motor Vehicles* (Cincinnati, OH: US Department of Health and Human Services, 1984); Vernon Mogensen, *Office Politics: Computers, Labor, and the Fight for Safety and Health* (New Brunswick: Rutgers University Press, 1996), 35–50, 109–25; National Association of Working Women, *The 9 to 5 National Survey on Women and Stress: Automation Addendum* (Cleveland: 9 to 5 National Association of Working Women, 1984).
44 Don Sneed, "VDTs as Potential Health Hazards: A Critical Analysis," *Newspaper Research Journal* 6, no. 4 (June 1985): 66–72.
45 9 to 5 National Association of Working Women, Campaign on VDT Risks, February 1984, in U.S. Congress, "OSHA Oversight-Video Display Terminals in the Workplace: Hearings before the Subcommittee on Health and Safety of the Committee on Education and Labor, 1984" (Washington, DC: US Government Printing Office, 1985), 25, 34–48.
46 Statement of Stephen D. Channer, BIFMA, U.S. Congress, "OSHA Oversight-Video Display Terminals in the Workplace: Hearings before the Subcommittee on Health and Safety of the Committee on Education and Labor, 1984" (Washington, DC: US Government Printing Office, 1985), 118.
47 Statement of Vico E. Henriques, CBEMA, U.S. Congress, "OSHA Oversight-Video Display Terminals in the Workplace: Hearings before the Subcommittee on Health

and Safety of the Committee on Education and Labor, 1984" (Washington DC: US Government Printing Office, 1985), 301.
48 Mogensen, *Office Politics*, 75–6.
49 CBEMA, *Guide to the Draft American National Standard for Human Factors Engineering of Visual Display Terminal Workstations* (Washington, DC: CBEMA, 1985).
50 Etienne Grandjean, *Ergonomics in Computerized Offices* (New York: Taylor & Francis, 1987), 189–92.
51 Grandjean, *Ergonomics in Computerized Offices*, 6–7
52 Haworth, *Unitek Electronic Support by Haworth* (Holland, MI: Haworth, 1980s [exact date unknown]). Trade catalog from HML. Haworth, *Individually Unique*.
53 Herman Miller, *A Manageable Environment for Information Processing* (Zeeland, MI: Herman Miller, 1982). Trade catalog from HMCA.
54 Radio Shack, *"1989 Tandy Computer Catalog" RSC-20* (Fort Worth, TX: Tandy, 1989), 42; Computerland, *Accessories and Supplies Catalog* (Oakland, CA: Computerland, 1988), 10, 17; DEC, "Personal Computer Catalog'; William Howard, "Biotech Add-Ons," *PC Mag*, October 2, 1984, 153–5.
55 Sauter, Chapman, and Knutson, *Ergonomic Evaluation of VDT Workplaces*, 50.
56 Dean, "Pros and Cons of Affixing Lighting"; Douglas Gordon, "Lighting Requirements for VDTs,' *AIA Journal* (1987); Pulgram and Stonis, *Designing the Automated Office*, 86.
57 For example, in the State of Wisconsin, the new ergonomic policy established in 1985 prioritized intensive computer users. Memo from Helene Nelson to Tom Alt, May 31, 1985, DOA: Box 52 Folder 7.
58 Memo from Charles Abernathy to Dick Rubenstein on "Form Factor and Layout," September 18, 1980. DEC: Box 1 Human Factors Report 444/1208, Folder "Form Factor."
59 Robert Guinter et al., "AT&T Bell Lab's Ergonomic Program Aims to Cure VDT Workstation Ills," *Occupational Health and Safety* 64, no. 2 (1995): 32.
60 Paul Atkinson, "The (in)Difference Engine: Explaining the Disappearance of Diversity in the Design of the Personal Computer," *Journal of Design History* 13, no. 1 (2000): 59.
61 Davis, "Information Technology and White-Collar Productivity," 58.
62 Herman Miller, *Information Age* (Zeeland, MI: Herman Miller, 1990), 6–9, 11. Research report from the HMCA.
63 R. Oades, "Cabling in Intelligent Buildings," *Property Management* 7, no. 1 (1989): 27.
64 David Bernard Ciolkowski, "Upgrade Telecom without Rewiring," *Facilities Design and Management* 12, no. 7 (1993): 31.
65 Herman Miller, *Information Age*, 10.
66 Herman Miller, *Information Age*, 11.

Chapter 6

1 Quickborner Team, "10 General Maxims," 141–3.
2 Quickborner Team, "General Planning Goals," 1.
3 Propst, *The Office*, 66.
4 Propst, *The Office*, 66–7.

5 Donald Canty, "Landscaping: Idea to Industry in Ten Years," *AIA Journal*, October 1974, 44.
6 "Signage System Project for Action Office II" September 9, 1968, RP: Box 42 Folder "Signage and Signage System for Action Office II," December 9, 1969, RP: Box 42 Folder "AO2 Signage."
7 Office layout, John Deere, KRJDA: Box 325 Folder "Model Shots."
8 Herman Miller, "The Office in the Age of the Keyboard," *Ideas*, April 1978, 6. Magazine from the HMCA.
9 Brill, Margulis, and Konar, *Using Office Design to Increase Productivity*, vol. 2, 56–7.
10 Joanna Smith Bers, "ADA Means Watching Your FM Step," *Facilities Design and Management* 11, no. 2 (February 1992): 40–3; Cynthia Leibrock, "Dignified Options to ADA Compliance," *Facilities Design and Management* 13, no. 6 (June 1994): 56–9; Joanna Smith Bers, "Equal Footing for Disabled, Thanks to ADA," *Facilities Design and Management* 11, no. 2 (February 1992): 21.
11 Paul Arthur and Romedi Passini, *Wayfinding: People Signs and Architecture* (New York: McGraw-Hill Book, 1992), 64–7; "Signage Finding Your Way through ADA," *Facilities Design and Management* 11, no. 10 (October 1992), 68–9.
12 Joanna Smith Bers, "Removing ADA's Confusion Barrier," *Facilities Design and Management* 12, no. 3 (March 1993): 58–61.
13 Ruth Colker, *The Disability Pendulum: The First Decade of the Americans with Disabilities Act* (New York: New York University Press, 2005), 145–57.
14 Alfvin Toffler, *The Third Wave* (New York: Bantam, 1989), 210–17.
15 Reagan Mays Ramsower, *Telecommuting: The Organizational and Behavioral Effects of Working at Home* (Ann Arbor, MI: UMI Research Press, 1985), 12–13; Office of Technology Assessment, *Automation of America's Offices*, 189–97.
16 Franklin Becker and Fritz Steele, *Workplace by Design: Mapping the High-Performance Workscape* (San Francisco, CA: Jossey-Bass, 1995), 104–6.
17 Becker and Steele, *Workplace by Design*, 104–5.
18 Anthony DeMarco, "Home Is Where the Office Is," *Facilities Design and Management* 14, no. 11 (November 1995): 60.
19 "Bell Atlantic Asks Managers to Telecommute," *Facilities Design and Management* 11, no. 8 (August 1992): 12.
20 DeMarco, "Home Is Where the Office Is," 58–9.
21 Bill Stumpf, "The Nomadics: An Hypothesis for Office Work in the Present and Future," Report dated May 1995, WS: Box 21 Folder 2.
22 Lorel McMillan, "Ernst & Young Calculates a High Return from Hoteling and High-Tech," *Facilities Design and Management* 12, no. 4 (April 1993): 32–7.
23 Becker and Steele, *Workplace by Design*, 120–3; Franklin Becker, William Simms, and Bethany Davis, "Excuse Me. I Think That's My Desk," *Facilities Design and Management* 10, no. 2 (February 1991): 50–1.
24 Kirk Johnson, "In New Jersey, IBM Cuts Space, Frills and Private Desks," *New York Times*, March 15, 1994.
25 Mike Brill, "Brill's Last Word: The Emperor's New Virtual Office," *Interiors* 154, no. 5 (May 1995): 154.
26 Johnson, "IBM Cuts Space."
27 Marilyn Zelinsky, *New Workplaces for New Workstyles* (New York: McGraw-Hill, 1998), 82–5.
28 Becker and Steele, *Workplace by Design*, 120–3; Becker, Simms, and Davis, "I Think That's My Desk," 50–1.

29 Phil Patton, "The Virtual Office Becomes Reality," *New York Times*, October 28, 1993.
30 Ziva Freiman "Going Turfless," *Progressive Architecture* 75, no. 10 (October 1994): 92.
31 Richard Rapaport, "Jay Chiat Tears Down the Walls," *Forbes*, October 25, 1993, 25–8.
32 James Russell, "Virtually Brave New World," *Architectural Record*, September 1994, 88–97 Freiman, "Going Turfless," 90. Many of these doors have since been up for sale at online auction sites like 1stdibs and 20Wright, for example, "door from TBWA/Chiat/Day" at https://www.wright20.com/auctions/2018/05/furniture-pimp-the-collection-of-jim-walrod/140, accessed on November 15, 2018 and "door from TBWA Chiat Day New York by Gaetano Pesce" at https://www.1stdibs.com/furniture/building-garden/doors-gates/door-from-tbwa-chiat-day-new-york-gaetano-pesce/id-f_3438952/, accessed on November 15, 2018
33 Zelinsky, *New Workplaces for New Workstyles*, 74.
34 Russell," Virtually Brave New World," 92.
35 Mike Brill, "Brill's Last Word: A New Frankenstein's Monster Is Loose," *Interiors* 154, no. 10 (October 1995): 82.
36 Zelinsky, *New Workplaces for New Workstyles*, 72.
37 Warren Berger, "Lost in Space," *Wired*, February 1 1999, https://www.wired.com/1999/02/chiat-3/.
38 Zelinsky, *New Workplaces for New Workstyles*, 251.
39 Ellen Bruce Keable and Michael Brill, "Hoteling: Beyond Space Reduction," *Facilities Design and Management* 19, no. 6 (June 2000).
40 Berger "Lost in Space". Mitchell Pacelle, "Vanishing Offices," *Wall Street Journal*, June 4, 1993.
41 Zelinsky, *New Workplaces for New Workstyles*, 84–5.
42 Zelinsky, *New Workplaces for New Workstyles*, 224.
43 Franklin Becker and Fritz Steele, "Making Space for Teamwork," *Facilities Design and Management* 14, no. 7 (July 1995): 58; Zelinsky, *New Workplaces for New Workstyles*, 35; Francis Duffy, *The New Office* (London: Conran Octopus, 1997), 65.
44 Michael O'Neill, *Ergonomic Design for Organizational Effectiveness* (Boca Raton, FL: Lewis, 1998), 239–41.
45 Becker and Steele, "Making Space for Teamwork," 56; Becker and Steele, *Workplace by Design*, 70.
46 Becker and Steele, *Workplace by Design*, 71–7.
47 Duffy, *The New Office*, 72–5.
48 Jean Wineman and Margaret Serrato, "Facility Design for High-Performance Teams," in *Supporting Work Team Effectiveness*, ed. Eric Sundstrom (San Francisco, CA: Jossey-Bass, 1999), 282–5.
49 Becker and Steele, "Making Space for Teamwork," 80–1.
50 Becker and Steele, "Making Space for Teamwork," 58.
51 James Edward Sved, "Alcoa Recycles," *Building Design & Construction* 41, no. 6 (2000): 89; Duffy, *The New Office*, 166.
52 Frances Anderton, "'Virtual Officing' Comes in from the Cold," *New York Times*, December 17 1998; Nicolai Ouroussoff, "A Workplace through the Looking Glass," *LA Times*, January 31, 1999; Clifford Pearson, "After Trying the Virtual Clive Wilkinson Gets Real with New Offices for TBWA/Chiat/Day," *Architectural Record*, August 1999, 102–7.

53 Franklin Becker, *Offices at Work: Uncommon Workspace Strategies That Add Value and Improve Performance* (San Francisco, CA: Jossey-Bass, 2004), 51–2.
54 Becker and Steele, *Workplace by Design*, 79–81.
55 Duffy, *The New Office*, 237.
56 Duffy, *The New Office*, 78–81.
57 Becker, *Offices at Work*, 32–4.
58 Arthur Gensler, *Developing the Architecture of the Workplace: Gensler, 1967-1997* (New York: Edizioni Press, 1998), 116–21.
59 Gary Andrew Poole, "Nerds in Gilded Cubicles," *New York Times*, February 4, 1999.
60 Kwolek-Folland, *Engendering Business*, 137–9; Helena Chance, *The Factory in a Garden: A History of Corporate Landscapes from the Industrial to the Digital Age* (Manchester: Manchester University Press, 2017), 98–115.
61 Union Carbide, Project Statement, KRJDA: Box 424 Folder "Project Statements"; General Foods, "Meeting Notes," February 27, 1978, KRJDA: Box 521 Folder "Design Notes GF 6."
62 Union Carbide, *HQ News*, June 1982, 5, KRJDA: Box 424 Folder "Building Brochures."
63 Zelinsky, *New Workplaces for New Workstyles*, 109.
64 Steven Greenhouse, *The Big Squeeze: Tough Times for the American Worker* (New York: Anchor Books, 2009), 185.
65 Juriaan van Meel and Paul Vos, "Funky Offices: Reflections on Office Design in the 'New Economy'," *Journal of Corporate Real Estate* 3, no. 4 (2001): 326.
66 Greenbaum, *Windows on the Workplace*, 105.
67 Rapaport, "Jay Chiat Tears Down the Walls," 28.
68 Juliet Schor, *The Overworked American: The Unexpected Decline of Leisure* (New York: Basic Books, 1991), 28–32.
69 Kunda, *Engineering Culture*, 198–204.
70 Duffy, *The New Office*, 56–7.
71 Keable and Brill, "Hotelling," 26, 28.
72 Berger, "Lost in Space"; Russell, "Virtually Brave New World," 94.
73 Saskia Sassen, *Globalization and Its Discontents* (New York: New Press, 1998), 48.
74 Dana Dubbs, "Balancing Benefits of Outsourcing vs in-House," *Facilities Design and Management* 11, no. 8 (August 1992), 42–4.
75 Paul Tarricone, "Outsourcing on the Upswing," *Facilities Design and Management* 17, no. 12 (December 1998), 32–4.
76 "A Thriving Industry," *Facilities Design and Management* 19, no. 11 (November 2000), 34–8.
77 Gerald Hubbard, "How to Make That Tough Outsourcing Decision Work for You," *Facilities Design and Management* 12, no. 7 (July 1993).
78 Kunda, *Engineering Culture*, 209–12, 225.
79 "Klauser Orders His Own State Janitor," *Catch-All Gazette*, January 1991, DOA: Box 85 Folder 18. Letter to Governor Thompson from state employee, January 17, 1991, DOA: Box 85 Folder 18.
80 Hochschild, *The Time Bind*, 139–43.
81 Art Budros, "The Mean and Lean Firm and Downsizing: Causes of Involuntary and Voluntary Downsizing Strategies," *Sociological Forum* 17, no. 2 (2002): 312–13.
82 Hatton, *The Temp Economy*, 92.
83 Greenhouse, *The Big Squeeze*, 131–2.
84 Ron Lieber, "The Permatemps Contretemps," *Fast Company*, July 31, 2000, https://www.fastcompany.com/40787/permatemps-contretemps.

85 Greenhouse, *The Big Squeeze*, 131–2.
86 Stephen Barley and Gideon Kunda, *Gurus, Hired Guns, and Warm Bodies: Itinerant Experts in a Knowledge Economy* (Princeton, NJ: Princeton University Press, 2006), 184–7.
87 Greenbaum, *Windows on the Workplace*, 85–6.
88 Brendan Read, "Call Center Cool," *Facilities Design and Management* 17, no. 10 (October 1998): 56–7.
89 Gensler, *Developing the Architecture*, 174–7.
90 Greenhouse, *The Big Squeeze*, 11, 111–14.
91 Doreen Massey, *Space, Place, and Gender* (Minneapolis: University of Minnesota Press, 1994), 87–91.
92 MOMA, "Exhibition at MoMA features innovative design solutions for the workplace of the near future," January 2001, https://www.moma.org/documents/moma_press-release_387046.pdf.
93 Paola Antonelli, *Workspheres* (New York: Museum of Modern Art, 2001), 70–210.
94 Antonelli, *Workspheres*, 61.

Conclusion

1 Katharine Schwab, "The Slow Death of Open Offices,' *Fast Company*, February 2019, 10–12; Angus Montgomery, "Frank Gehry Works on Huge Open-Plan Office for Facebook," *Design Week*, August 28, 2012, https://www.designweek.co.uk/issues/may-2012/frank-gehry-works-on-huge-open-plan-office-for-facebook/. Lydia Lee, "Status Update," *Architectural Record*, August 2015, 86–93.
2 Facebook Headquarters Gensler website: https://www.gensler.com/projects/facebook-headquarters accessed on February 9, 2019.
3 Shannon Mattern, "Sharing Is Tables: Furniture for Digital Labor," *e-flux architecture* (2017), https://www.e-flux.com/architecture/positions/151184/sharing-is-tables-furniture-for-digital-labor/.
4 Nick Statt, "Facebook Rejects Female Engineers' Code More Often, Analysis Finds," *The Verge*, May 2, 2017, https://www.theverge.com/2017/5/2/15517302/facebook-female-engineers-gender-bias-studies-report.
5 Mario Koran, "Black Facebook Staff Describe Workplace Racism in Anonymous Letter," *Guardian*, November 13, 2019, https://www.theguardian.com/technology/2019/nov/13/facebook-discrimination-black-workers-letter.
6 Laurence Dodds, "Facebook Employee Blasts 'Black People Problem' at Social Network," *The Telegraph*, November 27, 2018, https://www.telegraph.co.uk/technology/2018/11/27/facebook-employee-blasts-climate-racial-discrimination/; F. B. Blind, "Facebook Empowers Racism against Its Employees of Color," *Medium*, November 7, 2019, https://medium.com/@blindfb2020/facebook-empowers-racism-against-its-employees-of-color-fbbfaf55ab76.
7 Sarah T. Roberts, *Behind the Screen: Content Moderation in the Shadows of Social Media* (New Haven, CT: Yale University Press, 2019), 68–70; Olivia Solon, "Underpaid and Overburdened: The Life of a Facebook Moderator," *The Guardian*, May 25, 2017, https://www.theguardian.com/news/2017/may/25/facebook-moderator-underpaid-overburdened-extreme-content; Colin Horgan, "Facebook Is Built on Inequality – Featured Stories," *Medium*, December 6, 2018, https://medium.com/s/story/facebook-is-built-on-inequality-6bb1e0fa27ea; Julia Angwin and Ariana Tobin, "Facebook (Still) Letting Housing Advertisers Exclude Users

by Race," *ProPublica*, November 21, 2017, https://www.propublica.org/article/facebook-advertising-discrimination-housing-race-sex-national-origin.

8. Mark Wilson, "Cubicles Are Back, and We Have Open Plan Offices to Thank," *Fast Company*, February 12, 2019, https://www.fastcompany.com/90305213/the-hip-new-open-plan-office-trend-cubicles; Rebecca Rosen, "Our Cubicles, Ourselves: How the Modern Office Shapes American Life," *The Atlantic*, April 14, 2014, https://www.theatlantic.com/business/archive/2014/04/our-cubicles-ourselves-how-the-modern-office-shapes-american-life/360613/; Alyse Kalish, "This Is Why So Many Companies Insist on Open Offices Now," *The Muse*, https://www.themuse.com/advice/history-of-the-open-offices-exist-cubicles; Hannah Ewens and Jamie Clifton, "Open Plan Offices Should Be Banned Immediately," *Vice* (blog), October 1, 2018, https://www.vice.com/en_uk/article/j54gv4/open-plan-offices-should-be-banned-immediately.

9. "Are Cubicles Preferable to the Open Layout?," *New York Times*, January 14, 2015; Michael Useem, "A First Generation Problem," *New York Times*, January 14, 2015; Nikil Saval, "Let Employees Decide," *New York Times*, January 14, 2015; Susan Cain, "Sharing Sunlight, Not Insanity," *New York Times*, January 14, 2015; Anne-Laure Fayard, "Balance Proximity and Privacy," *New York Times*, January 14, 2015; Adam Stoltz, "The Problem Isn't Openness, It's Noise," *New York Times*, January 14, 2015.

10. Kabir Sehgal, "Its Time to Bring Back the Office Cubicle," *Fortune*, January 18, 2017, https://fortune.com/2017/01/18/i-hate-open-offices/.

11. Matt Richtel, "The Pandemic May Mean the End of the Open-Floor Office," *New York Times*, May 4, 2020, https://www.nytimes.com/2020/05/04/health/coronavirus-office-makeover.html.

12. Renyi Hong, "Office Interiors and the Fantasy of Information Work," *tripleC: Communication* 15, no. 2 (2017): 556.

13. Geoffrey James, "How Open-Plan Offices Kill Diversity and Equality," *Inc.com*, October 10, 2018, https://www.inc.com/geoffrey-james/how-open-plan-offices-kill-diversity-equality.html; Nitasha Tiku, "Why Tech Leadership May Have a Bigger Race than Gender Problem," *Wired*, October 3, 2017, https://www.wired.com/story/tech-leadership-race-problem/.

14. Victor Ray, "Why So Many Organizations Stay White," *Harvard Business Review*, November 19, 2019, https://hbr.org/2019/11/why-so-many-organizations-stay-white.

15. Alison Hirst and Christina Schwabenland, "Doing Gender in the 'New Office'," *Gender, Work & Organization* 25, no. 2 (March 2018): 169–71.

16. Dean Nieusma, "Alternative Design Scholarship: Working toward Appropriate Design," *Design Issues* 20, no. 3 (Summer 2004): 16.

17. Franklin Becker, *Offices at Work: Uncommon Workspace Strategies That Add Value and Improve Performance* (San Francisco, CA: Jossey-Bass, 2004), 171–4.

Index

ableism 63–4, 69, 82, 153–4, 164
  See also disability; universal worker
access flooring 121
accessibility 22, 63–4, 84, 106–8, 169
accessories for the workstation 17, 43, 51, 89, 100, 134–6
Acoustic Conditioner (Herman Miller) 75–7
acoustics. *See* noise
Action Factory (Herman Miller) 94
Action Office. *See* Herman Miller
advertising 23, 81, 94–5, 114, 130, 166
aesthetic coherence 45, 86, 89–90, 101–2, 107, 110
alienation of work 58–9, 85–6, 159
alternative office 142, 151–8
amenities in office 31, 151, 155–8, 161
American Indian identity. *See* racial and ethnic identity
Americans with Disabilities Act (ADA) 145
Antonelli, Paola 163
Apple Computers (Cupertino) 155
architectural envelope 6, 16–17, 19, 33, 42–3, 55, 119–20
Arthur Andersen (San Francisco) 147–8
art in the office 131, 156
ASD Group (Westinghouse) 103, 131
Associated Space Design (ASD) 30–1
Asian American identity. *See* racial and ethnic identity
AT&T 136–7
automation of work 7, 52–3, 58–9, 100, 118, 122, 129–31, 146
Avis 24–5, 98

Bamforth, Ken 65
Becker, Franklin 30, 87, 151–2, 154–6
Bell Telephone Company 118, 146
Bertalanffy, Ludwig von 25

Black identity 21–3
  See also racial and ethnic identity
Blue Cross Blue Shield (New York City) 56
BOSTI (Buffalo Organizations for Social and Technological Innovation) 44, 81–5, 103, 106, 109, 144–5, 147
brainstorming 31–3, 94, 153–4
break space 31, 70, 152, 154–5
Brill, Michael 147, 149–150
  See also BOSTI
building systems 42
  cabling 120, 123–9, 137–8
  HVAC 60, 119–21
  lighting systems 80–1, 106, 136
  phone 49, 118, 138
  power 49, 119–20, 123–9
burolandschaft. *See* office landscape; Quickborner Team
Business and Institutional Furniture Manufacturers Association (BIFMA) 132–3

cabling 41, 49–50, 80, 118, 120, 123–9, 137–8
call center 161–3
CBS Building (New York City) 110–12
ceiling 6, 42, 50, 120–1, 136
CETRA (Kimball) 50–1, 124, 127
chairs. *See* seating
change over time 9–10, 25, 56–60, 106, 117–23, 138
change, planning for 39, 40–5, 52–6, 118–23, 129
Chiat/Day (California and New York) 148–50, 154–5, 157–8
Chiat, Jay 148–9
childcare 146
Citibank (New York City) 53, 58

Citizens and Southern National Bank (Atlanta) 28
clerical workers 22, 57–8, 68–9, 126, 129–31, 160
  demographics of 58, 84–5, 129
  treated as interchangeable 20, 35, 58
  See also hierarchy of workforce
club office 148–9, 151–4
clutter 27, 93–100, 104–5, 110
collaboration 6, 29, 64–5, 142, 151–4, 170–1
color
  changing palettes 103–4
  choice of 89, 101–3
  consistency of 41, 102–4
  visual interest and 15, 33, 72, 110, 112, 131, 149
communication
  as central function of office 64–70
  cross-disciplinary 152
  electronic 142
  environmental determinism of 26–8, 64–70, 141–5, 151–4
  information sharing 26, 65–7
  open plan facilitating 26, 30, 64–70, 141, 151–4
  as planning tool for office design 64–70
  and privacy 79–86
  unwelcome 69–70
Comprehensive Storage System (Herman Miller) 96
Computer and Business Equipment Manufacturer Association (CBEMA), 133
computer networks 93–4, 129, 137–8, 146, 149
computing, decentralized 122, 146
computing, history of 117–18
computing, mainframe 118–23
computing, personal
  equipment and furniture 124–6
  ergonomics 129–39
  mixing hardware systems 136–7
  portability of 127–8, 142, 149
  revolution of 118–19, 146
  shared terminals 127–8
  slow adoption 121–3
  standardization of 146, 149
  See also automation of work
Congress of the United States 132–3

connectors for furniture 45–52, 55
contract workers 41–2, 50, 123, 159–61
conventional office. *See* traditional office
copy room 119, 144
corporate bureaucracy 7, 18–19, 24–5, 68–9, 96–8
corporate culture. *See* organizational culture
corporate modernism 18
cost-saving strategies 7–8, 60, 120–1, 136–7, 166–7
  See also energy reduction efforts; retrofitting
countercultural movement 23–5, 30–3, 111–12
crowding in open plan 53, 148
cubicles 5, 85–6, 148, 167
cybernetics 8, 26, 65

Deering, Milliken and Co. (New York City) 17–18
dehumanization of work 59, 85–6, 118, 159
density in open plan 53, 148
departments 35, 66–8, 71–2, 103, 134
design as a social tool 79, 81–8, 93–4, 150–1, 165
  movement and communication 26–8, 64–70, 141–5, 151–4
  organization and storage 95–100, 150
  restrictions on personal decoration 107–11
desks, freestanding 55, 89–91, 106, 125–8
  See also systems furniture; workstation; work surfaces; *and specific product lines*
Digital Equipment Corporation (DEC) 122, 126, 136
disability 22, 63–4, 84, 106–8, 131, 146, 169
  auditory 79–80, 169
  cognitive 78–80, 153–4, 169
  physical 106–8, 145, 169
  visual 131, 153–4, 169
  wheelchair access 106–8
  See also ableism
discrimination
  by designing for universal worker 19–23, 37–8, 170

and hierarchy of workforce 16, 36, 57, 159–61, 170
  inequity and 159
  racial and ethnic identity 136, 169
  See also disability; gender; sexuality
disorder 27, 30, 63–7, 93–100, 104–6, 110
display, in workstation 92–3, 99–100, 105, 109–14
disruption 53, 69–70
distractions 70, 79–80, 144, 167
diversity and collaboration 152, 170–1
diversity and inclusion 15–16, 107
diversity of workforce. *See* universal worker
Divider Wall (E. F. Hauserman Company) 43–4
downsizing 8, 40, 160
  See also job insecurity
drawers 98–100, 104–5, 113
Drucker, Peter 24–5, 29, 44
Duffy, Francis (Frank) 30, 42, 151, 155, 158, 164
Dunlap, "Chainsaw Al" 160
DuPont (Wilmington, DE) 26–7

economic recession 7–8, 40, 52, 56–7
  See also job insecurity
efficiency 6, 52, 141, 152, 156–7
E. F. Hauserman Company 40–5
egalitarianism 7–8, 15–16, 25–33, 37–8
  See also hierarchy of workforce; hierarchy of workspace
Electronic Arts 157
enclosures. *See* partitions
energy reduction efforts 8, 60, 120
environmental determinism 64–70, 81–8, 165
environment and behavior 64–5, 80
  See also BOSTI
Ernst & Young (Chicago) 147, 150
Epic Records (New York City) 111–12
Eppinger Furniture 30–1
ERA-1 (Haworth) 50, 123–4
ergonomics 94, 129–39
ethnic identity. *See* racial and ethnic identity
Ethospace (Herman Miller) 51, 86, 107
exclusionary design 20, 33–5, 132–3, 137–9, 153
  See also universal worker
executive office in open plan 31, 33, 165
executive workers
  agency of 36–7
  executive dissatisfaction 34
  liberated from private office 68–9, 165
  open plan office of 31, 33, 165
  See also hierarchy of workforce; management and professional workers

Facebook (Menlo Park, CA) 165–6
facilities management 40, 52–6, 137, 159
  planning role of 111, 128–9
  and standardization 103–4, 107, 109
finishes, materials for 3, 48, 89, 102, 149
  acoustics and 74
  and hierarchy 17, 27, 30–1, 34–5, 102
fitness facilities 155–7
flexibility of workday 8, 15, 151, 157–8, 160
flexible use of space 43, 144, 148, 168
Freehafer Hall, Purdue University 1–4, 55, 65–72, 98, 125–6
furniture as interior architecture 51
furniture, freestanding 55, 89–91, 106, 125–8
furniture systems. *See* systems furniture
future of work 145–51, 163–4

Gehry, Frank 165
gender
  and discomfort 32
  expendability based on 57–8, 159
  and hierarchy of workforce 21, 35, 129
  physical appearance and 21, 72
  politics and 15, 23
  and sexual harassment 73
  and surveillance 72–3, 169
  White women 20
  and the workspace 63, 112–13
  See also universal worker
Gensler 150, 162, 166
Girard, Alexander 131
grid arrangement 15, 41, 141, 144

Hall, Edward 65, 109
hardware systems 45–52, 55
Hauserman Company 40–5
Haworth 50–1, 103, 107–8, 123–4, 134–5

Hawthorne study 80–1
Herman Miller 2, 26–9, 35, 54, 128, 138
　Acoustic Conditioner 75–7
　Action Factory 94
　Action Office (1) 26–9, 91–4,
　　96–100, 103
　Action Office (2) 28–9, 46, 92–3, 143–4
　Action Office 2, 39, 54, 71–2, 75–8, 90,
　　130–1, 134–5
　Ethospace 51, 86, 107
　Herman Miller Research 92–3, 103
hierarchy of workforce
　design and 17, 94, 101–3, 105, 163
　lack of mobility between 162
　lower status workers 35, 57,
　　142, 158–63
　lower vs upper 19, 69–70, 84–5,
　　112–13, 141–2, 158–63, 169
　varied agency in workplace 35–7,
　　121–2, 141–2, 146, 160, 170
hierarchy of workspace
　and design process 30–1, 37
　flattening of 7, 16, 29–30, 52, 94
　hidden hierarchy 30
　in organizational structure 17–19, 24
　rejection of 16, 25–33
　space 15, 17, 33, 101–2, 161
　space standards 17–19, 22, 34,
　　42, 111
Hiserman, Mary Ann 106–7
Hispanic identity. See racial and ethnic
　identity
Hoos, Ida Russakoff 118, 122
hoteling 147–8, 150
humanization of the office 129–39,
　146, 162

IBM 53, 146–7, 150
identity. See disability; gender; racial and
　ethnic identity; universal worker
interior scenery 42–3
intersectional identities 21–3, 88
inventory systems for components and
　hardware 54–5
IT departments 137
itinerant work 145–51

Jaeger, Dieter 26
JFN Associates 92–3
job insecurity 142, 158–62

and automation 118
expendability 69, 142, 158–63
layoffs and downsizing 8, 40, 160
reorganization 19–20, 35, 52–60,
　144
and upward mobility 29–30
John Deere (Moline, IL) 119–20, 144
Johnson Wax (Racine, WI) 6

Kimball 50–1, 83, 103, 124, 127
Knoll, Florence 17–18, 110–11
Knoll, Inc. 17–18, 47, 124
knowledge worker 7, 24–5
　and universal worker 160, 164, 168
　See also management and professional
　　workers
Krueger International 124–5

labor activism 56, 58, 132
Lanier, Susan 148
Larkin Building (Buffalo) 6
Latino/a identity. See racial and ethnic
　identity
layoffs 8, 40, 160
leisure and work boundaries, blurred
　156–8, 163–4
Lewin, Kurt 65
LGBT identity 73–4
lighting integrated into furniture 49–50,
　120, 136
long- vs. short-term planning 42–3, 49,
　118–23, 129
Lorenzen, Hans 26
Louis Harris and Associates 4–5, 34,
　57, 79, 87
Lubowicki, Paul 148

McDonald's (Oakbrook, IL) 30–3, 63, 72
McGregor, Douglas 24–5, 29, 44, 59
maintenance 40, 54, 101, 105, 119,
　150–1, 158–9, 169
　See also facilities management
management control of workers 89–90,
　107–9, 162, 164
management philosophy 6, 8, 16, 23–5,
　33, 64–5
management and professional workers
　agency of 36–7, 121–2, 160
　demographics of 16, 84–5, 113, 166
　See also hierarchy of workforce

marketing of systems furniture 81, 94–5, 114
Massachusetts Institute of Technology (MIT) 65
Mayo, Elton 80–1
meeting spaces 31–3, 70, 152–5
memos 68–9, 98, 143
men. See gender, universal worker
mental health 57–9, 78–80, 114, 129, 156–8
Meridian (Kimball) 103
Mills, C. Wright 19
Mobiles (Steelcase) 50, 99–100
mobility. See accessibility; hierarchy of workforce; job insecurity; movement
mock-up, for workstation 3, 36
modularity 41–2, 61, 96
   adaptability for individual 27–8, 89–96, 106–7
   enabling change 39, 45–7
   See also standardization; systems furniture
Montgomery Ward (Chicago) 35
Morrison Raceway (Knoll) 124
Moveable Wall (Steelcase) 45, 47–8, 99
movement
   circulation through office 25–7, 64–70, 141–5, 151–4
   spaces for 66–8, 143–5, 153, 156
   within workspace 85, 93–4, 133, 142, 155
   See also accessibility
Museum of Modern Art (MoMA) 163–4

Nelson, George 96
9 to 5 (labor union) 58, 132
noise 63, 77, 130, 149, 153, 169
   creating privacy 74–5
   controlling 70, 74–80, 167
non-territorial office 145–51
normate worker. See universal worker

Office Interior System (OIS, E. F. Hauserman Company) 44–5
office landscape 1, 6, 25–9, 33–4, 55, 66
   See also Quickborner Team
office layout 5, 27, 35, 66–8
off-site office 161–2
open plan office, defined 4–6 165–6, 168

failure to live up to ideals 145, 165–71
   See also universal worker
reinvented 142, 165–71
user resistance 33–4, 150
organizational culture 15–17, 111–12, 142, 151, 168
   centralization 7, 12, 58–9
   decentralization 25, 53, 58
   progressive ideals 8, 12, 15–16, 23–33, 106
   spatial structure echoing it 10, 17, 52–3, 66–8
organization man. See universal worker
outsourcing 158–63
overhead costs 7–8, 148
overwork 156–8
Owens-Corning Fiberglass Corporation 75

Packard, Vance 17
paperflow 19–20, 65–9, 94–6, 105, 149–50
paperless future 100, 149–50
partitions 1–4, 28, 31, 48, 51, 141
   ceiling-height 33, 40–3, 79
   changing heights of 3, 12, 80, 82–3, 152, 162, 167
   as display surface 9–10, 94, 106, 110–11, 113–15
   as isolating 63, 85–6
   labor to alter 41–2, 45–7, 50
   See also facilities management
   storage furniture used as 99–100
   as structural support for other elements 46, 50, 71, 77, 80, 93, 123–5, 136
   See also systems furniture, walls
part-time employment 57
personalization 104–5, 109–14
   customizable workstation 91–5
   display 92–3, 110–15
   emotional needs met by 112, 114
   personal items 4, 105, 110–14 147–8
   personal space 109–14, 163
Pesce, Gaetano 149
Pile, John 35–6, 50, 72, 79, 96–8, 109–10
Places (Haworth) 51
planning and design process 35–6, 170
   space standards 17–19, 22, 34, 42, 111
   user participation in 35–7, 66–7, 80–6, 170–1

plants 2, 71, 130–1
play at work 31–3, 148–9, 154–8, 161
pool 4–5, 17, 113, 129, 161–2
popular media representations of the office 15, 85–6, 167
Powell/Kleinschmidt 101–3, 110
privacy
　acoustic 74–80
　and enclosure 80–6
　and productivity 70–80
　suspicions about 72
　visual 70–4, 82–3
private offices 17, 29, 36, 69, 79
　elimination of 29, 33, 63–4, 68, 72–3
　desire to retain 29–30, 72
productivity 7–8, 40, 52, 59, 80–1, 98–9, 118, 156–8
Propst, Robert 26–9, 39, 71–2, 75–9, 90–4, 98–9, 143–4
Prudential (Merrilleville, IN) 101–3, 110
Pulgram, William 30–1, 100, 128
　See also Associated Space Design
Purdue University 1–4, 55, 65–72, 98, 125–6
purging of paper 99, 150

Quickborner Team 1, 25–8, 35, 39, 65–70, 74, 98, 143

raceways 41, 50, 124
racial and ethnic identity 21–3, 84
　and expendability 57, 159
　and hierarchy of workforce 22–3, 166
　and lower-tier labor 159
Ready Wall (E. F. Hauserman Company) 40–4
Research & Design Institute (REDE) 29
retrofitting 49, 55, 128–9, 136–7
road warriors 146–7
Roche, Kevin 8, 36, 42, 119–20, 144, 156
Rodgers (Sydney) and Associates 35, 68–9
rules and standards for workspace 107–11, 150–1

Saarinen, Eero 17–18, 110–11
safety 121, 123
Scandinavian Airline Systems (Stockholm) 155–6

Schnelle, Eberhard and Wolfgang 1, 26, 65
　See also Quickborner Team
seating 17–18, 23
　ergonomics 131, 133, 135–6
　lounge 31, 153
　privacy and 63, 83, 144
　and workstation 90, 101–3
secretaries 68–9, 126, 130–1, 160
secrets 73–4, 114, 166
security 72–3, 122, 159–60
segregation 21–2
service areas 96–7, 119, 144, 152, 162
service work 158–63
sexual harassment 73
sexual interactions at work 32, 73–4
sexuality 73–4
short- vs. long-term planning 42–3, 49, 118–23, 129
Silicon Valley 6, 31, 157, 159
Skidmore Owings & Merrill (SOM) 42
social nature of work 58–9, 63–70, 78–80, 81, 129, 143–4
Sommer, Robert 110
soundscapes 74–80
　See also noise
space, as temporary 147
space-saving with open plan 53, 148
space standards 17–19, 22, 34, 42, 111
space, social implications of 64–70
standardization
　and facilities management 103–4, 107–9
　and hierarchy of workforce 19
　in planning 17, 81–5, 168
　space standards 17–19, 42, 111
　in technology 60, 137–8, 146, 149
　workspace 34, 41
　workstation 89–90, 101–4, 106, 125–6
　See also accessibility; modularity; systems furniture
Steelcase 4–5, 34, 36, 57, 87, 100, 153
　Corporate Development Center 152
　lighting component 49
　Mobiles 50, 99–100
　Moveable Wall 45, 47–8, 99
　9000 35, 50, 94–5, 103
　3200 and 5200 31, 89
Steele, Fred (Fritz) 87, 110, 151–2, 154–6
Stephens (Knoll) 47

storage space 90, 95–100
Storagewall (George Nelson) 96
stress 57–9, 114, 129, 157–8
Stumpf, William 86, 147
Sundstrom, Eric 69–70, 79
supply area 96–7
support staff 158–63
surveillance 6, 59, 72–4, 162, 169
surveys of workers/users 4, 35–7, 66–7, 73, 80–6, 122, 132, 159
systems furniture 4–6, 27–8, 39–45, 90
    considerations when purchasing 46–7, 49
    flexibility 40–52, 93, 106–8
    hierarchy and 34–5, 89
    interchangeability of, within a single system 48
    limitations of 42, 48–9
    marketing and 81, 94–5, 114
    mixing systems 3–5, 10, 85, 128
    technology integrated into 120, 123–9, 136

Tandem Computers (Cupertino) 150
Task Response Module (TRM) 30–1
Taylor + Smith (Houston) 156
TBWA/Chiat/Day (Los Angeles) 154–5
teamwork 6, 64–5, 151–4, 170–1
technological change 6, 58, 100, 106, 118–23, 142
    See also computing
technology and health 129–39
technology, mobile 142, 145–6, 148–9
telecommuting 145–6
temperature 60, 119
temporary use of space 147
temporary work 57, 160
territoriality and ownership 169
    See also private offices
Theory X and Theory Y 24–5, 44, 59
Toffler, Alvin 145–6
Torp, Niels 155–6
total design approach 17, 36–7, 110–12, 156
Townsend, Robert 24–5, 98
traditional office 5, 17–23, 91
    CBS Building (New York City) 110–12
    desks, freestanding 55, 89–91, 106, 125–8
    partitions, ceiling-height 33, 40–3, 79

pool 4–5, 17, 113, 129, 161–2
space standards 17–19, 22, 34, 42, 111
total design approach 17, 37
Union Carbide (Danbury, CT) 36, 156
See also hierarchy of workforce; private offices
Trist, Eric 65

unemployment 7, 57
Unigroup (Haworth) 51, 107–8
Union Carbide (Danbury, CT) 36, 156
    See also Roche, Kevin
Union Carbide (New York City) 42
unions 56, 58, 132
United States Congress 132–3
United States Federal Agencies
    Federal Aviation Administration (FAA, Seattle) 36
    General Services Association (GSA) 36, 60
    Internal Revenue Service (IRS) 107
    National Institute for Occupational Safety and Health (NIOSH) 132
    Occupational Safety and Health Organization (OSHA) 132
UniTek (Haworth) 134–5
universal planning 137–9
universal worker 19–23, 63–4, 81–5, 104, 132–4, 153, 164, 169
urban-inspired office design 154–8

visual connections 69–70, 72, 82–3, 152–4, 169
visual continuity 45, 86, 89–90, 101–2, 107, 110
visual display terminal (VDT) 126 132–4
visual display terminal (VDT) corner 126–9

walls 69, 73, 165
    lack of 28 71–2, 86, 144, 168
    removal of 63, 82
    to support building systems 50, 75, 77, 121
    See also partitions
wayfinding 143–5
Welch, Jack 160
Westinghouse Electric Corporation 45, 103, 131
Weyerhaeuser (Federal Way, WA) 53

Whiteness 16, 20–2, 37, 83–4, 166, 169
  See also universal worker
Whyte, William 20
Wiener, Norbert 25
Wilkinson (Clive) Architects 154–5
windows 59, 106, 113, 138
wiring 41, 49–50, 80, 118, 120, 123–9, 137–8
Wisconsin, State of 10, 33–4, 52–3, 56, 59, 159–60
Wodka, Michael 75–8
women. *See* gender
Wooton desk 90
word processing 53, 58–9, 118, 122, 129–31, 146
work and leisure boundaries, blurred 156–8, 163–4
work as alienating 58–9, 85–6, 159
work, changing nature of 7, 11, 24–5
worker initiative
  agency 91, 104–9, 121–2, 150–2
  autonomy 7, 16, 25
  suppressed 89, 107–9
workers as individuals 11, 24, 102, 105–7, 109–14, 118, 138
  See also discrimination; diversity and inclusion; universal worker; *and specific identities*
worker satisfaction
  dissent 106–7, 111–14, 136, 150
  morale 33–36, 59
  needs not being met 69
  with the office space 33–7, 79, 167
  space disruptions and 54–5
workers' bodies
  discomfort 32, 54–5, 72–4, 131, 152
  height 70, 82–3
  physical appearance 72
  physical health 58, 60, 129–39
  See also disability
worker surveys 4, 35–7, 66–7, 73, 80–6, 122, 132, 159
workforce hierarchy. *See* hierarchy of workforce
working from home 145–6
workspace rules and standards 107–11, 150–1
workstation 90–5
  accessories for 17, 43, 51, 89, 100, 134–6
  as basic unit of office planning 101–4
  change over life of 104–9
  flexibility of 91–5, 106–7
  as interface 90, 93–4
  L-shaped 126–7
  mock-up 3, 36
  rules and standards for 107–11, 150–1
  standardization and 101–104
  user adjustments to 91–5, 104–14
work surface 92–3, 126–7, 134
  See also desks, freestanding; systems furniture
Wright, Frank Lloyd 6

Yamasaki, Minoru 35
Young and Rubicam (New York City) 53
youth culture 23–5, 30–3

Zelinsky, Marilyn 151
Zuckerberg, Mark 165–6

www.ingramcontent.com/pod-product-compliance
Lightning Source LLC
Chambersburg PA
CBHW070815250426
43672CB00030B/2687